Lecture Notes
in Business Information Pro 111

Series Editors

Claes Wohlin (Ed.)

Agile Processes in Software Engineering and Extreme Programming

13th International Conference, XP 2012
Malmö, Sweden, May 21-25, 2012
Proceedings

 Springer

Volume Editor

Claes Wohlin
Blekinge Institute of Technology
School of Computing
Karlskrona, Sweden
E-mail: claes.wohlin@bth.se

ISSN 1865-1348   e-ISSN 1865-1356
ISBN 978-3-642-30349-4   e-ISBN 978-3-642-30350-0
DOI 10.1007/978-3-642-30350-0
Springer Heidelberg Dordrecht London New York

Library of Congress Control Number: 2012937367

ACM Computing Classification (1998): D.2, K.6

Typesetting: Camera-ready by author, data conversion by Scientific Publishing Services, Chennai, India

Printed on acid-free paper

Springer is part of Springer Science+Business Media (www.springer.com)

Preface

In the last decade, we have seen agile and lean software development strongly influence the way software is developed. Agile and lean has moved from being a way of working for a number of pioneers to becoming, more or less, the expected way of developing software also in industry. The transition to more agile and lean practices is not easy and any expected benefits do not come automatically. Thus, there is a great need for research and practice to work together to understand, evaluate and improve software development.

An important starting point is to study agile and lean software development both academically and in close collaboration between academia and practice. This book presents a number of research contributions in relation to these ways of developing software. More specifically, the book includes a number of chapters on different themes related to agile and lean software development. The themes include general aspects of agility, agile teams, studies related to release and maintenance, and research on specific practices in agile and lean. The four themes are complemented with four shorter chapters capturing some additional aspects on agile and lean software development.

The target audience of the book is researchers, teachers and practitioners who would like to gain insight into some contemporary research that most likely will affect both future research and practice in relation to agile and lean software development.

The chapters represent a selection of the papers submitted to the 13th International Conference on Agile Software Development (XP 2012). The strong submissions from researchers and practitioners, as well as the informed reviews, were a prerequisite for the book. The reviewers include members of the Program Committee and a set of additional reviewers supporting the Program Committee. Thus, I would like to extend my sincere gratitude to all contributors, both authors and reviewers. Thanks!

The editing of this book was supported by the BESQ+ project, which is funded by the Knowledge Foundation in Sweden under the Grant 20100311.

March 2012   Claes Wohlin

Organization

Research Paper Program Committee

Pekka Abrahamsson	Free University of Bozen-Bolzano, Italy
Muhammad Ali Babar	IT University of Copenhagen, Denmark
Aybüke Aurum	University of New South Wales, Australia
Robert Biddle	Carleton University, Canada
Luigi Buglione	Engineering Ingegneria Informatica, Italy
Ivica Crnkovic	Mälardalen University, Sweden
Torgeir Dingsøyr	SINTEF ICT, Norway
Tore Dybå	SINTEF ICT, Norway
Amr Elssamadisy	Wireless Generation, USA
Hakan Erdogmus	Kalemun Research Inc., Canada
Steven D. Fraser	Cisco Research Center, USA
Juan Garbajosa	Universidad Politecnica de Madrid, Spain
Alfredo Goldman	University of São Paulo, Brazil
Des Greer	Queen's University Belfast, UK
Orit Hazzan	Technion - Israel Institute of Technology, Israel
Rashina Hoda	The University of Auckland, New Zealand
Helena H. Olsson	Gothenburg University, Sweden
Martin Höst	Lund University, Sweden
Gargi Keeni	Tata Consultancy Services, India
Kirsi Korhonen	NSN, Finland
Philippe Kruchten	University of British Columbia, Canada
Pasi Kuvaja	University of Oulu, Finland
Stig Larsson	Effective Change, Sweden
Casper Lassenius	Aalto University, Finland
Kalle Lyytinen	Case Western Reserve University, USA
Lech Madeyski	Wroclaw University of Technology, Poland
Michele Marchesi	University of Cagliari, Italy
Grigori Melnik	Microsoft, USA
Alok Mishra	Atilim University, Turkey
Nils Brede Moe	SINTEF ICT, Norway
Ana M. Moreno	Universidad Politecnica de Madrid, Spain
Oscar Nierstrasz	University of Bern, Switzerland
Nilay Oza	VTT, Finland
Maria Paasivaara	Aalto University, Finland
Jennifer Pérez	Universidad Politécnica de Madrid, Spain
Kai Petersen	Blekinge Institute of Technology, Sweden
Adam Porter	University of Maryland, USA
Outi Salo	Nokia, Finland

Helen Sharp	The Open University, UK
Alberto Sillitti	Free University of Bozen-Bolzano, Italy
Darja Smite	Blekinge Institute of Technology, Sweden
Giancarlo Succi	Free University of Bozen-Bolzano, Italy
Marco Torchiano	Politecnico di Torino, Italy
Stefan van Baelen	K.U. Leuven, Belgium
Xiaofeng Wang	Free University of Bozen-Bolzano, Italy
Hironori Washizaki	Waseda University, Japan
Barbara Weber	University of Innsbruck, Austria
Werner Wild	Evolution, Austria
Laurie Williams	North Carolina State University, USA
Agustín Yagüe	Universidad Politecnica de Madrid, Spain
Pär Ågerfalk	Uppsala University, Sweden

Additional Reviewers

Wojciech Biela
Dibyendu Biswas
Mahesh Kuruba
Jorge Ressia Moreno
Fabrizio Perin
Viviane Santos
Erwann Wernli
Mansooreh Zahedi

Table of Contents

Specific Agile Practices

Short Papers

Agile Principles as Software Engineering Principles: An Analysis

Normand Séguin, Guy Tremblay, and Houda Bagane

Département d'informatique, Université du Québec à Montréal
C.P. 8888, Succ. Centre-ville
Montréal, QC, Canada, H4G 2C1
{seguin.normand,tremblay.guy}@uqam.ca

Abstract. Ever since software engineering was born, over 40 years ago, *hundreds* of "fundamental principles" for software engineering have been proposed. It is hard to believe that such a young discipline—in fact, any discipline—would rest on such a large number of "fundamental" principles. A few years ago, Séguin and Abran indeed showed, through a detailed analysis of the various principles proposed in the software engineering literature during the 1970–2003 period, that many—in fact most!—of the statements proposed as "fundamental principles" could not be considered as *software engineering principles*. The analysis method proposed by Séguin and Abran provides, among other things, a rigorous definition of term *principle* along with a set of criteria allowing to verify whether or not a statement is a *software engineering principle*. In this paper, we apply this method to the *agile principles*. More specifically, we examine the principles proposed by the Agile Manifesto as well as those from three well-known agile methods: XP, Scrum, and DSDM. Our analysis results show that many of the statements proposed as *agile principles* are in fact also *software engineering principles*.

Keywords: Agile Principles, Software Engineering Principles.

1 Introduction

Software engineering was born about forty years ago and has since become a better defined discipline: new development methods have been proposed, new tools, theoretical as well as practical, have been developed, including a *Guide to the software engineering body of knowledge* [1]. In fact, some even claim that "Software engineering has, indeed, become a profession [...] [although] what it has not become is part of the engineering profession" [2].

While various researchers and practitioners are working to develop new methods, techniques and tools, others are attempting to define the discipline's foundations. Such foundations must be enduring, relatively insensitive to technological changes, thus independent of the techniques or technologies that are *la mode du jour*. Among these foundational elements are *principles*.

The software engineering literature contains multitudes of statements that were claimed to be "*fundamental principles*" of software engineering [3, 4, 5, 6,

C. Wohlin (Ed.): XP 2012, LNBIP 111, pp. 1–15, 2012.

7, 8, 9, 10]. In previous work, Séguin and Abran [11] presented a first analysis that identified the statements that could indeed be considered *software engineering principles*. More precisely, they proposed a rigorous definition of the term *principle* along with a set of criteria allowing to verify if a statement proposed as a software engineering principle was, in fact, such a principle. They then used these criteria to analyze numerous statements—over 300!—that had been proposed as software engineering principles. Their analysis identified 34 such principles: 24 were totally independent from each other, whereas the remaining 10 could be deduced from the other, more general, principles. In other words, only 24 statements among the (more than) 300 analyzed (i.e., only 8 %) were in fact *software engineering principles*.

Among the noticeable events that marked the software engineering discipline over the last decade is, most certainly, the emergence of the *Agile* development methods. These methods claim to share a common set of ideas, stated in what is known as the *Manifesto for Agile Software Development* [12]. This manifesto expresses four key *values*, that are common among the various methods, values that stress the priority that must be given to individuals and their interactions, to working software, to customer collaboration, and to change responsiveness. From these values result a set of *principles*—12 of them—that are also presented in the *Agile Manifesto* and that are supposedly shared by the various agile methods. In the present paper, we analyze those 12 principles to determine whether these statements are *software engineering principles*.[1]

Although the various agile methods share several values and principles, they differ from each other not only by the practices they use, but also by various additional principles on which they rest. Thus, we also analyze the principles proposed by three well-known agile methods: XP [15], Scrum [16] and DSDM [17].

Our paper is organized as follows. Section 2 presents our conceptual framework as well as the research method used to analyze the various statements proposed as principles. The following sections then present our analysis results for the Agile Manifesto principles (Sect. 3) and the principles of XP, Scrum and DSDM (Sect. 4). Finally, Section 5 provides a general discussion of the analysis results, and Section 6 concludes and presents some possible future work.

2   Conceptual Framework and Methodology

When one looks into the software engineering literature that deals with principles, one can see that numerous authors use the following terms without making a clear distinction between them: *principle, concept, law,* etc. Such a terminological confusion definitely has negative consequences on the wording and interpretation of statements. Hence, statements proposed as principles are generally worded in one of three different ways: (*i*) a single term, usually denoting a concept; (*ii*) a *descriptive* statement; (*iii*) a *prescriptive* statement.

---

[1] Some of the results we present have initially been described, *in French only*, in a *Mémoire de maîtrise* [13] and in a paper published in *Génie logiciel* [14].

Most authors, except for a few [3, 4], did not explicitly present or describe the method or the criteria used to identify principles and justify their selection. Thus, most of the principles lists presented in the literature essentially represent *the authors' opinions*. This is most certainly why the software engineering literature contains such a large number of statements proposed as "principles"—over 300!—and why there is no clear consensus on those principles.

In what follows, we briefly present the key elements of the method proposed by Séguin [18] and Séguin and Abran [11] to identify software engineering principles. We do not present the complete method but only the first phases, which are those we applied to analyze the principles proposed by the Agile Manifesto and by various agile methods. But first, some terminology.

2.1 Three Key Concepts: Value, Principle, Practice

Agile methods, including the Manifesto, make a clear distinction—in fact, suggest a hierarchy—among the notions of *value*, *principle*, and *practice*. These key concepts may be defined as follows.

According to the Oxford English Dictionary (OED) [19], one definition for *value* is the following:

> The relative worth, usefulness, or importance of a thing or (occas.) a person; the estimation in which a thing is held according to its real or supposed desirability or utility.

Another definition, for the plural form *values*, is the following:

> The principles or moral standards held by a person or social group; the generally accepted or personally held judgement of what is valuable and important in life.

Similarly, Power [20] defines *values* as *ideals* shared and embraced by a group. These values, positive or negative, are generally implicit, part of the individuals' personality or the group's culture. Furthermore, "values are often emotive—they represent driving forces behind people" [20].

According to the OED [19], some definitions for *principle* are the following:

> A fundamental truth or proposition on which others depend; a general statement or tenet forming the (or a) basis of a system of belief, etc.; a primary assumption forming the basis of a chain of reasoning.

> *Science*. A general or inclusive statement about an aspect of the natural world that has numerous special applications or is applicable in a wide variety of cases.

> A general law or rule adopted or professed as a guide to action; a settled ground or basis of conduct or practice; a fundamental motive or reason for action, esp. one consciously recognized and followed.

The latter definition is particularly interesting and is reflected in the definition used by Séguin [18] in his work on software engineering principles, as he gave the following definition of a *principle*:

> A principle is a first and fundamental statement of the discipline worded in a prescriptive manner in order to guide action, that can be verified in its consequences and by experiments.

Accordingly, by itself, a single concept cannot be considered as a principle. Furthermore, being "a fundamental truth [or] motive," a principle should not be derived and, therefore, is intrinsically *fundamental*—so the term *fundamental principle* is redundant.

A principle should also be some kind of rule, law or general truth [19, 21], that provides ground and guidance for action. This latter aspect is particularly significant in our context (*software engineering* principles), as principles are expected to be the foundation on which *practices* rest. Furthermore, as the third OED definition states, a principle is a rule "adopted or professed as a guide to action [that is] consciously recognized and followed." This means that it should be possible to observe, in practice, whether or not a principle has been applied and followed. As we will see below, all these various aspects will be present in our criteria for identifying software engineering principles.

As for *practice*, Aubry [22] defines it as follows (our translation): "A practice is a concrete and proven approach that allows to solve typical problems or to improve how software is developed." He adds that "values and principles are from the cultural level and should not change from one project to another, whereas practices are application of principles in specific context" [22]. In other words, it is values and principles that should guide the choice of practices.

2.2   Principles Analysis Method

The method proposed by Séguin and Abran to analyze software engineering principles consist of four key phases [11]. For our analysis of agile principles, we used the first phases dealing with *individual criteria analysis*. Table 1 shows the individual criteria for identifying software engineering principles. These criteria

Table 1. Individual criteria for identifying software engineering principles

1.	A principle is a statement worded in a prescriptive manner [18].
2.	A principle should not be directly associated with, or rise from, a technology, a method, or a technique, nor be a specific software engineering activity (adapted from [4]).
3.	A software engineering principle should not state a compromise (or a mix) between two actions or concepts (adapted from [4]).
4.	A software engineering principle should refer to concepts related with the SE discipline [4].
5.	A principle should be worded in such way that it is possible to test it in practice or to observe some of its consequences [4].

are said to be *individual* as they are applied to each principle independently from each other.[2] We briefly explain them below—for more details, see [4, 11].

The first criteria states that a principle should be worded as a *prescriptive* statement. Thus, it should provide guidance with respect to some action, without saying explicitly how to do it. The second criteria states that a principle should neither be expressed in terms of a specific technique or method, nor be a specific activity—although applying the principle could lead to performing some appropriate activities. To apply this identification criteria, we used the ISO/IEC 12207 standard [23] as reference framework, as it describes standard software engineering processes and activities. The third criteria states that a principle should not express a *compromise* between two actions (or concepts) nor should it suggest a mix between actions. As originally expressed by Bourque et al. [4]: "[a] principle should not attempt to prioritize or select among various qualities of a solution; the engineering process should do that." The fourth criteria requires that the statement should contain or explicitly refer to software engineering concepts; if not, then although the statement might be a *general principle*, it is not specifically a *software engineering principle*. To apply this criteria, we used the *Guide to the SWEBOK* [1] as reference framework, as it defines the key SE knowledge areas. Finally, the fifth criteria states that a principle should be observable or verifiable, or as expressed by Bourque et al. [4]: "A fundamental principle should be precise enough to be capable of support or contradiction." In other words, applying, or not, the principle should have some consequences. For example, "*Don't believe everything you read.*" could not be retained as a principle because the consequences of applying this prescription cannot be verified.

The procedure we used to analyze agile principles is the following. First, we analyzed each principle based on the five individual criteria. Then, if only the first criteria (prescriptive wording) was not satisfied and a *minor rewording* could turn the statement into a prescriptive form, we retained the principle with the new wording. We applied this procedure for the principles proposed in the Agile Manifesto [12] as well as those proposed by XP [15, 24], Scrum [16, 22, 25, 26] and DSDM [17]. In the following sections, we present the results of our analysis.

3   Analysis of the Agile Manifesto Principles

Since the early '80s, a large number of software development methods—too numerous to cite—have been proposed to face "*The Software Crisis.*" Many of these methods relied on a strict and detailed software process, that put much emphasis on *following a plan* to alleviate the difficulties and problems associated with software development. By contrast, many of the methods proposed in the late '90s aimed at using simpler and lighter development processes. Thus, initially, the term *lightweight process* was often used, to contrast with the *heaviness*

---

[2] Séguin and Abran [11] also introduce two overall criteria, that allow to check the global coherence of various principles. However, given the limited number of principles we analyzed (32 vs. 313), we only used the individual criteria.

of formal software processes—later called *plan-driven* by Boehm and Turner [27]. However, as expressed by Hunt on the tenth anniversary of the Agile Manifesto:

> But "light-weight," while perhaps technically correct, carried connotations of insufficiency. So after some discussion, we all agreed on coining the term agile. And thus the Agile Manifesto and the eponymous movement were born.[3]

The *values* expressed in the Agile Manifesto, which are shared by numerous agile methods, appear in Table 2.

Table 2. Manifesto for Agile Software Development [12]

We are uncovering better ways of developing software by doing it and helping others do it. Through this work we have come to value:

– Individuals and interactions over processes and tools
   – Working software over comprehensive documentation
   – Customer collaboration over contract negotiation
   – Responding to change over following a plan

That is, while there is value in the items on the right, we value the items on the left more.

From the Agile Manifesto's four values have been derived a set of 12 principles. These principles can be seen as operationalization of the four fundamental values; they emphasize collaboration, interaction, frequent deliveries, continuous validation, etc. Table 3 shows these 12 principles [12].[4] Each of these 12 principles were analyzed using the five individual criteria described in Section 2.2. Table 4 shows the results of this analysis.

Criterion no. 1, which states that a principle must be expressed in a prescriptive manner, rejected 6 principles. As suggested by our analysis method, if a principle is rejected only because of this criterion, a *minor* rewording can be performed. Principle no. 7, can thus be reworded as *Measure the progress primarily through working software.* Seven principles (six unchanged, one with a minor rewording) satisfy the first criterion, whereas five others are worded in a purely descriptive manner.

The 12 principles satisfy criterion no. 2 which states that a principle must not result from a technology, a method, a technique or an activity. Rather, it is activities that should result from principles. They also satisfy criterion no. 3, which states that a principle must not suggest a compromise or trade-off between two actions or concepts.

---

[3] http://blog.toolshed.com/2011/01/why-johnny-cant-be-agile.html, January 10th, 2011.

[4] In this table and the followings, the statements retained as software engineering principles have been shown *in italics*.

Table 3. The 12 principles from the Agile Manifesto

	Proposed principles
1	*Our highest priority is to satisfy the customer through early and continuous delivery of valuable software.*
2	*Welcome changing requirements, even late in development. Agile processes harness change for the customer's competitive advantage.*
3	*Deliver working software frequently, from a couple of weeks to a couple of months, with a preference to the shorter timescale.*
4	*Business people and developers must work together daily throughout the project.*
5	*Build projects around motivated individuals. Give them the environment and support they need, and trust them to get the job done.*
6	The most efficient and effective method of conveying information to and within a development team is face-to-face conversation.
7	*Working software is the primary measure of progress.*
8	*Agile processes promote sustainable development. The sponsors, developers, and users should be able to maintain a constant pace indefinitely.*
9	Continuous attention to technical excellence and good design enhances agility.
10	Simplicity—the art of maximizing the amount of work not done—is essential.
11	The best architectures, requirements, and designs emerge from self-organizing teams.
12	At regular intervals, the team reflects on how to become more effective, then tunes and adjusts its behavior accordingly.

Table 4. Analysis of the 12 principles from the Agile Manifesto based on the individual criteria—*Retained* as worded, *Retained** with minor rewording, or Rejected

Principle	Criteria					Result
	1	2	3	4	5	
1	+	+	+	+	+	*Retained*
2	+	+	+	+	+	*Retained*
3	+	+	+	+	+	*Retained*
4	+	+	+	+	+	*Retained*
5	+	+	+	+	+	*Retained*
6	-	+	+	-	+	Rejected
7	-	+	+	+	+	*Retained**
8	+	+	+	+	+	*Retained*
9	-	+	+	+	-	Rejected
10	-	+	+	-	-	Rejected
11	-	+	+	+	-	Rejected
12	-	+	+	-	-	Rejected

Criterion no. 4 states that a principle wording must include concepts related with software engineering [1]. Three principles (6, 10 and 12) are rejected because they do not contain such explicit reference.

Criterion no. 5 states that a principle must be testable. For example, principle 4 can be verified by determining whether meetings between the two groups are held and how frequently. It should also be possible to observe the results when such meetings never occur. Four principles do not satisfy this criterion.

Following the application of the five individual criteria, seven principles proposed by the Agile Manifesto are retained as software engineering principles.

Table 5. Correspondence between Agile Manifesto values and principles

Manifesto Values	Agile Manifesto Principles											
	1	2	3	4	5	6	7	8	9	10	11	12
1. *Individuals and interactions over processes and tools.*				+	+	+		+			+	+
2. *Working software over comprehensive documentation.*	+		+				+		+	+	+	
3. *Customer collaboration over contract negotiation.*	+	+		+				+				
4. *Responding to change over following a plan.*	+	+	+									+

Before examining the principles proposed by some Agile methods, it is interesting to examine the correspondence between the Agile Manifesto principles and values, shown in Table 5: We note a complete coverage of both values and principles, i.e., each value is associated with at least one principle, and vice-versa.

4   Analysis of Three Agile Methods Principles

In this section, as we did for the Agile Manifesto principles, we analyze the principles proposed by three well-known agile methods: XP, Scrum and DSDM.

4.1   eXtreme Programming

eXtreme Programming (XP) was developed in the late '90s by Beck, Jeffries and Cunningham [15]. XP values are expressed quite succinctly by Beck [15]:

1. Simplicity
2. Communication
3. Feedback
4. Courage

However, Beck also notes that values are too vague to help decide which practices should be used, so those values must be refined into more concrete principles [15]. Beck thus expresses the same idea mentioned earlier, namely, that it is principles that guide the choice of practices.

XP five principles as initially expressed by Beck are the following:

1. Rapid feedback
2. Assume simplicity
3. Incremental change
4. Embrace change
5. Quality work.

Table 6. The five XP principles as expressed by Cohn [24]

	Proposed principles
1.	*Provide rapid feedback to its customers and learn from that feedback.*
2.	Favor simplicity and always attempt a simple solution before moving to a more complex one.
3.	*Improve the software through small, incremental changes.*
4.	Embrace change because they know they are truly adept at accommodating and adapting.
5.	*Insist that the software consistently exhibits the highest level of quality workmanship.*

A few years later, Cohn [24] expressed XP principles as shown in Table 6. Cohn's wording follows the spirit of Beck's principles, although Cohn's wording is more complete and explicit. Thus, it is Cohn's principles that we analyzed. Table 7 shows the analysis results.

Table 7. Analysis of the five XP principles using the individual criteria—*Retained* as worded, or Rejected

Principle	Criteria					Result
	1	2	3	4	5	
1	+	+	+	+	+	*Retained*
2	+	+	+	-	-	Rejected
3	+	+	+	+	+	*Retained*
4	+	+	+	+	-	Rejected
5	+	+	+	+	+	*Retained*

XP's foundations consist of 4 values, 5 principles and 12 practices. However, Beck's original principles are mostly concepts, that do note guide action—e.g., *Rapid feedback*. Cohn's rewording of XP principles provide a better ground for action and have a better fit with our criteria for software engineering principles. Thus, three out of five XP principles as expressed by Cohn are retained as SE principles, whereas all of Beck's original principles would be rejected.

4.2   Scrum

The term *Scrum* first appeared in 1986 [28], where the authors introduced new *product* development practices—not yet specifically targeted to software products. A few years later, Schwaber [16], who would be one of the Agile Manifesto's signatories, proposed the Scrum method, subsequently described in more detail by Schwaber and Beedle [25]. Scrum rests on the following five values [25]:

1. Commitment
2. Focus
3. Openness
4. Respect
5. Courage

Scrum also rests on six principles, presented in Table 8. According to Schwaber and Beedle [25], these principles can be summarized by the following ideas: "Scrum is a management and control process that cuts through complexity to focus on building software that meets business needs. Scrum is superimposed on top of and wraps existing engineering practices, development methodologies, or standards. [...] Scrum deals primarilary at the level of the team. It enables people to work together effectivily, and by doing so, it enables them to produce complex, sophisticated products."

Table 8. The six Scrum principles

	Proposed principles
1.	Built-in instability.
2.	Self-organizing project teams.
3.	*Overlapping development phases.*
4.	Multilearning.
5.	Subtle control.
6.	Organizational transfer of learning.

Table 9. Analysis of Scrum six principles based on the individual criteria—*Retained* as worded, *Retained** with minor rewording or Rejected

Principle	Criteria 1	2	3	4	5	Result
1	-	+	+	-	-	Rejected
2	-	+	+	+	-	Rejected
3	-	+	+	+	+	*Retained**
4	-	+	+	-	-	Rejected
5	-	+	+	-	-	Rejected
6	-	+	+	+	-	Rejected

Table 9 shows the analysis result for the Scrum principles: Only one principle is retained, no. 3, but with a minor rewording—*Use overlapping development phases*. The other Scrum principles are mostly conceptual and descriptive. They do not guide action and it would be difficult in practice to check—as implied by Scrum's commitment value itself—if they have been followed or not.

4.3   DSDM

DSDM (*Dynamic System Development Method*), developed in the UK, is a descendant of the RAD method (*Rapid Application Development*) [29].

DSDM proposes nine principles [17], presented in Table 10, whereas Table 11 shows our analysis results. One principle satisfied all criteria, whereas seven satisfied all but the first (prescriptive wording). Since it was possible to (easily) reword each of the latter—e.g., *Focus on the frequent delivery of products.*—they were all retained as SE principles.

Table 10. The nine (9) DSDM principles

	Proposed principles
1.	Active user involvement is imperative.
2.	DSDM teams must be empowered to make decisions.
3.	The focus is on frequent delivery of products.
4.	Fitness for business purpose is the essential criterion for acceptance of deliverables.
5.	Iterative and incremental development is necessary to converge on an accurate business solution.
6.	All changes during development are reversible.
7.	Requirements are baselined at a high level.
8.	Testing is integrated throughout the life cycle.
9.	A collaborative and cooperative approach between all stakeholders is essential.

Table 11. Analysis of the nine DSDM principles using the individual criteria—*Retained* as worded, *Retained** with minor rewording or Rejected

Principle	Criteria 1	2	3	4	5	Result
1	-	+	+	+	+	Retained*
2	+	+	+	+	+	Retained
3	-	+	+	+	+	Retained*
4	-	+	+	+	+	Rejected
5	-	+	+	+	+	Retained*
6	-	+	+	+	+	Retained*
7	-	+	+	+	+	Retained*
8	-	+	+	+	+	Retained*
9	-	+	+	+	+	Retained*

Compared to XP (3 out of 5) and Scrum (1 out of 6), almost all of DSDM principles (8 out of 9) have thus been retained. Among the three agile methods, DSDM thus appears to be the one whose underlying principles are the most faithful to our definition of software engineering principles.

5 Discussion

Proponents of agile software development methods have proposed various principles to use as foundations of their methods. However, much like proponents of more classical software engineering methods, they did not necessarily ensure that the "principles" they proposed were, indeed, principles. For lack of a clear and unambiguous definition of the notion of principle and lack of a set of well-defined criteria, similar confusion appears in the specification of *Agile principles* as observed for *Software engineering principles*. Thus, many statements proposed as agile principles are worded either as simple concepts (one or a few words) or in a descriptive manner.

For example, XP principles [15] are mostly concepts (e.g., *Quality work*). Such wording provides little guidance for software developers that want to put these "principles" in practice, possibly leading to confusion, indecision, or contradictory actions. However, we noted that Cohn [24] managed to reword XP principles to provide better guidance. As for Scrum principles, again these are mostly simple concepts, that provide little guidance (e.g., *Multilearning, Subtle control*). Again, it is neither clear to what actions should lead such principles, nor how to verify if these principles have been applied or not in a Scrum-based software development project. On the other hand, DSDM principles appear to better obey the criteria for being software engineering principles.

More generally, if we examine the relationships among the various criteria and the 32 principles we analyzed, we note the following:

- (Prescriptive wording) This criterion led to the rejection of numerous principles. However, quite often, minor rewording allowed to satisfy this criterion.
- (Technology/method independence) All the analyzed statements satisfied this criterion. This characteristic implies, as some have claimed, that many agile *principles* may indeed be appropriate for various software development approaches and methods.
- (Lack of compromise/tradeoff) All analyzed statements satisfied this criterion.
- (Software engineering) This criterion led to the rejection of seven statements. Thus, even though some of these statements may be *general principles*—e.g., "Simplicity [...] is essential"—we cannot consider them to specifically be *software engineering principles*.
- (Verifiable) This criterion led to the rejection of 11 principles. Statements rejected because of this criterion are thus too imprecise to be refutable—e.g., "Continuous attention to technical excellence and good design enhance agility."

The analysis of the various statements proposed in the mainstream software engineering literature as *software engineering principles* [18] showed that most of these statements were not principles, at least not software engineering principles: 313 principles were analyzed and, based on the individual criteria, only 34 of them (11 %) were retained (including some with minor rewording). Interestingly, among the 32 agile principles we analyzed, 19 were retained *as software engineering principles* (59,4 %), even though the proposed agile principles did not intend *a priori* to be *SE principles*—contrary to the 313 principles analyzed by Séguin, that all claimed to be SE principles!

Table 12. Correspondance between the *Guide to the SWEBOK* knowledge areas and the agile principles retained as software engineering principles (AM = Agile Manifesto). The ten knowledge areas are the following: 1.SR=Software Requirements, 2.SD=Software Design, 3.SC=Software Construction, 4.ST=Software Testing, 5.SM=Software Maintenance, 6.SCM=Software Configuration Mangagement, 7.SEM=Software Engineering Management, 8.SEP=Software Engineering Process, 9.SETM=Software Engineering Tools and Methods, 10.SQ=Software Quality.

Principles		Knowledge areas									
		1. SR	2. SD	3. SC	4. ST	5. SM	6. SCM	7. SEM	8. SEP	9. SETM	10. SQ
AM	1	X	X	X				X	X		X
AM	2	X									
AM	3	X	X	X	X			X	X		X
AM	4	X						X	X		
AM	5							X		X	
AM	7							X	X		
AM	8							X			
XP	1	X									
XP	3			X							
XP	5										X
Scrum	3							X	X		
DSDM	1	X									
DSDM	2										
DSDM	3			X					X		
DSDM	5			X				X	X		
DSDM	6						X				
DSDM	7	X									
DSDM	8				X						
DSDM	9	X									

It is interesting to establish a tentative mapping between the Agile principles that were retained as SE principles and the 10 knowledge areas from the *Guide to the SWEBOK*—see Table 12.

None of the principles explicitly touch upon the *Software maintenance* knowledge area, and only one implictly touches upon the *Software configuration management* area (*All changes should be reversible*). This is a bit *ironic* knowing the emphasis put on the latter aspect by the various agile practices: "Agile methods consist of individual elements called *practices*. Practices include using version control, setting code standards, and giving weekly demos to your stakeholders." [30]. It is as though such aspects were so *intrinsic* to agile methods that... expressing them as principles was unnecessary.

More generally, our analysis shows that the Agile movement and methods definitely rest on a set of principles and that most of these principles are, in fact, *software engineering principles*. Although agile methods were—and sometime still are—considered outside of "mainstream software engineering," our analysis shows that such is not the case.

6   Conclusion

Our goal, when we started this work, was to determine whether the *agile principles* proposed in the Agile Manifesto and by some agile methods were *software engineering principles*. To attain this goal, we used the method and criteria described by Séguin [18], who analyzed numerous statements that claimed to be *fundamental principles of software engineering*. Séguin found that few (11 %) of those statements could be considered software engineering principles. Based a similar analysis of agile principles, it turned out that even though the agile principles did not claim to be software engineering principles, most of them (59 %) were!

As future work, it would be interesting to analyze the principles proposed by various other agile methods—including the lesser-known XP principles [15, 31]. With a larger number of statements, the collective criteria proposed by Séguin and Abran [11] could then be applied. This would then help to understand how well the Agile Manifesto principles indeed represent, or not, principles common to many agile methods. The criteria used in our analysis could also serve as general guidance for "methodologists" who intend to develop new methods, agile or not, that rest on a set of well-defined principles.

References

1. Abran, A., Moore, J., Bourque, P., Dupuis, R. (eds.): Guide to the Software Engineering Body of Knowledge (2004 Version). IEEE Computer Society Press (2004)
2. Davis, M.: Will software engineering ever be engineering? Commun. ACM 54, 32–34 (2011)
3. Boehm, B.W.: Seven basic principles of software engineering. Journal of Systems and Software 3(1), 3–24 (1983)
4. Bourque, P., Dupuis, R., Abran, A., Moore, J.W., Tripp, L., Wolff, S.: Fundamental principles of software engineering—A journey. J. Syst. Softw. 62, 59–70 (2002)
5. Davis, A.M.: 201 principles of software development. McGraw-Hill, Inc. (1995)

6. Ghezzi, C., Jazayeri, M., Mandrioli, D.: Fundamentals of Software Engineering, 2nd edn. Prentice Hall (2003)
7. Lehman, M.M.: On understanding laws, evolution, and conservation in the large-program life cycle. Journal of Systems and Software 1, 213–221 (1979-1980)
8. Ross, D., Goodenough, J., Irvine, C.: Software engineering: Process, principles, and goals. Computer 8(5), 17–27 (1975)
9. Royce, W.W.: Managing the development of large software systems: concepts and techniques. In: Proc. 9th Int'l Conf. on Soft. Eng., pp. 328–338 (1987)
10. Wasserman, A.: Toward a discipline of software engineering. IEEE Software 13(6), 23–31 (1996)
11. Séguin, N., Abran, A.: Les principes du génie logiciel: une première analyse. Génie Logiciel (80), 45–51 (2007)
12. Beck, K., et al.: Manifesto for Agile Software Development (February 2001), http://agilemanifesto.org
13. Bagane, H.: Analyse des principes du génie logiciel au niveau du développement agile. Master's thesis, Dép. d'Informatique, UQAM (March 2011)
14. Bagane, H., Tremblay, G., Séguin, N.: Principes de génie logiciel et développement agile : une analyse. Génie Logiciel (98), 43–51 (2011)
15. Beck, K.: Extreme Programming Explained—Embrace Change. Addison-Wesley (1999)
16. Schwaber, K.: Scrum development process. In: ACM Conf. on Obj. Oriented Progr. Syst., Lang., and Applic. (OOPSLA), pp. 117–134 (1995)
17. Stapleton, J.: DSDM: Dynamic Systems Development Method: The Method in Practice. Addison-Wesley Professional (1997)
18. Séguin, N.: Inventaire, analyse et consolidation des principes fondamentaux du génie logiciel. PhD thesis, École de Technologie Supérieure, Montréal, QC (2006)
19. Oxford English Dictionary Online project team: Oxford English Dictionary (November 2011), http://www.oed.com
20. Power, G.: Values, practices & principles, http://www.energizedwork.com/weblog/2006/12/values-practices-principles (Visited on April 2011)
21. Bunge, M.: Philosophical Dictionnary. Prometheus Book, New York (2003)
22. Aubray, C.: Scrum: le guide pratique de la méthode agile la plus populaire. Dunod (2010)
23. ISO/IEC: Information technology—software life cycle processes. Technical Report ISO/IEC Std 12207: 1995, ISO/IEC (1995)
24. Cohn, M.: User Stories Applied—For Agile Software Development. Addison-Wesley Professional (2004)
25. Schwaber, K., Beedle, M.: Agile Software Development with Scrum. Prentice-Hall (2001)
26. Schwaber, K.: Agile Software Development with Scrum. Microsoft Press (2004)
27. Boehm, B., Turner, R.: Balancing Agility and Discipline—A Guide for the Perplexed. Addison-Wesley (2004)
28. Takeuchi, H., Nonaka, I.: The new new product development game. Harvard Business Review (1986)
29. McConnell, S.: Rapid Development: Taming Wild Software Schedules. Microsoft Press (1996)
30. Shore, J., Warden, S.: The art of agile development. O'Reilly Media (2007)
31. Fowler, M.: Principles of XP (October 2003), http://martinfowler.com/bliki/PrinciplesOfXP.html

Agile Software Development Practice Adoption Survey

Narendra Kurapati[1], Venkata Sarath Chandra Manyam[1], and Kai Petersen[1,2]

[1] Blekinge Institute of Technology, 37140 Karlskrona, Sweden
[2] Ericsson AB, Box 518, SE-371 23, Karlskrona, Sweden
{naku10,vemc10}@student.bth.se, kai.petersen@bth.se,
kai.petersen@ericsson.com

Abstract. Agile methodologies are often not used "out of the box" by practitioners, instead they select the practices that fit their needs best. However, little is known which agile practices the practitioners choose. This study investigates agile practice adoption by asking practitioners which practices they are using on project and organizational level. We investigated how commonly used individual agile practices are, combinations of practices and their frequency of usage, as well as the degree of compliance to agile methodologies (Scrum and XP), and as how successful practitioners perceive the adoption. The research method used is survey. The survey has been sent to over 600 respondents, and has been posted on LinkedIn, Yahoo, and Google groups. In total 109 answers have been received. Practitioners can use the knowledge of the commonality of individual practices and combinations of practices as support in focusing future research efforts, and as decision support in selecting agile practices.

Keywords: Software Development, Agile Practices, Adoption, Survey.

1   Introduction

In response to the need of reacting to changes in customer needs quickly agile methodologies have gained considerable importance in the software development industry. A variety of software development methodologies (e.g. Scrum, Extreme Programming (XP, etc.) and their related practices have gained attentions from research, with the majority of empirical research focusing on XP [2]. Overall, many practices are considered as being part of the agile toolbox, different articles identifying 21 [9] up till 32 [12] agile practices.

Given that companies work in different contexts the "out of the box" agile methodologies are often not followed as they are described in the books. Instead, companies select the practices that fit their needs [5,12,11]. As the main focus of past research was on individual case studies [2] there is a research gap with regard to which practices the software industry at large is using. We only identified two surveys of relevance focusing on agile practices [1,10]. The survey by [1] focuses on which methodologies were used, but does not ask for actual usage on

C. Wohlin (Ed.): XP 2012, LNBIP 111, pp. 16–30, 2012.

practice level. Sochova [10] only included a very limited number of agile practices in her survey. Overall, this raises the need for a survey study on agile practice adoption to better understand, which agile practices are actually used in industry.

In response to the above mentioned research gap we conducted a survey to find out which agile practices are used in industry. In particular, the survey aims at answering the following research questions:

- *RQ1:* How commonly used are individual agile practices?
- *RQ2:* Which agile practices are used together by practitioners, and how common are the combinations?
- *RQ3:* To what degree does the software industry comply to Extreme Programming (XP) and Scrum?
- *RQ4:* As how successful do the practitioners perceive the adoption of agile practices in terms of customer satisfaction and employee satisfaction?

The remainder of the paper is structured as follows: Section 2 presents related work. Section 3 describes the research design. Section 4 contains the results of the survey. Section 5 concludes the paper.

2   Related Work

The related work focuses on the identification of agile practices and related methodologies, and population oriented studies that have a specific focus on agile practice adoption.

2.1   Literature on Agile Practices

Dybå et al. [2] conducted a systematic review on empirical research investigating agile software development. They found that the main focus of past research was on XP, while very few studies targeted other methodologies, such as Scrum. With regard to classification of research methods four surveys were identified, none focusing on agile practices used within the methodologies.

Williams [12] conducted a literature review and identified 32 agile and lean software development practices that are related to well known agile methodologies, namely XP, Scrum, feature driven development (FDD), and Lean. Some practices are cross-referenced given that the practices are similar, but have different names in different agile methodologies. She also points out that organizations tend to select practices creating hybrid methodologies.

Shashank and Darse [9] conducted a systematic literature review focusing on the identification of agile practices and how they are adapted, e.g. different ways of how pair programming is done. They identified 21 different practices and their adaptations in form of sub-practices.

Petersen [8] identified 22 agile practices and 4 lean practices. The practices have been mapped to agile and lean principles to highlight the differences and similarities between lean and agile software development.

Jalali and Wohlin [3] identified 25 agile practices used in global software development through a systematic review of literature.

Koch [6] provides a summary of agile methodologies and practices. After presenting the agile principles and practices he links the practices to different software development methodologies.

The studies [12,9,8,3] have been used as input for the construction of the agile survey used in this study. The practice list used in the survey presents a consolidated view of agile practices, where some practices were merged and others split. The linkage of agile practices used in our survey and agile methodologies was based on descriptions in [6,12].

2.2   Agile Surveys

We identified two surveys focusing on the adoption and use of agile practices in industry.

Dogs and Klimmer [1] conducted a survey in 2004 where they received 84 responses. The goal of the survey was to capture which agile methodologies are most frequently used, success with respect to defects and user experience, and the perceived usefulness of different agile practices. The most commonly used methodology was XP (38.6%) followed by FDD (14.55%), RUP (11.9%) and Scrum (7.2%). Furthermore, a number of methodologies with less than 5% of all answers were identified. A ranking of how many responses state that a practice was used successfully showed that more than half of the identified practices received more than half of the total number of responses. However, the study does not look into which practices are actually selected independently of a methodology.

Sochova [10] conducted a survey on agile adoption receiving 181 responses in a three month period in 2009. The survey focused on reasons to start agile, difficulty of using agile practices, and actual usage of agile practices. The focus was on 9 agile practices (stand-up meeting, backlog, burn-down, pair-programming, TDD, estimations in points, planning poker, customer demo, and retrospective). With respect to ease of use Scrum, backlog, and burn-down, retrospective, and customer demo were perceived as the easiest. Pair programming, TDD, and estimation were perceived as hard to learn. With regard to usage the least used practices are planning poker, TDD, pair programming with more than 30 people not using them. Scrum standup (not used by 2) and customer demo (not used by 3) are used by almost all of the respondents. The survey is limited in the sense that it only focuses on very few practices.

Korhonen [7] surveyed three agile teams with regard to their agile adoption in different points in time. The practices considered were daily practices (user stories, product backlog, and short iteration), team practices (refactoring, Scrum, self-organized teams), and programming practices (collective code ownership, pair programming, refactoring, tests written at the same time as code, TDD, and continuous integration). The specific focus was on determining, which practices were used by teams without programming responsibility. Their general findings were that teams with no direct responsibility for programming adopted agile practices related to daily practices and team practices. Only the programming team would in addition to that also adopt programming practices, but at the same time rely on the other two categories of practices as well.

Overall, the related work shows that there are investigations on agile practices, where the practices are mostly investigated through case studies. We found very few surveys, where one (Sochova [10]) was of limited rigor, not discussing e.g. validity threats. This motivates the work presented in this paper, focusing on agile practice adoption in software industry through a survey to get a broader picture of what practices are actually used in the industry. Finding this out is of interest as several researchers recognized that companies tailor their practice selection to their needs [5,12,11].

3   Survey Design

Sampling and Population: The survey was sent out to 600 practitioners that were sampled by diversity (different countries, companies, and domains), and was posted on LinkedIn, Yahoo, and Google groups. The population comprises software industry practitioners who are experienced in agile software development. In total we received 109 valid answers from practitioners.

Survey Structure: The survey consisted of six different parts, namely introduction, demographics, agile practice adoption, agile practice adaptation, employee and customer satisfaction, and contact details. In total the survey comprised of 217 questions.

Part 1: Introduction: The introduction shortly explained the purpose, benefits for the respondents, definition of population (who should fill in the survey), estimated duration of the survey (30 Minutes), and information about the researchers conducting the study.

Part 2: Demographics: This part captured information about the respondent and his/her organization. The practitioners also selected whether they want to answer the survey for a single project or their organization. The reason for doing so was that many roles in software organizations are not necessarily involved in the project work. For example, in market-driven development market analysts package requirements and based on the availability of requirements one or several projects are initiated, i.e. there is a pre-activity before the actual development projects start.

Part 3: Agile Practice Adoption: The respondents got a list of agile practices with a short description of the practice, and selected those that they use. An overview of the practices is given in Table 1. As mentioned earlier, several reviews on agile practices have been conducted [12,9,8,3], these have been used to create a consolidated list of practices for the survey. The mapping of the practices to the two methodologies checked for level of adoption is based on the book by Koch [6] on agile software development (see Appendix E for XP and Appendix H for Scrum) and the analysis of compliance is based on this book.

ID	25 Agile Practices	XP	SCRUM
Of	Office (office structure that supports agile development)	√	
PP	Pair Programming (two people communicate and program on the same computer)	√	
PG	Planning Game/On-site customer (Interaction between customer and developer for effort estimation, scope, and timing of release)	√	
TP	Tracking Progress (tracking of progress of project)		√
40H	40 Hour Week (number of working hours for project per week)	√	
Ref	Refactoring (Restructuring code for better understandability and reduced complexity)	√	
Ret	Retrospective (Discussing good and weaker aspects at the end of the iteration)		
SR	Short/small Releases (Delivering less more often to the customer)	√	
SD	Simple Design (Goal to design the simplest solution)	√	
Sp	Sprint/Iteration (Iterative development considering a sprint/time box)		√
SPM	Sprint Planning Meeting (Meeting to select features for following sprint/iteration)		√
SRM	Sprint Review Meeting (Review meeting to discuss about the work after each sprint/iteration)		√
S-ups	Stand-ups (Short every-day meeting to discuss what was done the last day)		√
St	Stories/Features (Feature/Stories are short statements of the functionality desired by the system user/customer)		√
Team	Team (Work in teams, e.g. co-located, distributed, project manager, SCRUM Master)	√	√
TDD	Test Driven Development (Unit tests developed before coding the software)	√	
Testing	Testing (Continuous testing, unit, integration, acceptance)		
CS	Coding Standards (Coding rules followed by programmer)	√	
CO	Collective Ownership (Anyone can change code, not owned by individuals)	√	
Comm	Communication (Different channels of communication among team members, e.g. face to face, Skype, etc.)		
C&CM	Configuration and Change Management (Enables identification of historical tracking/versioning and change management process)		
CI	Continuous Integration (Regular integration of code)	√	
Doc	Documentation (Importance/emphasis on documentation, e.g. architecture)		
IW	Informative Workshops (Feedback mechanism among agile teams which supports in the daily work)		
Me	Metaphors (Terms used to define the system between customer and developer for reduction of ambiguities)	√	

Fig. 1. Identified Practices and their Mapping to XP and Scrum

Part 4: Agile Practice Adaptation: For each practice selected in Part 3 the practitioners provided answers of how they adapted the practice to their organization by choosing sub-practices.

Part 5: Employee satisfaction and customer satisfaction: This part focused on the outcome achieved when using the agile practices with respect to perceived employee and customer satisfaction. Only a sub-set of the respondents answering Part 1, Part 2, and Part 3 completely answered with respect to customer satisfaction. In our analysis, hence only a sub-set of the answers is reprsented.

Part 6: Contact details: The respondents were free to provide their contact details so that the results of the survey can be made available to them. Furthermore, getting the contact details allowed us to ask further questions with respect to the answers received.

The focus of the study presented here was on agile practice adoption, which makes use of the answers received in Part 2, 3, and 5 of this survey.

Prior to running the survey from October 11, 2011 till November 11, 2012 the survey was reviewed from two researchers (one full professor and one PhD student) and two practitioners, who in informal interviews provided feedback and suggested changes, that were incorporated.

Analysis: The analysis for RQ1 was done using descriptive statistics. As RQ2 is focusing on combinations of agile practices used in industry, we used hierarchical cluster analysis and agglomerative clustering to find similar groups of practices. As a distance measure Euclidean distance was used. RQ3 was also analyzed through descriptive statistics.

Validity Threats: In surveys there is always a risk that questions are misunderstood. In order to reduce the risk we conducted interviews with two practitioners and two researchers who work/do research in agile software development.

Furthermore, the outcome might be biased with respect to similarities of the respondents. However, respondents from different domains, experience levels, etc. answered the survey, even though a limited number of responses was obtained. Hence, this threat is partially reduced. One threat remaining is that respondents represent different roles and project types. Given that a previous study (cf. [7]) showed that depending on the type of project there are different usages of agile practices, there might be a risk that the results are biased towards programming oriented projects, as the majority of respondents were programmers. With regard to the project managers, we also do not know whether they used agile in a programming project.

Evaluation apprehension was avoided by guaranteeing anonymity to the respondents, and not forcing them to provide their contact details if they do not want to.

Hypotheses guessing is a threat, which means that the practitioners might provide answers the researcher wants to hear. However, we only revealed the information that we are seeking to find which practices are used in industry; not, for example, that we intend to check conformance to development methods, which would likely have biased the practitioner to select certain practices.

Given that a web survey was posted in on-line communities, and requests for filling in the survey by e-mail were sent, there was no control for the researchers with respect to external validity (i.e. the general applicability of the results). What can be observed is that few practitioners from military domain have answered the survey, however, for other domains such as information systems, outsourced, commercial, end-user, and embedded several answers have been received.

The survey is long and hence maturation is a threat to validity. Given that we captured not only practice adoption, but also adaptation (how each individual practice is used by them), there is a risk that the practitioners might get bored. Though, in order to get a complete picture of agile practice adaptation there is a need to ask detailed questions of how agile practices are used. This is more a threat for the overall survey, as the questions relevant to this study were asked in Part 3, which was very early in the survey. Hence, for the results presented in this paper the threat of maturation is low.

Only a sub-set of the respondents answered questions with respect to their satisfaction with respect to agile, so they do not represent the full set of respondents based in which we captured agile practice adoption. However, we decided to still present the results as they give some indication of whether the agile practice adoption as presented in this survey was a success.

4   Results

4.1   Survey Demographics

Table 1 shows the results of system type for projects and organizations. When defining the system types we followed the recommendation by Jones [4]. Observe that the total number of responses is higher than 109 as an organization or team can work on different types of systems at the same time (e.g. a commercial end user system). What can be observed is that the majority of the responses come from the information system domain (38%), followed by outsourced (20%) and commercial (19%). All types are accounted for with regard to the total responses. On project level, no answers have been received from the military domain.

Table 1. Number of Responses per System Type

System type	Project	Organization	Responses Total	Percentage Total
Information Systems	16	50	66	38%
Outsourced (developed under contract)	7	28	35	20%
Commercial (marketed to external client, e.g. sold on CD)	8	25	33	19%
End user (private, for personnel use, e.g. banking software)	4	11	15	9%
Embedded	2	12	14	8%
Other	3	4	7	4%
Military	0	4	4	2%
Total	40	134	174	100%

Table 2 shows the distribution of responses by role, showing that all roles are covered in the survey, in particular programmers, project managers, agile coaches, and business analysts are well represented. Furthermore, the respondents are experienced in software development, which is indicated by the average experience.

Table 2. Respondents and Experience

Role	Responses	Percentage	Avg. exp (years)
Programmer	55	24.34	11
Project Manager	52	23.01	10
Agile Coach	29	12.83	4.7
Business Analyst	27	11.95	9.7
System Designer	20	8.85	11.8
System Analyst	18	7.96	8
Quality Assurance	14	6.19	5
Researcher	11	4.87	9.75
Total	226	100.00	

4.2   Commonality of Agile Practice Usage

Here we investigated the commonality of each individual agile practice, as is shown in Figure 2. As a means for structuring the data we define three categories, namely:

- Common: Used by > 2/3 of the respondents (represented by black bars).
- Less common: Used by [1/3;2/3] of the respondents (represented by gray bars).
- Seldom: Used by < 1/3 of the respondents (represented by white bars).

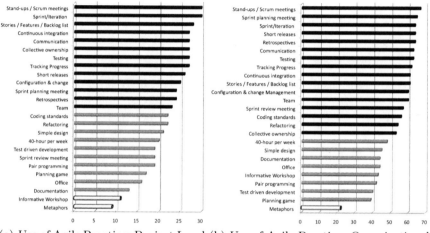
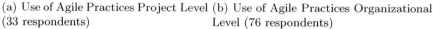

(a) Use of Agile Practices Project Level (33 respondents)

(b) Use of Agile Practices Organizational Level (76 respondents)

Fig. 2. Frequeny of Agile Practice Usage

Project: Common practices are stand-ups, sprint and iteration, stories and features, continuous integration, communication, collective ownership, testing, tracking progress, short releases, configuration and change management, sprint planning meeting, retrospectives, and team.

Less common practices are coding standards, refactoring, simple design, 40-hour week, test-driven development, sprint review meeting, pair programming, planning game, office, and documentation.

Seldom practices are informative workshop and metaphors.

Organization: Common practices are stand-ups, sprint planning meeting, sprint and iteration, short releases, retrospectives, communication, testing, tracking progress, continuous integration, stories and features, configuration and change management, team, sprint review meeting, coding standards, refactoring, and collective ownership.

Less common practices are 40-hour week, simple design, documentation, office, informative workshop, pair programming, test-driven development, and planning game.

Metaphors is a practice applied rarely.

Comparison: Comparing the responses on project and organizational level we can see that the answers show a high level of agreement with respect to how commonly the practices are used. With regard to common practices on organizational level we find sprint review meeting, coding standards, and refactoring, which are less common practices on project level. Otherwise, the common practices are the same. With regard to the less common practices there is also a high agreement, project level having coding standards, refactoring, and sprint review meeting in that category, while organizational level has informative workshop, which is rated less common on project level. Metaphors fall in the seldom category for projects and organizations, while informative workshops are seldom for project level, but not organizational level.

4.3   Combination of Agile Practices

Table 3 shows the results of the hierarchical cluster analysis on project and organizational level for practices. The data is sorted in ascending order for distance. If many respondents choose a similar set of practices they are likely to end up in one cluster. Overall, the table shows which practices are used together on project and organizational level. The following information shown in the table should be highlighted:

- When comparing project and organization, the distance between items on organizational level is larger than on project level. One possible explanation might be that practices on organizational level are more spread as an organization might run projects with varying practices in each project.
- Similarities between project and organization: Test driven development (TDD) and pair programming (PP) are in the same cluster for project and organization, even though the distance is much lower on project level (2.236 on project level in comparison to 4.472 on organizational level). Cluster 7 (Stand-ups, Sprint/iteration, Sprint planning meeting, retrospective) for project is the same as Cluster 3 for organization with similar distance values (3,073 on project level and 3,231 on organizational level) that are both relatively low given that the largest distance is 4.144 and 6.476 for project and organization, respectively. The identity of clusters 3 and 7, while having low distance values at the same time, would indicate that the clusters are distinctive when combining practices.

After identifying similar groups we investigated the frequency of responses that fell into the previously identified clusters, as shown in Table 3. The goal is to identify the most frequently used combination of agile practices.

For structuring the data (Figure 3) we divide the usage of combinations of practices in three categories, namely:

- Common: Used by $> 2/3$ of the respondents.
- Less common: Used by $[1/3;2/3]$ of the respondents.
- Seldom: Used by $<1/3$ of the respondents.

Table 3. Cluster Analysis

	Project				Organization		
Cluster	1st item	2nd item	Distance	Cluster	1st item	2nd item	Distance
1	S-ups	Sp	1.414	1	SPM	Sp	2.236
2	SD	Ref	1.732	2	S-ups	Ret	3.000
3	Testing	St	2.000	3	Cluster 2	Cluster 1	3.231
4	TDD	PP	2.236	4	St	TP	3.317
5	Cluster 1	SPM	2.236	5	CI	Ref	3.317
6	CI	SR	2.449	6	Testing	Team	3.317
7	Cluster 5	Ret	2.641	7	C&CM	Comm	3.317
8	Cluster 3	C&CM	2.646	8	Cluster 6	Cluster 4	3.532
9	Cluster 6	TP	2.828	9	Cluster 8	Cluster 3	3.766
10	CS	40H	2.828	10	Cluster 5	CO	3.803
11	Team	SRM	2.828	11	Cluster 9	SR	4.023
12	Cluster 8	Cluster 2	2.911	12	Cluster 11	Cluster 7	4.040
13	Cluster 4	Of	2.914	13	Cluster 10	CS	4.320
14	Cluster 9	CO	2.940	14	Cluster 12	SRM	4.356
15	IW	PG	3.000	15	TDD	PP	4.472
16	Me	Doc	3.000	16	Cluster 14	Cluster 13	4.516
17	Cluster 14	Cluster 12	3.067	17	Cluster 15	SD	4.996
18	Cluster 11	Cluster 7	3.073	18	IW	Of	5.000
19	Cluster 17	Comm	3.328	19	Cluster 16	40H	5.137
20	Cluster 19	Cluster 10	3.381	20	Cluster 18	Cluster 17	5.334
21	Cluster 20	Cluster 18	3.481	21	Doc	PG	5.385
22	Cluster 21	Cluster 13	3.705	22	Cluster 20	Cluster 19	5.493
23	Cluster 22	Cluster 15	3.837	23	Cluster 22	Cluster 21	5.560
24	Cluster 23	Cluster 16	4.144	24	Cluster 23	Me	6.476

Project: On project level common combinations of practices are represented by clusters 1 (stand-ups, Sprint/iteration), 3 (testing, stories/features), 6 (continuous integration, short releases), and 5 (stand-ups, sprint/iteration, and sprint planning meeting).

Less common combinations are represented by clusters 9 (continuous integration, short releases, tracking progress), 8 (testing, stories/features, change and configuration management), 7 (retrospective, sprint planning meeting, stand-ups, sprint/iteration), 2 (simple design, refactoring), 14 (continuous integration, short releases, tracking progress, collective ownership), 11 (team, sprint review meeting), 10 (coding standards, 40 hour week), 4 (test-driven development, pair programming), 18 (team, sprint review meeting, stand-ups, sprint/iteration, and sprint planning meeting, sprint planning meeting), 12 (testing, stories/features, change and configuration management, simple design, refactoring), and 13 (test-driven development, pair programming, and office).

Seldom combinations of practices, which contain a larger set of practices, are represented by clusters 17, 19, 15, 16, 20, 23, 22, 21, and 24.

Organization: Common practice combinations on organizational level are clusters 1 (sprint planning meeting), 2 (stand-ups, retrospective), 4 (stories and features, tracking progress), 7 (change/configuration management, communication), 6 (testing, team), 3 (stand-ups, retrospective, sprint planning meeting), and 5 (continuous integration, retrospective).

Clusters 8 (testing, team, stories/features, tracking progress), 10 (continuous integration, retrospective, collective ownership), 13 (continuous integration, retrospective, collective ownership, coding standards), 9 (testing, team, stories/features, tracking progress, stand-ups, retrospective, sprint planning meeting), 18 (Informative workshop,office), 15 (test-driven development, pair programming), 12 (testing, team, stories/features, tracking progress, stand-ups, retrospective, sprint planning meeting, short releases, change/configuration management, communication), 11 (testing, team, stories/features, tracking progress, stand-ups, retrospective, sprint planning meeting, short releases), 21 (documentation, planning game), 17 (test-driven development, pair programming, simple design) represent less common practice combinations.

Seldom combinations contain many practices and are represented by clusters 14, 16, 20, 19, 22, 23, 24.

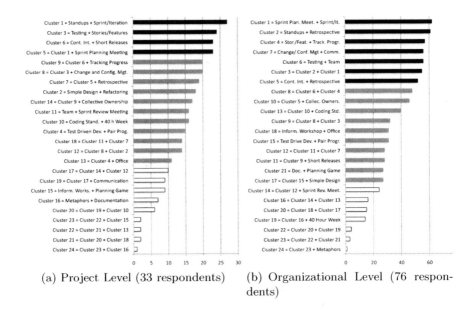

(a) Project Level (33 respondents)   (b) Organizational Level (76 respondents)

Fig. 3. Cluster Analysis for Agile Practice Combination - Frequencies

4.4   Compliance to Agile Development Processes (XP and Scrum)

The compliance is measured as the number of practices adopted belonging to the XP and Scrum methodologies, both containing a different number of practices (see Table 1). The compliance is structured as follows for XP and Scrum:

- Full compliance: All practices are fulfilled, which means 13 practices for XP and 7 practices for Scrum.
- Strong compliance: Most of the practices are fulfilled, which means 8-12 practices for XP and 4-6 practices for Scrum.
- Weak compliance: Few practices in relation to the total number of practices are fulfilled, which means for XP 4-7 practices and for Scrum 2-3 practices.
- No compliance: None or very few practices are fulfilled, meaning 0-3 for XP and 0-1 for Scrum.

Project: Figure 4 shows the compliance to XP and Scrum on project level. It is visible that Scrum has a higher compliance level than XP. For Scrum 33.33% of all respondents are fully compliant, and 45.45% are strongly compliant. Only few projects have weak (12.12%) or no (9.09%) compliance. For XP only 6.06% are fully compliant, while 54.55% are strongly compliant. There are, however, more projects that have weak (24.24%) or no (12.12%) compliance to XP.

Table 4 shows a cross-analysis of the compliance to Scrum and XP. It, for example, shows that one project using Scrum with full compliance is also fully compliant to XP, 10 projects using Scrum with full compliance are strongly compliant with XP, and so forth. The interesting observation here is that around 50 % of all projects are at least strongly compliant to both methodologies. There are few projects that use one of the methodologies and then have a weak compliance to the other (see e.g. strong compliance to XP and weak compliance to Scrum), showing clearly that neither of the methodologies is used in isolation from others.

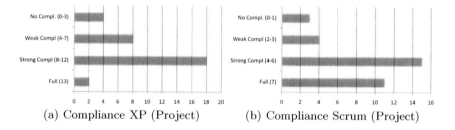

(a) Compliance XP (Project)   (b) Compliance Scrum (Project)

Fig. 4. Compliance to XP and Scrum (Project Level)

Table 4. Compliance on Project Level: Cross-Analysis

		XP			
		Full	Strong	Weak	No
	Full	1 (3.03)	10 (30.30)	1 (3.03)	0
SCRUM	Strong	0	7 (21.21)	7 (21.21)	1 (3.03)
	Weak	0	3 (9.09)	0	1 (3.03)
	No	0	0	0	2 (6.06)

Organization: Figure 5 shows the compliance to XP and Scrum on organizational level. A similar pattern to the one on project level can be observed. That is, organizations are more compliant to Scrum than to XP. For Scrum 50.00% are fully compliant, 39.47% are strongly compliant, 3.95% are weakly compliant, and 6.58% are not compliant. For XP, 5.25% of the organizations are fully compliant, 57.89% are strongly compliant, 27.63 are weakly compliant, and 9.21 are not compliant, showing the lower degree of compliance.

Table 5 shows that over 50% of the organizations are at least strongly compliant to Scrum and XP, which is a similar observation as for the project level. This also applies to the overall pattern that companies do not seem to concentrate solely on one of the development methods.

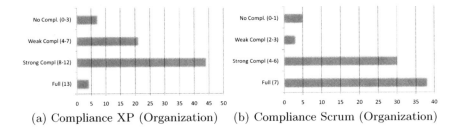

(a) Compliance XP (Organization)   (b) Compliance Scrum (Organization)

Fig. 5. Compliance to XP and Scrum (Organizational Level)

Table 5. Compliance on Organizational Level: Cross-Analysis

		XP			
		Full	Strong	Weak	No
	Full	3 (3.95)	27 (35.53)	7 (9.21)	1 (1.32)
SCRUM	Strong	1 (1.32)	17 (22.37)	10 (13.18)	2 (2.64)
	Weak	0	0	3 (3.95)	0
	No	0	0	1 (1.32)	4 (5.26)

4.5 Success of Adoption

Table 6 shows the responses for six factors with respect to employee satisfaction. Overall, the majority of the respondents perceives the agile adoption as positive, the factor with the highest agreement was related to reduction of stress and workload due to agile practice use.

Table 6. Employee Satisfaction

Employee satisfaction factors	Positive (agree/strongly agree)	Neither agree nor disagree	Disagree Strongly disagree	Do not know	Total
Adaptation of practices helps employee in reaching their goals and eventually the teams goals	61 (92%)	2 (3%)	1 (2%)	2 (3%)	66
The adapted practices increase individual and team morale.	62 (91%)	5 (8%)	0 (0%)	1 (1%)	68
The adapted combination of practices has increased/increases productivity.	58 (89%)	4 (6%)	1 (2%)	2 (3%)	65
Stress and workload on the employee decreases with this adapted set of practices.	45 (68%)	9 (14%)	9 (14%)	3 (4%)	66
The adapted combination of practices increased/increases internal work motivation.	55 (82%)	9 (13%)	2 (3%)	1 (2%)	67
High attendance and increase in productivity has observed with this adapted set of practices.	47 (70%)	15 (22%)	3 (5%)	2 (3%)	67

Table 7. Customer Satisfaction

Customer satisfaction factors	Positive (agree/strongly agree)	Neither agree nor disagree	Disagree Strongly disagree	Do not know	Total
Customers had/has an opportunity to select methodology or practices.	23 (34%)	8 (12%)	32 (48%)	4 (6%)	67
Customer had/has an opportunity to give rapid feedback	60 (90%)	4 (6%)	2 (3%)	1 (2%)	67
Customer has satisfied with the output through frequent deliveries	55 (83%)	8 (12%)	3 (5%)	0 (0%)	66
Customer has constant insight and control over the development process	45 (68%)	9 (14%)	12 (18%)	0 (0%)	66
This adapted combination of practices created positive response form customers	55 (83%)	6 (8%)	4 (7%)	1 (2%)	66

Table 7 shows the results with respect to customer satisfaction. The results show that the aspects that were most positively perceived were related to that the customer could provide rapid feedback, and is satisfied with the output of frequent deliveries, which also resulted in a high percentage of people answering positive with respect to positive responses from customers customers.

5   Conclusion

We conducted a survey of agile practice adoption, which was sent to over 600 practitioners and posted on LinkedIn, Yahoo groups and Google groups. The survey contained questions regarding demographics, agile practice adoption and adaptation, and outcomes of agile practice usage. This study focused on the agile adoption part of the survey. In the following answers to the research questions are presented.

RQ1: How commonly used are individual agile practices? With regard to usage of individual practices we identified three groups of practices based on their commonality for projects and organization (see Section 4.2. for the frequencies).

Knowledge of the commonality of practices has important implications for practice and research. From a practitioner point of view this knowledge provides pointers of which agile practices to consider for their own development organization, given that other practitioners learn and adapt their practice selection accordingly based on their experience.

RQ2: Which agile practices are used together by practitioners, and how common are the combinations? In order to answer RQ2 we conducted a cluster analysis to determine which agile practices are used together, and investigated the frequency of practice usage in each cluster (see Section 4.3.).

It was apparent that the combinations of practices belonging to clusters with low distance (i.e. they are very similar) and that are frequently used are very rational. This adds further to the validity of the survey. For example, on project level clearly stated stories and features support testing, continuous integration facilitates short releases, and sprint/iterations are strongly connected to a sprint planning meeting.

The analysis of the commonality further supports practice selection, as it supports further investigations in research and practice not just which practices to choose based on overall frequency, but how the selection of one practice might depend on one or more other practices.

RQ3: To what degree does the software industry comply to Extreme Programming and Scrum? Overall, we found that Scrum has a higher compliance than XP on project and organizational level, both levels showing very similar patterns (see Section 4.4). The result was that practices from Scrum and XP seem to be used together, i.e. both methodologies are used complementary. From a research perspective this means that it would be interesting to investigate how to integrate agile methodologies in the best possible way. It also means that future research needs to not only focus on single methodologies, given that the majority of past research has an XP focus.

RQ4: As how successful do the practitioners perceive the adoption of agile practices in terms of customer satisfaction and employee satisfaction? Overall, we found that the impact of agile practices was perceived as positive on customer satisfaction and employee satisfaction (see Section 4.5). It is important to highlight that these results have limitations as only a sub-set of the respondents answered this question.

Future Work: In future work the reasons of why certain agile practices and the combination thereof are chosen more frequently has to be investigated in further detail. Furthermore, as the scope of the survey also contained parts on practice adoption and outcome of agile practice usage, we will investigate how each individual practice is adopted by the companies, and with what success.

References

1. Dogs, C., Klimmer, T.: An evaluation of the usage of agile core practices. Master's thesis, Blekinge Institute of Technology, Sweden (2011)
2. Dybå, T., Dingsøyr, T.: Empirical studies of agile software development: A systematic review. Information & Software Technology 50(9-10), 833–859 (2008)
3. Jalali, S., Wohlin, C.: Agile practices in global software engineering - a systematic map. In: Proceedings of the 5th IEEE International Conference on Global Software Engineering (ICGSE 2010), pp. 45–54 (2010)
4. Jones, C.: Software assessments, benchmarks, and best practices. Addison-Wesley, Boston (2000)
5. Kniberg, H., Farhang, R.: Bootstrapping scrum and xp under crisis a story from the trenches. In: Proceedings of Agile Development Conference (AGILE 2008), pp. 436–444 (2008)
6. Koch, A.S.: Agile software development: evaluating the methods for your organization. Artech House, Boston (2005)
7. Korhonen, K.: Adopting Agile Practices in Teams with No Direct Programming Responsibility – A Case Study. In: Caivano, D., Oivo, M., Baldassarre, M.T., Visaggio, G. (eds.) PROFES 2011. LNCS, vol. 6759, pp. 30–43. Springer, Heidelberg (2011)
8. Petersen, K.: Is lean agile and agile lean? a comparison between two software development paradigms. In: Dogru, A.H., Bicer, V. (eds.) Modern Software Engineering Concepts and Practices: Advanced Approaches, pp. 19–46 (2010)
9. Shashank, S.P., Darse, D.H.P.: Finding common denominators for agile practices: A systematic literature review. Master's thesis, Blekinge Institute of Technology, Sweden (2011)
10. Sochova, Z.: Agile adoption survey (2009)
11. Vriens, C.: Certifying for cmm level 2 and iso9001 with xpatsignscrum. In: Proceedings of the Agile Development Conference (ADC 2003), pp. 120–124 (2003)
12. Williams, L.: Agile software development methodologies and practices. Advances in Computers 80, 1–44 (2010)

Applying Agile Development in Mass-Produced Embedded Systems

Ulrik Eklund and Jan Bosch

Chalmers University of Technology
Software Engineering Division, Dept. of Computer Science & Engineering
Göteborg, Sweden
ulrik.eklund@ituniv.se, jan.bosch@chalmers.se

Abstract. The paper presents a method to manage critical interactions to manage when introducing agile software development in mass-produced embedded systems. The method consists of a context model together with a set of measures, and is validated by empirical evidence from three cases.

From an industrial perspective, the paper provides a prescription on how to implement agile software development outside the typical domains for agile, in this case for mass-produced products with embedded software governed by a stage-gate process for mechanics and hardware.

From a research perspective, the paper provides an analysis of the software development cycle for products with embedded software, especially where product development as a whole is driven by a plan-driven process. The main contribution is a method for introducing agile in areas where by necessity the full R&D process cannot be agile.

Keywords: embedded systems, agile software development, case study.

1 Introduction

Agile software development is quite pervasive today in several domains, even if it is still not the norm. Agile methods are a mandatory part of university curricula in software engineering and used in project courses. But agile development has not taken the same hold in embedded systems, even though it promises business benefits also attractive in this domain. The reason is that there are factors that distinguish embedded systems from other domains where agile software development has proven its value.

In this paper, we provide an overview of the problem context and support it both by empirical evidence from three cases at Volvo Car Corporation (VCC) as well as published literature. We then present a method with measures that address found obstacles to introducing agile development in the embedded systems context focusing on successful product ownership. Finally we validate the method through one finished and two on-going cases of agile development in the context above.

The contributions of this paper are twofold: First, from an industrial perspective a set of factors that must be considered if implementing agile software

C. Wohlin (Ed.): XP 2012, LNBIP 111, pp. 31–46, 2012.

development outside the common domain for agile, in this case for mass-produced products with embedded software governed by a stage-gate process for the hardware. In addition, the paper prescribes a set of measures that must be considered by an original equipment manufacturer (OEM).

Second, from a research perspective the paper provides an analysis of the software development cycle for products with embedded software, especially where product development as a whole is driven by a plan-driven process. The main contribution is a method for introducing agile development in domains where by necessity the full R&D process cannot be agile, including (1) some subcontractors not working agile, (2) interface with hardware and mechanics and (3) certification processes. The method provides guidance how to manage the interface between agile and non-agile parts of R&D. In addition, the paper provides a rich insight into the challenges for development of automotive software through a number of cases.

2   Context and Problem Statement

Several studies report on successful implementation of agile methods in new development of software systems with strong user interaction, e.g. web-based shops[1,2]. However there are several domains where agile software development practices is not nearly as pervasive, such as mass-produced embedded systems[3]. Examples of products in this domain are cars and trucks, micro-wave ovens and other home utensils, sewing machines, printers and copying machines.

The relevance of the context and the research question is validated through three case studies at VCC as well as cases found in published literature. In addition to these cases there are also three validation cases, also from VCC, making a total of six cases providing empirical evidence.

2.1   Case 1: Introduction of Distributed Software Architecture

Case description: VCC as OEM introduced a distributed software architecture for the first time, in late 1998. This was in contrast to the previous generation of cars where each feature was realised by a single micro-controller with very limited interaction between the features.

Found issues: The distributed architecture allowed more integrated functionality between components that previously were stand-alone from a functional viewpoint. Most of the electronic and software design of the micro-controllers were outsourced to a number of suppliers responsible for both hardware and software co-design. Function decomposition was deployed between the outsourced micro-controllers and definition of interfaces between them had to be done by the Electric and Electronics Systems Engineering (EESE) department of VCC. Since user features were realised by cooperating software from different teams, the development process required synchronisation of all developed software.

Goal of the case study: Identifying factors influencing three key designs of the software architecture: In-vehicle network topology, software variability mechanisms, and split of responsibility among development teams for requisitions elicitation and system definition.

Research problem relevance: The case confirms the research question by giving an example of greenfield software development. Factors that were critical to manage for the project were e.g. distributed functionality affecting integration and validation of the complete product, interaction between development teams both technically & planning-wise according to stage gates, technical standards to simplify integration, and subcontracting software development according to fixed schedules & fixed requirements specifications.

2.2 Case 2: Architecture Maintenance Process

Case description: Managing architectural changes in a controlled way at VCC when releasing new or updated products.

Found issues: Over time the development process in the previous case had some unintended side effects; design documents became very large, were difficult to comprehend and were difficult to maintain. It was difficult to find design contradictions in the system because of high coupling and low cohesion that led to increased integration efforts for verification and validation. While it was still quite easy to add new functionality it was becoming successively hard to change existing software. The architects seemed to be mostly evaluating various design proposals from development teams (suppliers when software and hardware development is outsourced, which was quite common). An issue in the change management process was to achieve informed consent from all concerned stakeholders.

Goal of the case study: Identifying the actual architecture change process(es), how well it worked and what artefacts/information was used.

Research problem relevance: The case gives some examples of critical factors needed to manage for software development in this context, e.g. overview of the implemented functionality, integration & validation between different subsystems, and change management.

2.3 Case 3: Development Project of an Infotainment System

Case description: VCC decided to deliver a new generation of infotainment systems to extend its competitive position. The development organisation had to deal with several prerequisites which had a major effect on the project: The systems were to be sold by more than one brand within Ford Motor Company and developed components were to be shared between brands (both hardware and software) while maintaining a brand-specific HMI. This was to leverage sourcing with other (unrelated) components from new suppliers. All software was also to be outsourced while in the previous system generation the software for the main micro-controller was developed in-house at VCC. There was also a desire to minimise the requirements elicitation effort in terms of spent man-hours.

Found issues: Initially the focus was on component development, i.e. on each micro-controller with its deployed software. The software specifications for each micro-controller were also reused from the previous generation to minimise the effort in writing new specifications. Some of the complex customer features were distributed between two micro-controllers, which led to a complicated interface shared between two software suppliers. The project progress was initially measured in implemented customer features that meant that delivery of platform software necessary for integration and testing was initially de-emphasized.

The setup of the teams changed in the middle of the project, from being focused on component development to being focused on feature development with cross-functional teams. It was difficult to plan and manage the integration occasions necessary for validation and verification since there was no overall view of feature realisation and development at both VCC and the involved suppliers was based on incorrect assumptions about the architecture. The project also started midway with shorter sprints with a limited set of features verified after each sprint rather than planning against large integration occasions. These changes probably were key contributions in keeping the launch date.

Goal of the case study: A post mortem analysis to identify the major factors influencing the architecture and the causal relationships between them and the used process. Management at the concerned department at VCC ordered the study to learn from this case and avoid similar issues in future R&D efforts.

Research problem relevance: The case serves as an example where initial approach was typical for waterfall development, but could have benefited from agile practices, e.g. requirements were not fully known from the beginning, integration & validation was no sufficiently planned, the architecture was complex and the feature content constantly changed during development.

2.4   Research Problem

Based on cases 1-3 we define the domain of mass-produced embedded systems by four characteristics:

- Deep integration between hardware and software for significant parts of the functionality
- Strong focus on manufacturing aspects of the product in the development (e.g. by project gates)
- Strong supplier involvement
- Some parts realise safety-critical functionality

The research problem is "What are the critical interactions for a team doing agile software development within a plan-driven project in this context, and how can these interactions be facilitated?"

3   Research Methodology

The research followed a process of Context and problem identification → Model and method development → Method validation. Both the problem identification and the validation were done through six qualitative case studies.

All cases were captured in a qualitative manner and analysed with an interpretative approach[4]. The studies took advantage of the fact that the first author was native[5] to VCC, and acted as a participant/observer. The main data sources in case 1, 2 and 3 were interviews, either recorded and transcribed or with notes taken during the interview.

The selection of interviewees in all cases was made as a purposive sample[6] to ensure in cases 1 and 3 that all key developer roles were represented. In case 2 more than half of the architects at VCC participated in the interview study. An overview of used data sources and the author role in each case is seen in Table 1.

Table 1. Case data and author involvement

Case	Data sources	Author role
1	Interviews with 20 developers + design documents	Insider observer
2	Interviews with 6 architects + design documents + personal notes	Participant / insider observer
3	Interviews with 6 key developers + design documents	Insider observer
4	All project & design documents of both product owner and Scrum team + personal notes	Participant / insider observer
5	Official meeting notes and presentations + personal notes	Insider observer
6	Official meeting notes and presentations + personal notes	Participant / insider observer

The main data source in case 4 was the complete project and design documentation contained in two project sites, augmented by the personal notes of the first author, who was a stakeholder at the product owner side. In case 5 and 6 the data consists of process documentation, meeting notes and presentations at VCC as well as the first author's personal notes as a change agent.

The analysis of the data sources in cases 1-3 focused on identifying the context of software development in mass-produced embedded systems. The analysis in cases 4-6 focused on identifying a set of measures facilitating agile development in this context and a model describing the types of interaction between agile teams and the rest of the R&D organisation. The context model and the measures of the method were derived largely following the theory described by Mintzberg[7].

4   Method for Introducing Agile Software Development in Mass-Produced Embedded Systems

A typical development process for mass-produced embedded systems is to follow a traditional stage-gate process, where the gates are driven by decisions and investment in the manufacturing of the product, i.e. driven by the hardware.

Gate progression corresponds to software artefacts, e.g. user requirements, system requirements, software architecture, component requirements, and software implementation, i.e. a waterfall process even if the artefacts are updated as the project progresses. Software requirements are the result from systems engineering work and are usually structured according to the hardware partitions if the system consists of several micro-controllers. It is quite common to outsource part of the software development to subcontractors, especially in the automotive domain, where most software is today subcontracted with a fixed price connected to one product line or sold together with a specific hardware solution.

There are several different development methods that can be described as agile, two of the most commonly used being XP[8] and Scrum[9]. Common for all agile methods are that they share a set of values[10]. We distinguish agile development from plan-driven or waterfall development through these values and a set of practices which are method agnostic:

– Software is iteratively developed in time-boxed periods of 2-6 weeks
– The result after each iteration is running software
– The content to be implemented, and therefore the final product content, is continuously decided in each iteration.

In order to accomplish agile development, a set of measures needs to be in place, regardless of context and domain. Examples of domain-independent measures include a product backlog, development team co-location and product owner involvement[11]. In the remainder of this section, we present context-specific measures required for mass-produced embedded systems.

The method for introducing agile software development consist of a model, seen in Figure 1, defining interactions necessary for agile teams together with a

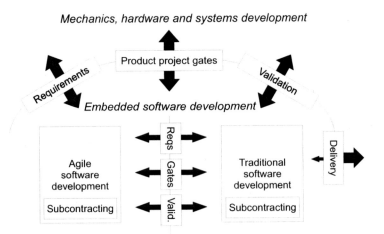

Fig. 1. The context of software development of mass-produces systems and the interactions between software development teams in general and agile teams in particular, to the rest of the organisation

set measures facilitating agile development in a context where the full product cannot be agile. The interactions between the development of embedded software and the entire product development can be classified as one of four categories; requirements, project gates, integration & validation, and delivery. The interactions between software teams doing agile development and those doing traditional development falls within the first three categories.

Based on the model a set of measures are prescribed, summarised in Table 2. Each measure is either a prerequisite for agile development, e.g. must be defined in the pre-game phase of Scrum, or an activity while doing the iterations, e.g. in the game phase of Scrum. Each measure targets a specific interaction relevant to the teams introducing agile development:

1. Interface to the rest of the organisation outside software development
2. Internal activity to the teams adopting agile development
3. Interface to the teams doing traditional software development.

Table 2. The measures of the four categories prescribed model

Phase	Category	Relationship	Measure to implement
Prerequisites	Requirements	Interface to the rest of the organisation	P1: Dedicated product owner
	Project gates	Interface to the rest of the organisation	P2: Clear structure and goal of the process improvement
		Interface to the rest of the organisation	P3: Involve the OEM project manager
		Interface to the rest of the organisation	P4: Connect agile roles to the rest of the organisation with an acceptable governance structure
	Validation	Internal activity	P5: Align pulse between OEM and subcontractor
	Internal	Internal activity	P6: An established platform used by the development team
		Internal activity	P7: Resource necessary agile roles
		Internal activity	P8: 1-to-1 mapping between OEM and subcontractor's development teams
Activity	Requirements	Interface to the rest of the organisation	A1: Gradual growth of requirements
		Interface to the rest of the organisation	A2: Interact with existing tools
		Internal activity	A3: Quality attributes and architecture in the product backlog
	Project gates	Interface to the rest of the organisation	A4: Project reports
	Validation	Interface to traditional teams	A5: Product technology standards
		Interface to the rest of the organisation	A6: Fulfil quality assessments
		Interface to the rest of the organisation	A7: Meet product integration test schedule
		Interface to traditional teams	A8: Definition of system anatomy
		Interface to traditional teams	A9: Interface definitions towards other sub-systems
	Internal	Internal activity	A10: Focus on enthusiasts
		Internal activity	A11: Implement refactoring as continuous activity

4.1   Requirements

This category encompasses how the software requirements implemented by the agile team relate to the requirements of the finished product, they typically contain both functional requirements experienced by the end-user, but also quality attributes, such as testability. The model also includes the methods and tools for capturing and transferring requirements in this category.

The measures prescribed to handle requirements, besides the common practices prescribed by the chosen agile approach, in the context of mass-produced embedded systems are:

Prerequisite 1: A positive product owner who is responsible for prioritising requirements, in a large project can be done by many different stakeholders resulting in unclear directions. This addresses the context of manufacturing focus in the product project and supports the agile value of Individuals and Interactions over Processes and Tools[10].

Activity 1: Gaining acceptance for gradual growth and polishing of requirements instead of waterfall development of artefacts. This also addresses the manufacturing focus and supports Responding to Change over Following a Plan.

Activity 2: Interact with the common project tools used beyond the agile development project teams. This also addresses the manufacturing focus.

Activity 3: Include quality attributes and architectural solutions in the product backlog if they are not resolved in the pre-game/planning phase. This menas that the architects must interact with the teams during the entire project instead of defining an architecture description as a development prerequisite.

4.2   Product Project Gates

This category focuses on the interface between the software development team and the full product project. This includes the static organisation of the project including governance and reporting, as well as basic principles for driving and measuring progress. The measures prescribed to agile team to operate within a plan-driven project context are:

Prerequisite 2: Clear structure and goal of the process improvement to establish consensus about the process improvement and empower the change agents. This addresses the manufacturing focus and supports the agile value of Responding to Change.

Prerequisite 3: Involvement of the project manager at the OEM at e.g. sprint demos to experience first hand the growth of implemented software. This supports the agile value of Individuals and Interactions.

Prerequisite 4: Connect the practices and roles of the agile method (e.g. Scrum) to existing roles and functions at the rest of the organisation with a governance structure acceptable to the line and project organisation, e.g. clarify where what type of decisions are taken by whom. This addresses the manufacturing focus and supports Individuals and Interactions.

Activity 4: Include the product project's demands for artefacts, milestones and gates in the work products from the agile software development teams. This addresses the manufacturing focus of the product project.

4.3 Validation

This category is concerned with the interface between agile software development and the validation of the product as a whole. The category includes activities necessary to integrate the various software and hardware parts to a whole, how this whole is verified against the requirements and the validation of the full product. The measures prescribed to agile team to successfully integrate with the full product and support validation are:

Prerequisite 5: Align OEM pulse and subcontractor's sprint intervals if development is outsourced to maintain development flow. This addresses the context of supplier involvement and supports the agile value of Customer Collaboration.

Activity 5: Verify and validate adherence to technical standards required by the product architecture platform, such as communication protocols, logging, power management and similar services. This addresses software and hardware integration and supports Working Software.

Activity 6: Fulfilment of required quality assessment of software, e.g. automotive SPICE[12]. This addresses the context of safety-critical functionality and supports Working Software.

Activity 7: Generate deliverables in time to scheduled product testing, e.g. HIL testing and integration testing on the complete product. This addresses the manufacturing focus and supports Working Software.

Activity 8: Define and update a system anatomy [13] to understand technical dependencies between what is implemented in each sprint. This addresses software and hardware integration and supports Working Software.

Activity 9: Define interfaces towards other sub-systems to alleviate the necessity of synchronised development of individual backlog items. This addresses the manufacturing focus and supports Working Software.

4.4 Software Delivery

This is category describes the principles for how the finished software is delivered to the end-user. In mass-produced embedded systems the software and the hardware is delivered as a single product and this is the only possibility if the software is stored in ROM. But other principles, such as continuous delivery or software updates, are conceivable and increasingly considered in the embedded systems industry. As the delivery of software is not changed, despite the adoption of agile software development internal to the organization, there are no specific measures to adopt. It is beyond the scope of this paper to fully explore the possibilities of post-deployment updates of software, but is left to be explored in future work.

4.5   Internal Activities

These are the measures that have no direct relationship to other software development teams or the rest of the organisation, and are thus up to the agile teams. However, in our experience, these are important for successful implementation of agile development in the context of mass-produced embedded systems.

Prerequisite 6: Guarantee the availability of an established platform used by the development team, including a software platform, development infrastructure and an integration environment. This addresses the context of software and hardware integration and supports the agile value of Working Software.

Prerequisite 7: Resource necessary roles to facilitate the development team(s), e.g. Scrum master, Product owner and Scrum coaches as well as roles required by mechanics, hardware and systems development, such as integration leader. This supports the agile value of Individuals and Interactions.

Prerequisite 8: Establish a direct, e.g. 1-to-1, mapping between OEM feature definition and integration testing teams and the subcontractor's development teams if programming is outsourced. This addresses the context of supplier involvement supports the agile value of Individuals and Interactions.

Activity 10: Introduce agile development only where the organisation is enthusiastic and make use of any previous experiences as product owners and developers. This supports the agile value of Individuals and Interactions.

Activity 11: Implement frequent refactoring and "clean-as-you-go" as an activity, even though it does not provide direct customer value. This addresses the manufacturing focus and supports the value of Working Software. In plan-driven projects these activities are either defined up-front or commonly "hidden" as feature development in sourcing agreements.

5   Method Validation

The method for introducing agile software development in mass-produced embedded systems was used in three projects where agile software development was used at VCC. Case 4 has concluded, while case 5 and 6 is still going on at the time this paper was written.

5.1   Case 4: Agile Development of an Infotainment Sub-system

Case description: Development project of a prototype to establish a proof-of-concept for some radically different development strategies compared to case 3 for a similar system, an infotainment system based on an open platform, Android. The project was executed in an industrial setting, but the resulting system was not intended to go into mass production and be sold to customers.

The primary goal of the project was to establish whether it was possible to do feature development with extremely short lead-times from decision to implementation compared to present industrial projects, e.g. case 3 above, from a nominal lead-time of 1-3 years to 4-12 weeks. The finished system was required to be open to 3rd party feature development, i.e. development not sourced or ordered by VCC, and as such form the basis for a software ecosystem around Volvo infotainment systems.

Agile context: The short lead-times were accomplished by a small development team using Scrum from EIS by Semcon[1], which had a supplier relationship to VCC as product owner. Working software was continuously validated in "real" environments, i.e. the infotainment system was installed in both a driving simulator and real test cars and users evaluated the system during the project.

All project information was centrally managed with Trac[2] with full access for both the team and the stakeholders supporting the product owner. The two sites stored the product backlog, design documentation, progress reports, sprint backlogs and burndown charts. The openness of the system was enabled by an open architecture based on Android with separation of feature development from platform and hardware development, this also enabled the ability of open innovation of features.

Goal of the case study: The goal of the case study was to evaluate alternative, i.e. agile, ways of working compared to "common practice" in the business domain.

Method relevance: The project was not connected to the release of new car models and therefore had no demands of gate reports or a large governance structure. Instead the governance was provided of a team of developers at VCC supporting the appointed product owner. The members of this team had mostly more than ten years of automotive experience, and met in bi-weekly half-day meetings. One major difference for the Scrum team compared to an industrial vehicle project was the smaller effort spent on testing and quality assessments, which partly explains the significant decrease in lead-time. The project used prerequisites 1, 2 and 4-8, and activities 1, 2, and 9-11 of the method.

5.2   Case 5: Climate Control Software

Case description: The studied project develops climate control software in-house at VCC, where it was previously outsourced.

Agile context: The development team applies most of Scrum practices since this is a natural evolution of present team practices. The product owner resides at the interior department, in cooperation with one person from product planning at VCC. The development team of nine persons and the Scrum master are part of the EESE department with extensive domain expertise of climate control. Most of the algorithms are developed in Simulink from which C code is generated.

---

[1] A local consultancy firm with thorough automotive software experience.
[2] http://trac.edgewall.org/

The software will run on a hardware platform with basic software delivered by the HVAC[3] hardware supplier. Both the control software and the standardised basic software are based on the AUTOSAR software architecture[14] and the interfaces to other systems, including HMI, are stable.

Goal of the case study: The study was performed as validation of the model in Section 4 and to provide feedback to software process improvements at VCC.

Method relevance: It was to difficult to find a willing person to act as a product owner towards the programming team, one can speculate if this is because the team was perceived as having better domain expertise than a prospective product owner from another department. There was little controversy in redefining existing requirements into a format suitable for a backlog. These requirements will also be stored in the engineering database at VCC when considered stable.

The governance structure was simple with few different concerned stakeholders, but still more complex than case 4. The team adjusted their sprint schedule to suit integration events of the complete electrical system. A set of project report templates was developed to fulfil the needs of the project management with the intention of report them after each sprint. An agile coach was involved the first months to get the team up to speed as quickly as possible. The project uses most of the measures prescribed by the method, i.e. prerequisites 1, 2, 4, 6, and 7 and activities 1-7 and 9-11.

5.3   Case 6: Next Generation Infotainment System

Case description: Development of next generation infotainment system at VCC, to be included in future car models. The system scope is similar to case 3 above, but with a major increase in feature content, especially for connected services.

Agile context: The concerned department at the OEM has already taken some steps towards agile methods compared to case 3: Software requirements are defined on a feature level rather than on a design or implementation level. Cross-functional development teams organised around features are responsible for defining, integrating and validating features in the vehicle. Development is made in 6 week increments with shorter turn-around time compared to the gate timing of the overall car project.

Goal of the case study: The study was performed as validation of the model in Section 4 and to provide feedback to software process improvements at VCC.

Method relevance: The product owner role is held by a duo, one from the department of product planning at VCC, the other from the EESE department.

---

[3] HVAC = Heating, Ventilating, and Air Conditioning.

In contrast to case 5, the governance structure guiding sprint planning is very complex but has a change control board as final focal point. We believe this is caused by the infotainment system realises much of the HMI and connectivity services, which means there are numerous concerned stakeholders interested in brand competitiveness. It is implied that the product owner will decide if red tape in the board risk postponing a sprint. The project report template is still not universally accepted by all stakeholders.

The agreement with the subcontractor was on iterations of six weeks. The ten feature teams have been organised to match the subcontractor's teams, but the sprints have not started at the time of writing. The initial sprint planning and goals were aligned with the test vehicle builds.

A system anatomy was defined by a group of key developers at VCC and will continuously be updated together with the subcontractor. The interfaces to other subsystems were identified with the help of the architecture group at the EESE department. The project used all Prerequisites and Activities prescribed by the method.

5.4   Method Use in the Three Cases

The method was developed to fulfil a practical need to systematically identify and implement necessary measures for successful agile development since no comparable method was found in published literature. The issues addressed in cases 4-6 are not of how a development team adapts to agile software development, but how such a team operates in a context of a much larger project developing a product with embedded software. To facilitate this, the method defines 19 measures concerning interaction addition to the practices prescribed by an agile method such as XP or Scrum.

Case 4, 5 and 6 were executed in roughly that chronological order, so it was natural to apply the measures of prescriptions in increments. The measures used in case 4 focused on how an OEM can act as a product owner towards a subcontractor using Scrum. Case 5 develops software in-house of the OEM and therefore some of the measures are not relevant. Using Scrum in this case was neither controversial nor perilous and fitted well with the overall strategy of insourcing software. Case 6 wants to improved ways of working compared to the experiences from case 3. The measures used are there both to support the subcontractor using iterative development and to achieve a more lucid management of project compared to case 3.

In all cases the proposed measures addressed real concerns voiced by various stakeholder at VCC. In case 4 and 5 the measures seems to satisfy the stakeholders, while in case 6 there is still discussions suggesting that some stakeholders are still not comfortable with an agile approach to software development.

6   Related Work

The context described in Section 2.4 is supported by literature, for example Ebert & Jones[15] mentions factors contributing to the complexity in their survey of the present state of embedded software development: "combined software/hardware systems equipped with distributed software, computers, sensors, and actuators" which directly corresponds to the integration aspect. Ronkainen & Abrahamsson[16] emphasise that embedded systems are characterised by the concurrent co-design of hardware and software, same as seen in Section 2.4. Manhart & Schneider[17] describes agile development of software in buses at Daimler-Chrysler. They mention for example that "equipment, functions, or parameter sets are implemented by integrating different proportions of third party- and OEM manufactured components" indicating the supplier involvement.

The method above addresses issues also found in literature. Boehm & Turner[18] describes challenges of introducing agile software development in organisations using traditional or plan-driven software development. They identify three areas of conflicts when trying to introduce agile development in traditional organisations; "development process conflicts, business process conflicts, and people conflicts". Of these the method in Section 4 focuses on the first and the last and provides measures to handle those conflicts. Kruchten[19] explores the context of agile development, providing an analysis framework, but has no explicit prescription on how to introduce agile development outside what he calls "the agile sweet-spot". Turk et al.[20] identifies a set of six limitations with agile development. Four of them are addressed by the method described in this paper; subcontracting, building reusable artefacts, development involving large teams and development of large complex software.

The method above provides guidance on how to implement agile development on the team level where the organisation at large cannot adopt agile practices while Lanti[21] describes how to scale agile practices, specifically program management and product backlog administration, in large organisations with several development teams contributing to the final product. Savolainen et al.[22] list three requirement engineering practices required when implementing agile development of embedded systems; highly skilled people especially in requirements engineering, understanding the type of the system, and preserving existing key practices when making the transformation. The method here complements their work by also including measures beyond requirements.

7 Summary

The method presented in the paper was developed as an answer to "What are the critical interactions for a team doing agile software development within a plan-driven project in the context of mass-produced embedded systems, and how can these interactions be facilitated?" This context is defined by four characteristics; deep integration between hardware and software, strong focus on manufacturing aspects (e.g. by process gates), strong supplier involvement, and some parts realise safety-critical functionality.

The method consists of a context model describing four categories of interaction between the development of embedded software and the entire produce development together with a set of measures facilitating these interactions when agile development is introduced in a team. The identified interaction categories are requirements, project gates, integration & validation and delivery.

The prescribed set of measures in the method are of two kinds, the first being prerequisites for successful implementation of agile software development in organisations where by necessity the full R&D process cannot be agile. The second being a set of activities necessary for the teams doing agile development to both successfully interact with the non-agile parts of the organisation and internal activities to the teams. The research problem was found both in empirical evidence from three cases at VCC as well as in published literature. The method was also validated through one finished and two on-going cases of agile development in the context above.

The contributions of this paper are twofold: From an industrial perspective it provides a set of measures on how to implement agile software development outside the common domain for agile, in this case for mass-produced products with embedded software governed by a stage-gate process for the hardware. From a research perspective the paper provides a method with a context model for introducing agile in domains where the product as a whole is driven by a plan-driven process. Finally the paper provided a rich insight into the challenges for automotive software development through a number of cases.

Acknowledgements. This work has been financially supported by the Swedish Agency for Innovation Systems (VINNOVA) and Volvo Car Corporation within the partnership for Strategic Vehicle Research and Innovation (FFI).

The authors would like to thank developers at Volvo Cars and EIS by Semcon for participating in valuable discussions.

References

1. Goodman, D., Elbaz, M.: "It's not the pants, it's the people in the pants" learnings from the gap agile transformation - what worked, how we did it, and what still puzzles us. In: Proceedings of the Agile Conference, pp. 112–115. IEEE (2008)
2. Chung, M., Drummond, B.: Agile at Yahoo! from the trenches. In: Proceedings of the Agile Conference, pp. 113–118. IEEE (2009)
3. Salo, O., Abrahamsson, P.: Agile methods in european embedded software development organisations: A survey on the actual use and usefulness of extreme programming and scrum. IET Software 2(1), 58–64 (2008)
4. Walsham, G.: Interpretive case studies in IS research: nature and method. European Journal of Information Systems 4, 74–81 (1995)
5. Brannick, T., Coghlan, D.: In defense of being "Native", the case for insider academic research. Organizational Research Methods 10(1), 59–74 (2007)
6. Robson, C.: Real World Research: A Resource for Social Scientists and Practitioner-Researchers, 2nd edn. Blackwell (2002)
7. Mintzberg, H.: Developing theory about the development of theory. In: Great Minds in Management: The Process of Theory Development. Oxford Handbook of Management Theory, pp. 355–372. Oxford University Press (2005)

8. Beck, K.: Extreme Programming: A Humanistic Discipline of Software Development. In: Astesiano, E. (ed.) ETAPS/FASE 1998. LNCS, vol. 1382, pp. 1–6. Springer, Heidelberg (1998)
9. Schwaber, K.: Scrum development process. In: Proceedings of the ACM Conference on Object Oriented Programming Systems, Languages, and Applications, pp. 117–134 (1995)
10. Beck, K., Beedle, M., van Bennekum, A., Cockburn, A., Cunningham, W., Fowler, M., Grenning, J., Highsmith, J., Hunt, A., Jeffries, R., Kern, J., Marick, B., Martin, R.C., Mellor, S., Schwaber, K., Sutherland, J., Thomas, D.: Manifesto for agile software development (2001)
11. Kniberg, H.: Scrum and XP from the Trenches. Lulu.com (2007)
12. McCaffery, F., Pikkarainen, M., Richardson, I.: Ahaa –agile, hybrid assessment method for automotive, safety critical smes. In: Proceedings of the International Conference on Software Engineering, pp. 551–560. IEEE (2008)
13. Taxén, L. (ed.): The system anatomy - Enabling agile project management, 1st edn. Studentlitteratur (2011)
14. Fürst, S., Mössinger, J., Bunzel, S., Weber, T., Kirschke-Biller, F., Heitkämper, P., Kinkelin, G., Nishikawa, K., Lange, K.: AUTOSAR - a worldwide standard is on the road. In: International VDI Congress Electronic Systems for Vehicles, Baden-Baden, Germany (2009)
15. Ebert, C., Jones, C.: Embedded software: Facts, figures, and future. Computer 42(4), 42–52 (2009)
16. Ronkainen, J., Abrahamsson, P.: Software Development Under Stringent Hardware Constraints: Do Agile Methods Have A Chance? In: Marchesi, M., Succi, G. (eds.) XP 2003. LNCS, vol. 2675, pp. 73–79. Springer, Heidelberg (2003)
17. Manhart, P., Schneider, K.: Breaking the ice for agile development of embedded software: An industry experience report. In: Proceedings of International Conference on Software Engineering, pp. 378–386. IEEE, Washington, DC (2004)
18. Boehm, B., Turner, R.: Management challenges to implementing agile processes in traditional development organizations. IEEE Software 22(5), 30–39 (2005)
19. Kruchten, P.: Contextualizing agile software development. Journal of Software Maintenance and Evolution: Research and Practice (2011)
20. Turk, D., France, R., Rumpe, B.: Limitations of agile software processes. Systems Engineering 43, 43–46 (2002)
21. Laanti, M.: Implementing program model with agile principles in a large software development organization. In: Proceedings of the International Conference on Computer Software and Applications, pp. 1383–1391. IEEE, Turku (2008)
22. Savolainen, J., Kuusela, J., Vilavaara, A.: Transition to agile development - rediscovery of important requirements engineering practices. In: Proceedings of the Requirements Engineering Conference, pp. 289–294. IEEE (2010)

Understanding Team Dynamics
in Distributed Agile Software Development

Siva Dorairaj, James Noble, and Petra Malik

School of Engineering and Computer Science,
Victoria University of Wellington,
Wellington, New Zealand
{siva.dorairaj,james.noble,petra.malik}@ecs.vuw.ac.nz

Abstract. Team dynamics are patterns of interaction among team members that determine the performance of the team. Success of Agile software development depends on team interaction. Team interactions are, however, affected in distributed teams. Through a Grounded Theory study that involved 40 Agile practitioners from 24 different software companies in the USA, India, and Australia, we investigate the key concerns of distributed Agile teams. We found Agile teams depend significantly on team interaction, and adopt six strategies that promote effective team interaction in distributed software development.

Keywords: Team Dynamics, Team Interaction, Agile Methods, Grounded Theory, Distributed Teams.

1 Introduction

Team dynamics are patterns of interaction among team members that determine the performance of a software development team [1]. Several studies assert that team dynamics are important characteristics of high performance teams [2,3]. Effective team interaction provides avenues for team members to state ideas and opinions without barriers, listen actively to understand the concerns of other team members, and provide timely suggestions to the problems faced by the team [4,5]. Success of Agile software development depends significantly on team interaction [6,7,8].

Agile teams in distributed software development interact over time and space through technology-mediated communication such as telephone and e-mail [2,9]. Non-verbal communication such as facial expression and hand gestures that are often missing in technology-mediated communication, decreases the awareness of team member actions [2]. Team interactions are affected in distributed Agile teams [2,3,10]. This raises a critical question: *How do Agile teams promote team interaction in distributed software development?* Through a Grounded Theory study that involved 40 Agile practitioners from 24 different software companies in the USA, India, and Australia, we found six strategies that promote effective team interaction in distributed Agile teams: *'one team' mindset, personal touch, open communication, team collocation, team ambassadors,* and *coach travels.*

C. Wohlin (Ed.): XP 2012, LNBIP 111, pp. 47–61, 2012.

2   Research Method

2.1   Grounded Theory

Grounded Theory (GT) is a systematic research method that emphasises the generation of theory derived from systematic and rigorous analysis of data. GT was originally developed by Barney G. Glaser and Anslem L. Strauss [11]. We chose GT as our research method for two main reasons. Firstly, GT is suitable to be used in areas that are under-explored or where a new perspective might be beneficial, and the literature on distributed Agile software development, particularly on team dynamics in distributed teams, is still scarce [6,12]. Secondly, GT allows researchers to study social interactions and the behaviour of people in the context of solving problems, and Agile methods focus on people and their interactions in software development teams [13]. Notably, GT is increasingly being used successfully to study the social nature of Agile teams [14,15,16]. Using Glaser's guidelines, we commenced our research with a general area of interest (i.e distributed Agile software development) because beginning a GT study with specific research questions can lead to preconceived ideas or hypotheses of the research phenomenon [17,18]. Glaser [17,19] asserts that problem and its key concerns will emerge in the initial stages of data analysis – and it did.

2.2   Data Collection

Data collection in GT is guided through *theoretical sampling* whereby researchers iteratively collect and analyze their data, and decide what data to collect next and where to find the data [18,20]. A GT study requires the theoretical sampling to be continued until *theoretical saturation* [11] is reached – that is when no more new concepts or categories emerge from the data, and further data collection would be a waste of time.

We collected data through interviewing Agile practitioners. We started out data collection in the USA where several Agile practitioners had agreed to participate in our study. We conducted face-to-face, one-on-one, semi-structured interviews with our participants. We prepared a set of questions for the initial interviews to develop a smooth discussion with the participants. The interview questions focused on the challenges that teams face in distributed Agile projects, and the strategies adopted to overcome them. The interviews lasted for at least an hour, and were conducted at a mutually agreed location. Interviews were voice-recorded with consent from the participants. Voice recording the interviews helped us to concentrate on the conversation and understand participant's main concerns in distributed Agile projects. The ongoing interview and analysis guided the evolution of interview questions and choice of future participants. Over the past two years, the primary researcher has travelled twice to the USA, three times to India and once to Australia, for the purpose of interviewing participants for this study until the theoretical saturation has been reached.

Table 1. Participant and Project Details. (Agile Position: Scrum Master (SM), Agile Coach (AC), Developer (DEV), Business Analyst (BA), Quality Analyst (QA), Senior Management (MGT)).

Participant (code)	Agile Role	Project Distribution	Agile Method	Team Size	Project Duration (months)	Sprint (weeks)
P1	DEV	USA-India	Scrum	8 to 10	10	2
P2	AC	USA-India	Scrum & XP	12 to 14	12	2
P3	SM	USA-Western Europe-India	Scrum	10	8	3
P4	AC	USA-China	Scrum & XP	10	8	2
P5	AC	USA-India	Scrum & XP	8	12	2 to 3
P6	DEV	USA-UK	Scrum & XP	20 to 22	8	2
P7	AC	USA-Argentina-India	Scrum & XP	18	6	2
P8	DEV	USA-Australia-India	Scrum & XP	9 to 10	8	2
P9	DEV	Western Europe-Brazil	Scrum & Lean	14	24	2 to 3
P10	SM	USA-Argentina-India	Scrum	10 to 12	8	3
P11	SM	USA-Middle East-India	Scrum & XP	13	10	2
P12	DEV	USA-India	Scrum & XP	12	18	2
P13	SM	USA-India	Scrum & XP	17 to 20	5	2
P14	DEV	USA-India	Scrum & XP	16 to 17	36	2
P15	QA	USA-India	Scrum & XP	16	18	2
P16	SM	USA-India	Scrum & XP	16	18	2
P17	DEV	USA-India	Scrum & XP	16	18	2
P18	BA	UK-India	Scrum & XP	8	12	2
P19	DEV	USA-India	Scrum	8 to 10	10	3
P20	MGT	Australia-India	Scrum & XP	9 to 12	12	2 to 3
P21	SM	USA-Australia	Scrum	15	9	2
P22	SM	Australia-India	Scrum & XP	9 to 12	12	2 to 3
P23	QA	Japan-India-China	Scrum	7 to 8	4	2
P24	AC	Western Europe-India	Scrum & XP	9	5	2
P25	SM	USA-India	Scrum & XP	24	6	3
P26	AC	USA-India	Scrum & XP	16	(3) ongoing	3
P27	SM	USA-Brazil	Scrum & XP	30	6	2
P28	MGT	USA-India	Scrum	20	18	3
P29	SM	USA-India	Scrum & XP	14	10	2
P30	AC	Western Europe-India	Scrum & XP	8 to 10	(5) ongoing	2 to 3
P31	AC	UK-India	Scrum & XP	15 to 20	(7) ongoing	3
P32	MGT	UK-South Africa	Scrum & XP	12	18	2
P33	AC	Australia-Eastern Europe-India	Scrum & XP	50	24	3
P34	AC	USA-India	Scrum & XP	6 to 8	10	2
P35	AC	USA-India	Scrum & XP	8	18	3
P36	QA	Canada-India	Scrum & XP	10 to 15	18	2
P37	DEV	Western Europe-India	Scrum & XP	16	4	2
P38	BA	USA-India	Scrum & XP	28	(2) ongoing	2
P39	AC	USA-India	Scrum & XP	22 to 25	6 to 7	2
P40	DEV	Australia-India	Scrum & XP	7	6	1

2.3   Participant and Project Details

We interviewed 40 Agile practitioners from 24 different software organisations in the USA, India, and Australia. Participants adopted Agile methods, primarily Scrum and XP, in their distributed software development projects. We interviewed participants from a range of different roles within the distributed Agile projects: Scrum Masters, Agile Coaches, Developers, Quality Analysts, Business Analysts, and Senior Management (e.g. Vice President, Human Resource Manager, Director of Technology).

Table 1 shows participant and project details. Projects were distributed between 2 or 3 countries, iteration varied from 2 to 5 weeks, and project duration varied from 6 to 24 months though some projects were still ongoing when we interviewed the participants. Projects often started with a small team size of 6 to 12 members, but some teams had scaled through up to 50 members to accomodate the increasing complexity of their projects. Due to privacy and ethical consideration, we will only identify our participants using the codes P1 to P40.

2.4   Data Analysis

We transcribed the interviews, and used *open coding* to analyse the interview transcripts [18]. Open coding breaks down, examines, compares, conceptualises, and categorises the data [20]. We assigned a *code* or a summary phrase to each key point. Using GT's *constant comparison method* [21], we constantly compared each code with the codes from the same interview, and those from other interviews. The codes that are related to a common theme were grouped together to produce a second level of abstraction called a *concept*.

As we continuously compared codes, many fresh concepts emerged. These concepts were themselves analysed using constant comparison method to produce a third level of abstraction called a *category*. Several categories emerged from analysis of the interviews: *trust, communication, cultural differences* and *team interaction*. We wrote-up memos on the ideas about the codes, concepts and categories, and their inter-relationships with one another. We sorted the collection of the theoretical memos and used them to understand the research phenomenon. We intend to generate a *substantive theory* that explicates the research phenomenon using an emergent *theoretical code* [20]. Since the codes, concepts, and category emerge directly from the data, our findings are grounded within the context of the data. We have presented several findings in different papers [22,23,24]. In this paper we describe how distributed Agile teams build team interaction. Figure 1 shows the concepts *'One Team' Mindset, Personal Touch, Open Communication, Team Collocation, Team Ambassadors,* and *Coach Travels* that gave rise to the category *Building Team Interaction*.

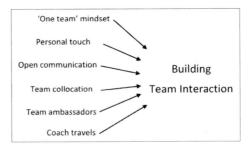

Fig. 1. Emergence of category *Building Team Interaction* from concepts

3   Results

In this section we present the strategies that promote team interaction in distributed Agile teams: the category *Building Team Interaction* and its underlying concepts. We have selected quotations from our interviews to illustrate the emergent concepts.

3.1   'One Team' Mindset

In Agile software development, team members need to interact frequently with the entire team during meetings, pair-programming, or discussions throughout the project:

> *"Working on a Agile project requires team members to work collaboratively with other people, talking and interacting whether it's in meetings, pairing, [or] talking to people one on one. The social interaction is so important."* —P20, Management Team.

Crucially, all team members from every location participate in a 'daily stand-up meetings' using technology-mediated communication. Teams prefer video conferencing over telephone conferencing during daily meetings to increase interaction among the team members:

> *"Daily stand-up meetings are mandatory for all team members. We often do Skype video calls. We feel that if we see team members face-to-face, we'll have better interaction with them."* —P36, Quality Analyst.

Teams understand that the daily standup meetings are important to the entire team, and therefore joint standup meetings are scheduled so that members from all locations are able to participate in the meeting:

> *"When we have a daily standup meeting, we talk about what everyone was doing, we get to know about who is doing what, what are the issues, what happened at the end of our day, and what we need to do for today. We definitely have a joint standup meeting [though] over different time zones, it can be difficult. "* —P11, Scrum Master.

When the team members are separated across several time zones, the daily stand-up meetings with the entire team causes difficulties for team members. Often, team members from one location have to stay back till late at night, while team members from another location have to come in to work very early in the morning:

> *"We have some people, with abnormal working hours, who come after lunch and work till late night."* —P4, Agile Coach.

Despite the difficulties interacting with one another, distributed teams try to keep a 'one team' mindset to foster their interaction:

> "*We are working as a team in Agile. The team knows that they are not separated just because they are in another building, or another location with some time zone difference. It's only one team.* " —P24, Agile Coach.

In this 'one team' mindset, project team members and customer understand that they all belong to one single team despite working from different locations:

> "*We have absolutely one team [but] we are working in different locations. And, the client is definitely part of the team.*" —P16, Scrum Master.

This 'one team' mindset is the fundamental factor that fosters effective interaction between team members and improve team performance:

> "*We have a one whole team mindset. The team is distributed but it is one whole team. Everyone works as one team, and there is one team performance.*" —P7, Agile Coach.

Participants P1, P3, P7, P16, P18, P20-P29, P32, P33, and P35-P38 explicitly discussed the 'one team' mindset where the members of the distributed team strive to interact and perform as one team.

3.2   Personal Touch

Distributed team members often have difficulties getting to know each other, or even just to 'put a face to the name':

> "*We were working together with Sebastian but we didn't know who is Sebastian. We have not even seen [his] face. It is hard to get the feeling of teamness when you don't know whom you are working with.*" —P9, Developer.

Teams are encouraged to keep photographs of all the members on a wall to get a 'team presence' that helps the members to recognise one another:

> "*It's very important to take pictures of [team member] and put them up on a card wall so that these people actually exists and become real in teams.*" —P2, Agile Coach.

Teams also create online repositories or Wikis, where the photographs of the entire team and description of each member, are shared with the team. The Wiki gives a personal touch to the team members, and fosters more meaningful interaction:

> "*We have a "team place" or Wiki where we upload the photographs of the team members, and share some moments of [our] personal life which will help us move forward in our professional interaction.*" —P24, Agile Coach.

Some teams allocate a short duration of time before daily meetings for team members to talk about personal matters, or to have some fun conversation:

> "*We need to have some personal time with other team members. We have 15 minutes before the daily meeting to speak freely to each other in the team.* " —P24, Agile Coach.

Teams exhibit strong dynamics when members are interacting without barriers. This kind of frequent interaction promotes team building:

> "*... the first 15 minutes [of daily meetings] was open time, and we could talk about anything we want. And, that's when we started seeing a very strong team building.*" —P1, Developer.

Knowing members personally promotes better understanding in the team where team members from all the locations are better able to understand the difficulties faced by other members:

> "*Team members understand and value the other team member's life, had the rapport with all team members, [and] team members [were] well jelled with each other.*"—P24, Agile Coach.

Teams need to participate in daily standup and retrospective meetings. The understanding established between team members allows them to 'share the pain' when working across different time zones:

> "*We start rotating the standup meeting [that is] for one month it is going to be at night [in India], and the next month it will be in the morning.*" —P18, Business Analyst.

The interaction of the team improves significantly when team members know each other. The team should have seen all the members of the team, talked to them, and possibly worked with them in close proximity to develop strong team dynamics.

3.3 Open Communication

Participants encourage open communication in distributed teams — team members keep direct and honest communication within project team, and also with customers and management:

> "*Communication needs to be kept as open as possible, and there should not be any hierarchy so that [team members] can communicate directly with customers and management.*" —P29, Scrum Master.

Open communication improves team interaction, and encourages team members to be involved in decision making for the project:

> "*The project team believed in communicating very openly and transparently. So, all decisions were made in consultation with the entire project team.*" —P38, Scrum Master.

Participants realised that frequent open communication fosters good understanding between project team and management:

> "*The more we have open conversations, [the] better we understand the management, [and] then we are able to suggest better alternatives to them.*" —P17, Developer.

As a result of a good understanding between project team and management, participants were able to communicate directly with the management to make a request for the team:

> "*[When] I had to negotiate with the management, it was not a challenging thing [because] management well understood us. So it became easier for them to give [the request].*" —P34, Agile Coach.

Some team members, however, face difficulties in engaging courageously in open communication with other members from different locations and the customers. Western participants described that their Indian counterparts unrealisticly agree to every request from the customers because it is typically not in the Indian culture to say 'No' to elders in a family, or superiors in an organisation:

> "*The Indians don't say 'No' to anything. That's one of the major problems faced by all the western customers. This is because of the culture [that] you should always obey the seniors.*" —P33, Agile Coach.

In order to address this concern, some teams engage in coaching to grow courage for team members to speak up, and improve interaction in the team:

> "*Here in India, trying to grow the courage for people to speak out and ask for what they need and be honest about what they can sustain, is something that I'm coaching a lot.*" —P31, Agile Coach.

Participants recognise that Agile methods value courage and open communication. Team members should be honest and transparent in all the levels of interactions, especially with customers:

> "*Most of the time, the members [in India] have a tendency to follow [requests] from the onsite members, but the onsite members are often more interested to know what other options are available. Agile taught them courage in speaking openly with the clients [sic].*" —P24, Agile Coach.

Teams members should understand that courage is the foundation of open and honest communication — both within the project team, and with customers and management — and should strive to grow courage to facilitate communication.

3.4   Team Collocation

Agile methods prefer collocated teams to allow frequent interaction between the team members. While a distributed development team is not (by definition) collocated, many projects choose to collocate all the team members at the beginning of a project:

> "At the beginning of the [distributed] project, it's important for the entire team and the customer to be collocated for the [first] few weeks of the project. That's really important." —P20, Management Team.

Some teams collocate at the customer location for the first iteration to allow frequent interaction between the project team and customer:

> "The idea was to start all together as a whole team here [at customer location] for the first iteration in order to have direct interaction with customer." —P7, Agile Coach.

Collocating for the first iteration, or for a couple of weeks, helps the team to establish trust and build team relationships. When the members are sent back to their distributed locations, the trust and team relationships that have been developed during the collocation help them to interact effectively:

> "I would collocate a team for the first few weeks of the project [until] the team is able to build trust, build relationships, [and] build shared understanding. It is much easier to have conversations with team members on the phone if you've met them previously in person." —P22, Scrum Master.

There are some teams that rotate the location for team collocation between the customer location, and project team locations for a specified time duration:

> "We prefer to collocate. The first set of collocation involved the delivery team [from India]. Then the second time is the team from the USA, the customers and all the stakeholders came down here [to India] and worked from the same location for a month." —P18, Business Analyst.

Team collocation develops strong team relationships that increase team performance when team members get distributed in different locations:

> "When we started, we moved everyone to client site, [and] worked collocated. When we moved back to [our] site, there was a very natural bonding between the entire team, and we were doing an excellent job." —P35, Agile Coach.

Teams that are not able to collocate all the members for the first iteration would at the least send the senior members to initiate team interaction between members in all the locations:

"Some of the senior members in the team go there [to other location] just to have a feel about the team members there." —P24, Agile Coach.

When team members travel to different locations, some team members were willing to spend personal time to get to know others and build strong team relationships:

"Apart from work, we spend a lot of good time with them. Some were keen to see our village life [in India] and come to our home." —P26, Agile Coach.

Some teams organise team building activities to accommodate the team members whom travel from other location. Team building activities encourage team members to interact comfortably, motivate them to develop good teamwork, and inspire them to work effectively as an Agile team.

"If other team members from onsite [are] coming here, we plan our team building activities so that we do that activities in that part of the month so that we can create a rapport with the onsite team." —P24, Agile Coach.

Realising the benefits of team collocation, some teams go so far as to move to the client's location for the entirety of short projects:

"We may not do the work offshore for the projects running for a smaller duration. We do it at the onsite [customer location] itself. We finish up the project from the client's site, and then come back [to our location]." —P36, Quality Analyst.

Overall, participants found that team collocation, even for a short duration, facilitates team interaction that develops good teamwork and establishes trust across the whole team, supporting the 'one team' mindset that is crucial in a distributed Agile development project.

3.5   Team Ambassadors

Rather than collocating the whole team, individual team members can travel to the other team locations, to interact closely with the team members there. These team members, referred to as 'team ambassadors', travel solely to foster interpersonal relationships within the team. Team Ambassadors do not act as a managers or liasions between separate teams — the 'one team' mindset helps ensure team coordination and decision making is shared across the whole distributed team, primarily via the daily distributed meetings.

Participants describe that the main responsibility of the team ambassadors are to understand the team members in the location to which they have been sent:

"We wanted mainly to understand the team. When I went there, I started observing people and their way of interacting with each other. We started understanding each other, and started to work as a team." —P33, Agile Coach.

While working in the other location, the team ambassadors develop good relationships with the members there, promoting the dynamics of the entire team:

> "*When you send people over, you work with them, you go out with them, drink with them. In that way, you build this friendship, [and] you understand the people that you work with. So the interaction improves a lot.*" —P12, Developer.

Some teams rotate team ambassadors between the offshore and onsite locations:

> "*Developers will rotate with developers, and rotations happens between Business Analysts also. We have people from here rotating for some duration. And, this [rotation] promotes team dynamics here.*" —P16, Scrum Master.

and this rotation provides opportunities for more team members to act as ambassadors:

> "*We rotate [team ambassadors] to facilitate more conversations [with team] and be able to understand them better.*" —P37, Developer.

Participants P1, P3, P11-P20, P24, P27, P33, P36-P38 understand the importance of team ambassadors for distributed teams. The team ambassadors promote interaction, create rapport within the 'one team', helping members to work effectively together, even though they are distributed.

3.6   Coach Travels

The role of an Agile Coach, though self-descriptive, is to help a team or individual adopt and improve Agile methods and practices. A coach helps team members reflect and improve the activities involved in software development, and often withdraws from the team when the time is right and let the team continue:

> "*I coach the team who are adopting Agile. Often I guide others to deal with the situation at hand, but I want them to be in-charge of their own situation, and be independant of the coach.*" —P2, Agile Coach.

Coaches typically emphasize the importance of working together as 'one team', cultivating team spirit, and engaging team members to improve the team dynamics:

> "*[After] we had the coaching activities, we were successfully able to form the teams, and I could see good team dynamics happening. That [coaching] brought in a lot of changes within the team.*" —P33, Agile Coach.

Agile coaches travel around all the team's locations to meet all the team members and establish good relationships with them. The personal interaction and the bonding with team members allows the coach to engage in coaching activities even from remote locations:

"It is very difficult to coach someone [whom] you don't have any personal connection [with]. So, I think that going to other country and meeting the team members helps me to keep on coaching daily from here. You need to keep a team relationship and travel as much as possible if you are coaching." —P7, Agile Coach.

Coaches improve interaction amongst team members and develop team understanding in different locations:

"We had a coach from onsite who came here [to India] for several weeks. That coaching improved the interaction with remote team because the coach helped them to understand the working style of the remote team members. We prefer that the coach from remote location visits our team frequently." —P28, Management Team.

Coaches travelling allows them to appreciate the wider environment at each location. This allows the coach to have more informed conversations with customers or the rest of the team:

"I have met more people in India, and I actually know more about what India is like. And knowing that gives me better empathy and sympathy for the team that work under [difficult] conditions. " —P22, Agile Coach.

Coaching activities can also foster effective interaction between project team and support groups in the organisation:

"... make sure that interaction between development team and the support groups enable cross-communication. So, if something goes wrong, there are different groups within the same organisation to support [the team]." —P34, Agile Coach.

Participants P1, P2, P7, P22, P24, P28, P31-P35 and P39 acknowledge that mentoring or coaching provided by Agile Coaches increased team interaction within the project team, and with other groups in the organisation. Coaches need to travel to all the distributed locations so that personal connections can be maintained between coach and team members.

4   Discussion

Distributed teams should maintain as far as possible a single team identity across all locations to promote interaction and encourage cooperation amongst team members [25]. Loss of 'teamness' could pull distributed projects apart as it is often difficult to integrate separate independent teams into a coherent team. We found that the 'one team' mindset is the fundamental strategy that brings together the team members across different locations and encourages cooperation between the team and the customer.

Distributed team members often leverage technology-mediated communication for team interaction. Non-verbal communication such as body language, hand gestures, facial expressions, and eye-contacts that forms 93% of communication are, however, missing in technology-mediated communication [26]. Fiore et al. [2] asserts that team interaction in distributed teams affects teamwork and team performances. Team building and establishing trust are difficult when team members do not work together in close proximity.

While most teams used video-conferencing, collocation, or team ambassadors to bind teams together, we found that some team members (P6, P8, P9, P25) have not even seen the faces of all members in the team. This is mainly because some team members did not get to travel to different locations to meet other members, and the technology-mediated communication between members in different locations were limited to phone calls or emails, but not video-conferencing. We found that teams need to create 'team presence' to allow the natural bonding between members in different locations. Practices such as keeping photographs of all the members on a wall, or maintaining Wikis with the photographs and description of the members create 'team presence' and build team ties.

Layman et al. [9] describe that a key member of the distributed Agile team who is physically located with the other team can provide an essential two-way communication conduit. This key member acted as a communication bridgehead between team members from different locations, and played the advocate for both groups on a daily basis. Braithwaite and Joyce [25] describe that local representatives travel from one location to another for an extended period to understand the members in that location, and share business domain knowledge between locations. We found that team ambassadors travel from one location to another, and work in close proximity with team members for a period of time. Unlike Layman et al., and Braithwaite and Joyce, these team ambassadors do not act as communication conduits but rather the teams members communicate directly with each other, using video, audio, messaging, and email to contact remote team members, both in the daily stand-up meetings, and whenever other interactions are required. The ambadassors carry out their own development tasks, and strive to develop good team relationships and to promote direct interaction between local and remote team members.

5   Limitations

The inherent limitation of a Grounded Theory (GT) study is that the results are grounded in the specific contexts explored in the research. These contexts were dictated by the availability of the participants, and by our choice of research destinations. We do not claim that our results are universally generalisable to all distributed Agile software development projects, but rather our results accurately characterize the contexts studied.

6   Conclusion

We investigated distributed software development from the specific perspective of Agile practitioners through a Grounded Theory study that involved 40 participants from 24 software companies in the USA, India, and Australia. We found distributed teams adopt six strategies to promote effective team interaction: *'one team' mindset, personal touch, open communication, team collocation, team ambassadors,* and *coach travels.* The teams that we studied were found practicing at least one of these strategies to promote team interaction between members in different locations. Some teams proactively adopted these strategies to work efficiently in distributed Agile projects, and some teams adopted them as solution strategies when problems around team interaction arise. We are mindful that there can be other strategies to promote team interaction that can be useful and effective in their own contexts, but did not emerge from our analysis. Future studies can compare and contrast team dynamics for distributed teams against team dynamics for collocated Agile teams.

Acknowledgments. Thanks to the Agile practitioners who participated in this study. Thanks to Dr. Rashina Hoda, Dr. Angela Martin and several anonymous reviewers. This study is supported by UNITEN (Malaysia) Ph.D. scholarship.

References

1. Castka, P., Bamber, C., Sharp, J., Belohoubek, P.: Factors affecting successful implementation of high performance teams. Team Performance Management 7, 123–134 (2001)
2. Fiore, S.M.: Distributed coordination space: Toward a theory of distributed team process and performance. Theoretical Issues in Ergonomics Science 4, 340–364 (2003)
3. Espinosa, J.A., Slaughter, S.A., Kraut, R.E., Herbsleb, J.D.: Familiarity, complexity, and team performance in geographically distributed software development. Organization Science 18, 613–630 (2007)
4. Johnson, D.W., Johnson, F.P.: Joining Together: Group Theory and Group Skills, 4th edn. Prentice-Hall, Englewood Cliffs (1991)
5. Katzenbach, J.R., Smith, D.K.: The Wisdom of Teams: Creating the High-performance Organization. Harvard Business School Press, Boston (1993)
6. Korkala, M., Abrahamsson, P.: Communication in distributed Agile development: A case study. In: 33rd EUROMICRO Conference on Software Engineering and Advanced Applications, pp. 203–210 (2007)
7. Korkala, M., Pikkarainen, M., Conboy, K.: Distributed Agile Development: A Case Study of Customer Communication Challenges. In: Abrahamsson, P., Marchesi, M., Maurer, F. (eds.) XP 2009. LNBIP, vol. 31, pp. 161–167. Springer, Heidelberg (2009)
8. Prikladnicki, R., Audy, J.L.N., Damian, D., de Oliveira, T.C.: Distributed software development: Practices and challenges in different business strategies of offshoring and onshoring. In: International Conference on Global Software Engineering, pp. 262–274 (2007)

9. Layman, L., Williams, L., Damian, D., Bures, H.: Essential communication practices for Extreme Programming in a global software development team. Information and Software Technology 48, 781–794 (2006); Special Issue Section: Distributed Software Development

10. Moe, N.B., Dingsoyr, T., Dyba, T.: A teamwork model for understanding an Agile team: A case study of a Scrum project. Information and Software Technology 52, 480–491 (2010)

11. Glaser, B.G., Strauss, A.L.: The Discovery of Grounded Theory: Strategies for Qualitative Research. Sociology Press, Aldine (1967)

12. Paasivaara, M., Lassenius, C.: Could global software development benefit from Agile methods? In: IEEE International Conference on Global Software Engineering, pp. 109–113. IEEE Computer Society, Washington, DC (2006)

13. Schwaber, K., Beedle, M.: Agile Software Development with Scrum. Prentice Hall PTR, Upper Saddle River (2001)

14. Hoda, R., Noble, J., Marshall, S.: Organizing self-organizing teams. In: Proceedings of the 32nd ACM/IEEE International Conference on Software Engineering, New York, USA, pp. 285–294 (2010)

15. Whitworth, E., Biddle, R.: The social nature of Agile teams. In: Proceedings of the AGILE, pp. 26–36. IEEE Computer Society, Washington, DC (2007)

16. Martin, A., Biddle, R., Noble, J.: The XP customer team: A grounded theory. In: Proceedings of the AGILE Conference, pp. 57–64 (2009)

17. Glaser, B.: Doing Grounded Theory: Issues and Discussions. Sociology Press, Mill Valley (1998)

18. Urquhart, C., Lehmann, H., Myers, M.D.: Putting the 'theory' back into grounded theory: guidelines for grounded theory studies in information systems. Information Systems Journal 20, 357–381 (2010)

19. Glaser, B.: Basics of Grounded Theory Analysis: Emergence vs Forcing. Sociology Press, Mill Valley (1992)

20. Glaser, B.: Theoritical Sensitivity: Advances in Methodology of Grounded Theory. Sociology Press, Mill Valley (1978)

21. Glaser, B.G.: The constant comparative method of qualitative analysis. Social Problems 12, 436–445 (1965)

22. Dorairaj, S., Noble, J., Malik, P.: Understanding the Importance of Trust in Distributed Agile Projects: A Practical Perspective. In: Sillitti, A., Martin, A., Wang, X., Whitworth, E. (eds.) XP 2010. LNBIP, vol. 48, pp. 172–177. Springer, Heidelberg (2010)

23. Dorairaj, S., Noble, J., Malik, P.: Bridging cultural differences: A grounded theory perspective. In: Proceedings of the 4th India Software Engineering Conference, ISEC 2011, pp. 3–10. ACM, New York (2011)

24. Dorairaj, S., Noble, J., Malik, P.: Effective Communication in Distributed Agile Software Development Teams. In: Sillitti, A., Hazzan, O., Bache, E., Albaladejo, X. (eds.) XP 2011. LNBIP, vol. 77, pp. 102–116. Springer, Heidelberg (2011)

25. Braithwaite, K., Joyce, T.: XP Expanded: Distributed Extreme Programming. In: Baumeister, H., Marchesi, M., Holcombe, M. (eds.) XP 2005. LNCS, vol. 3556, pp. 180–188. Springer, Heidelberg (2005)

26. Bianchi-berthouze, N., Kleinsmith, A.: A categorical approach to affective gesture recognition. Connection Science 15, 259–269 (2003)

Information Flow within a Dispersed Agile Team: A Distributed Cognition Perspective

Helen Sharp[1], Rosalba Giuffrida[2], and Grigori Melnik[3]

[1] The Open University, Walton Hall, Milton Keynes, MK7 6AA, UK
[2] IT University of Copenhagen, Denmark
[3] Microsoft Patterns & Practices, USA
h.c.sharp@open.ac.uk, rogi@itu.dk, grigori.melnik@microsoft.com

Abstract. One of the hallmarks of a co-located agile team is the simple and open flow of information between its members. In a co-located setting, peripheral awareness, osmotic communication and simple information radiators support agile principles such as collective ownership, minimal documentation and simple design, and facilitate smooth collaboration. However in a dispersed agile team, where individual team members are distributed across several sites, these mechanisms are not available and information sharing has to be more explicit. Research into distributed software development has been tackling similar issues, but little work has been reported into dispersed agile teams. This paper reports on a field study of one successful partially dispersed agile team. Using a distributed cognition analysis which focuses on information propagation and transformation within the team we investigate how the team collaborates and compare our findings with those from co-located teams.

Keywords: Dispersed agile development, distributed cognition, qualitative study.

1   Introduction

Global Software Development (GSD) is increasingly becoming normal practice in the software industry [1]. Organizations establish global software projects distributed all over the world, involving multiple teams located at different sites. It is claimed that GSD has advantages but it is also challenging because teams have to deal with temporal, geographical and socio-cultural distance, resulting in difficulties with division of work, inadequate communication, knowledge management, project and process management issues and infrastructure problems [2]. Several strategies have been suggested to overcome these challenges including reduced intensive collaboration [3], reduced temporal distance [3], increased formal documentation [2] and organizational factors such as processes, structure and goal alignment [4]. In contrast, agile methods depend on close collaborations, frequent informal face-to-face communication rather than lengthy documentation, and self-organising teams.

Despite these apparent differences, interest has been shown in assessing the viability of agile in GSD. Some studies suggest that agile practices mitigate GSD

C. Wohlin (Ed.): XP 2012, LNBIP 111, pp. 62–76, 2012.

challenges, whilst others believe they emphasize the challenges [5, 6], yet others suggest that agile practices need to be modified for success.

Holmström et al. [7] specifically explored how agile practices can reduce three kinds of "distance" – temporal, geographical, and socio-cultural. They found specific agile practices to be useful for reducing communication, coordination, and control problems. Layman [8] suggests that methodologies dependent on informal communication can be used on GSD projects, despite geographic, technical, temporal and linguistic hurdles: an email listserv, globally-available project management tool, and an intermediary development manager who played a strong role in both groups.

Challenges of distributed agile build on those of GSD in general, and include lack of close proximity, lack of team cohesion, lack of shared context and knowledge and unavailability of team members [9]. Communication related issues are the major challenges when using distributed agile [5]. Several researchers claim that extending or modifying agile practices is necessary in GSD. Lee at al [10] reported that conventional agile methods must embrace more rigour and discipline in a distributed setting. Kirscher et al. [11] recommend Distributed eXtreme Programming (DXP), in which eight XP practices are seen as independent of the locality of the team and thus are practices that can be applied in GSD while four of them (planning game, pair programming, continuous integration, and on-site customers) are dependent on collocated team members and thus require alternative solutions to work in GSD.

As in GSD, much of the research so far into distributed agile teams focuses on the situation where multiple teams are distributed globally. To date, little research investigates dispersed teams [12] where most or all individual team members are alone, i.e. they are the only team member in any one location. This situation has become more relevant as experts are often widely distributed, and small open source projects [13] also have similarities to the dispersed model.

Previous analysis of co-located agile teams highlights that information flow within and around team members is simple and open, supported by few mediating artefacts that promote discussion [14]. In this paper, we use the same analysis approach to investigate information flow in a partially dispersed agile team and to compare the results. In the next section we describe the study situation including the team, the data gathering and analysis. The analysis itself is presented in Section 3, Section 4 discusses our findings in the context of co-located agile teams and the challenges of global agile development, and section 5 presents some conclusions and future work.

2   The Study

The project under study was to develop enterprise software components for use by software developers in their own organisations when building their cloud-based solutions. The deliverables are composed of binaries, tests and developer guidance.

The development, including 'spiking' iterations ran for 5 months from July 2011 to November 2011, although the initial product backlog had been developed over several months prior to this, through consultation with the user community and other development teams (this development is outside the scope of this study). The product backlog prioritization was heavily influenced by community votes.

2.1   The Team

The project team consisted of one core team, an additional offshore testing team and a network of advisers (which was also globally dispersed). This study focused on the core team, which was made up of nine members. Most team members had worked together on a couple of previous projects, and hence knew each other. The team was an example of an agile dispersed development team as described above, although it should be properly defined as a partially dispersed team i.e. only one member of the team was in any one location for the majority of the time, except for those based in the team room in Seattle. At critical times within the product development (such as kick-off/exploration, beta release, final release) all team members who could attend, would visit Seattle for one or two sprints. The two development leads based in Buenos Aires would also meet occasionally and work together, although they mainly worked in different locations. Other team members would frequently pair remotely. Cross-discipline pairing (e.g. technical writer with developer) would also take place. An overview of the team members' roles and their locations is given in Table 1 (the real names of team members are substituted by pseudonyms to protect their identity). Only the documentation lead was a native English-speaker, but the main project language was English.

Table 1. Team membership

Pseudonym	Role	Location	Time zone
David	Technical writer, documentation lead	Bristol, UK	GMT +0:00
Edwin	Technical writer, training materials	Hague, The Netherlands	GMT +1:00
Mamu	Test lead (the majority of the testing team were located in India)	Vancouver, Canada	GMT -8:00
Rina	Tester	Seattle, USA	GMT -8:00
Eliah	Developer and subject matter expert	Seattle, USA	GMT -8:00
Joe	Lead developer	Buenos Aires, Argentina	GMT -3:00
Frederico	Lead developer	Buenos Aires, Argentina	GMT -3:00
George	Product owner	Seattle, USA	GMT -8:00
Jon	Developer (& user interface designer)	Montreal, Canada	GMT -5:00

The team used the hybrid "XP@Scrum" [15] approach with Scrum project management practices and XP engineering practices. Specifically, they met for stand-up meetings every day, developed in 2-week sprints with an iteration planning meeting, customer demos (with the product owner and the members of the advisory board) and a retrospective at the end of every sprint, had requirements expressed in stories, followed test-first development and practiced continuous integration and pairing. Within the two-week sprints, the team met every day for a 15 minute stand-up at 9.30am Seattle time, which fell within the working day for all timezones represented in the team. The furthest away was Edwin, in the Netherlands, for whom this time translated into 6.30pm. This meeting was accomplished using Microsoft's Lync, with some team members dialing in via computer telephony and others via regular phone lines. As typical to Scrum, each team member would report what they did before this meeting ("yesterday" for some team members and "today" for others, depending on timezone), what they are doing after this meeting ("today" or "tomorrow"), and any blocking issues. The offshore test team could not be present at stand-ups due to timezones so Rina acted as their proxy. Even when travelling, team members would make every effort to attend the standup. Once each team member had reported the team decided whether there was a need for a further discussion about any issues that had arisen (which was typically the case), and also when to do a triage. If it was decided that a discussion was required then the meeting resumed after a 10 minute break (for coffee). Sometimes all team members would attend these meetings and sometimes only relevant participants. Important meetings were recorded for future viewing by team members who could not attend e.g. the testers and technical writers. All team meetings were supported by Lync, with screen sharing being used for demos or to share diagrams etc. It has been reported by a team member that occasionally video streaming was used. Microsoft's OneNote and Team Foundation Server supported knowledge sharing. OneNote is a collection of wiki pages which can be tailored to any situation according to needs. For this project a shared OneNote file with revision tracking and residing on a Skydrive was used, so that everybody could contribute. Team Foundation Server houses the source repository together with the product backlog and sprint backlogs with the current status of stories and bugs within the backlog. Skydrive, a shared network folder for large files, audio recordings and presentations, was used by the team as an additional project artefact repository.

2.2   Data Gathering

An ethnographically-informed approach was taken to data gathering [16]. One of the authors (the researcher) conducted an observational study of the agile team and one other author is a member of the team under study. The researcher observed all team members remotely, as a common practice in virtual ethnography [17], with the purpose of understanding team members' perspective of having virtual colleagues and virtual meetings. Additionally, following a strategically-situated approach [18], some sites have been visited in order to enhance the understanding of the team and to understand the role of physical artefacts in a partially dispersed agile team.

The researcher attended two or three stand-ups a week and eight iteration planning meetings over the project, joined three triage sessions and several ad hoc conversations, visited USA and UK sites and obtained photographs of the Argentinean environment. She also had access to the team's OneNote notebook which contained records of the team's retrospectives and many brainstorms and discussions. At the end of the project she was also given recordings of pairing sessions and other ad hoc meetings. The data collected included observation notes, screen captures of Lync conversations, still photographs, recordings of team conversations, pairing sessions and iteration planning meetings. In addition, as the issue of information sharing was a clear theme in the field study data, a short questionnaire was completed by each team member asking for details of how and when they shared information. The questions asked in this questionnaire are reproduced in Table 2.

Table 2. Questions asked of the team about information sharing

Information sharing questions
1.   How do you share information with your fellow team members?
2.   Apart from the daily stand-ups, how often do you contact your fellow team members, and how, e.g. telephone Joe every hour for 5 mins?
3.   Are there artefacts or items of information that you don't need to share? Please describe specific examples and indicate why you don't need to share them.
4.   If you come across something you don't understand, where do you go for help? Please provide three example sources and describe the kind of information you glean from each

2.3   Distributed Cognition

Distributed cognition theory [19] examines the cognitive processes that are dispersed among individuals and between individuals and artefacts in the external environment with and through which they interact [20]. Within CSCW and HCI it has been used to investigate collaborative working e.g. [21, 22]. This kind of analysis views a cognitive system as being distributed across individuals, artefacts, internal (i.e. cognitive) representations and external representations in the environment. It focuses particularly on how information is propagated and transformed within the system to achieve collaboration. Co-located agile teams have been analysed using this approach [14, 23], but its use in software development more widely has been limited (e.g. [24]). In this paper, we base our analysis on Distributed Cognition in order to investigate how information flows within, around and through a partially dispersed agile team, as compared with a co-located agile team. We draw on previous descriptions of distributed cognition, and a technique called DiCOT to analyse the team's information flows.

2.4   DiCOT (Distributed Cognition for Teamwork)

DiCOT [25] provides a structured approach to reasoning about a situation from a Distributed Cognition point of view. It draws on ideas and representations from Contextual Design [26], together with a series of principles that are central to distributed cognition. There are three main themes in DiCoT:

1. The *physical theme* focuses on the physical environment within which the cognitive system operates, at whatever level of granularity is relevant, from the building or office layout to the positioning of items on a desk or noticeboard.
2. The *artefact theme* focuses on the detail of artefacts that are created and used to perform the activity under study.
3. The *information flow theme* focuses on what and how information flows through the cognitive system, the media which facilitate that flow and how the information is transformed in the process.

Furniss and Blandford [25] identify 22 principles from distributed cognition which can be loosely categorised according to these three themes (see Table 3). Each theme can be investigated using these principles, an associated model, and a tabular representation to capture the detail of activity within a theme. Although further work has been done to extend DiCOT to two other themes, these three were used in the original analysis and for comparability we focus only on these three.

Table 3. The principles of Distributed Cognition underlying DiCOT

Physical Layout
• Space and cognition: considers the use of space to support activity, e.g. laying out materials
• Perceptual: considers how spatial representations aid computation
• Naturalness: considers how closely the properties of the representation reflect those of that which it represents
• Subtle bodily supports: considers what if any bodily actions are used to support activity, e.g. pointing
• Situation awareness: considers how people are kept informed of what is going on, e.g. through what they can see, what they can hear and what is accessible to them.
• Horizon of observation: considers what an individual can see or hear (this influences situation awareness)
• Arrangement of equipment: considers how the physical arrangement of the environment affects access to information.
Artefacts
• Mediating artefacts: are used to perform the activity
• Creating scaffolding: considers how people use their environment to support their tasks, e.g. creating reminders of where they are in a task
• Representation-goal parity: considers how artefacts in the environment represent the relationship between the current state and goal state.
• Coordination of resources: considers the resources (e.g. plans, goals, history and so on) that are co-ordinated to aid action and cognition.
Information flow
• Information movement: considers the mechanisms (representations and physical realisation) used to move information around the cognitive system
• Information transformation: considers when, how and why information is transformed as it flows through the cognitive system
• Information hubs: are a central focus where information flows meet and decisions are made.
• Buffers: hold up information until it can be processed without causing disruption to ongoing activity.
• Communication bandwidth: considers the richness of a communication channel, e.g. face-to-face communication imparts more information than email
• Informal and formal communication: recognises that informal communication can be very important
• Behavioural trigger factors: cause activity to happen without an overall plan needing to be in place.

3   DiCOT Analysis

3.1   Physical Layout to Support Cognition

In terms of the office or working environment, each location was different, but no evidence was found of the working environment being used to support activity. Most collaborative activity took place in a virtual setting, e.g. in a Lync meeting or through instant messaging. Very little collaborative activity had a physical aspect to it except the layout used in the software support tools (which we explore through the artefact theme below). To illustrate the physical environment of the team members, we consider the team room and two other example workspaces below.

Fig. 1. (a) The team room in Seattle; (b) David's office; (c) Frederico and Joe while pairing

The Team Room in Seattle. Fig 1 (a) illustrates the team room environment. The walls are covered in white boards and several sketches and lists were on these walls at the time of the researcher's visit. However, only two walls were related to the current project, one of which contained a list of topics which had been identified for team conversations and another one was used for design discussions and sketching of specific features. The focus of the team room was twofold: the large screen which was used to display screen sharing during meetings; and the conference telephone on the small round table in the middle of the room. During meetings, team members present in the team room would sit or walk around this table. There was also a music centre for streaming music, and it was reported to the researcher that the team had an M&M's dispenser and adopted the ritual of getting a candy when a bug was fixed. In terms of the seven principles of the physical layout theme, the team did not in general use *space* or physical layout in the team room to support their work. However it was reported to the researcher that during onsite working, when more of the team members were present in Seattle, the physical space and layout were important. As there are no physical representations, the *perceptual* and *naturalness* principles are not relevant. During the researcher's time in the team room, there was no evidence of the use of *subtle bodily supports, situation awareness*[1] or *horizon of observation* to support collaborative working. This is not surprising as the team focus was elsewhere – as the researcher's notes comment, they were "somewhere in the ether". Arranging the large screen and the

---

[1] However one team member reported that overhearing others' conversations did trigger decisions and other discussions.

conference phone *equipment* in the centre of the room meant that everyone has clear access to information being shared digitally or orally, although each member of the team could also log onto Lync through their own computers to join the meeting.

Individuals' Physical Setting. David was based in the UK and worked mostly from home. The researcher visited his location to observe a day's work. The most striking aspect of David's environment was his computing *equipment*: an array of three screens sitting on his desk. While working, David would have several windows open spread across the three screens. There was no other evidence of the use of physical *layout* to support David's working, and as he was on his own no other physical principles are relevant here. Frederico and Joe came together to pair occasionally, and the only support they had in their physical environment was their laptops. Fig 1 (b, c) shows David's environment, and that of Frederico and Joe when they came together to pair.

3.2   Artefacts Created or Used

Among the locations observed, physical artefacts supported the team's work only in the office in Seattle – most of the distributed team's work and all activity of dispersed team members were supported through electronic documents and diagrams. The team room walls in Seattle (which were made of whiteboard material) displayed the list of topics for discussion, checklists and other information such as login details and configuration lines. There were also notes from brainstorming and design sessions. These artefacts were present only in the team room. The posters and certificates hanging on the walls in David's office, were not related to his work and the only sign of a physical external artefact was a (clean) pad of paper on his desk. In the office of Frederico and Joe, no physical artefacts were present at all, neither on the desk nor on the walls.

Regarding electronic artefacts, two main repositories supported the team's work: OneNote which the team referred to as their "Knowledge Base", and Microsoft Visual Studio Team Foundation Server (TFS). The latter is a collaboration platform to support teams through the automation and integration of processes, tools and project artefacts built around a central repository (with version control, build automation, workitem tracking etc.) as well as powerful reporting that help analyze and track progress and quality of the projects in real-time[2]. Our team used the facilities within TFS to support an agile process, code sharing, bug tracking and to maintain the product backlog: the stories and their statuses (see Fig 2). OneNote is also a commercial tool, described as "a digital notebook" which supports the development and sharing of information using diagrams, text, schedules and so on. It also supports revision tracking, which is important for identifying updates made by collaborators. Several templates for OneNote are available, but custom structures can also be developed. The structure used by our team is illustrated in Fig 3.

---

[2] http://www.microsoft.com/visualstudio/en-us/products/2010-editions/team-foundation-server/overview

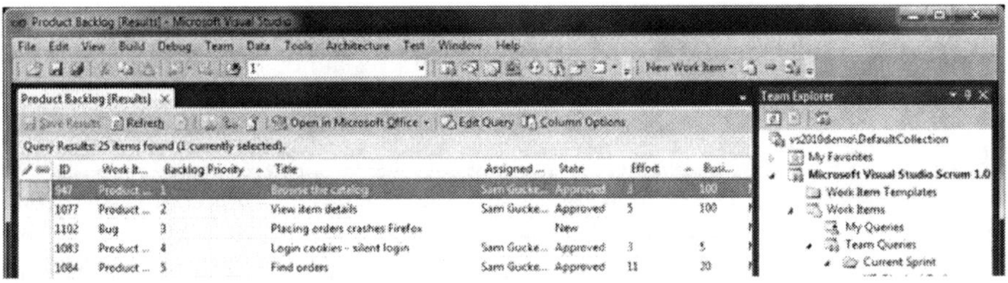

Fig. 2. Example screen shots of TFS (backlog view)

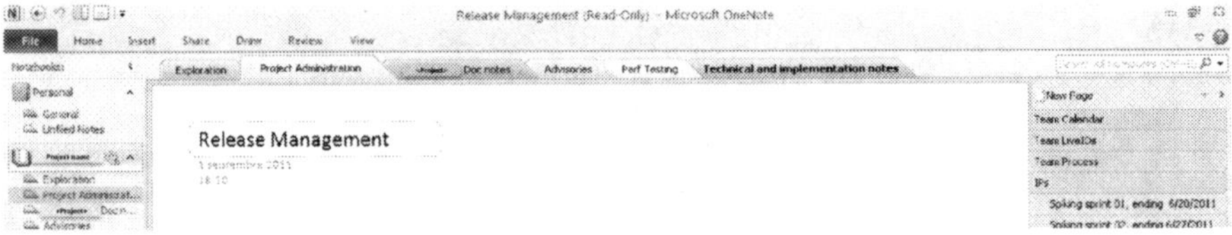

Fig. 3. Example screen shot of OneNote. The tab structure reads: Exploration, Project Administration, <Project> Doc Notes, Advisories, Perf Testing, and Technical and implementation notes.

Other artefacts were shared through Skydrive, a shared network folder for large files, audio recordings, presentations. OneNote, TFS and files shared on Skydrive were used to co-ordinate action. OneNote included a team diary showing when individuals were on leave etc, together with contact details, and the product backlog aspect of TFS included showed who was responsible for which story and kept a record of who created or edited any documents. TFS was also used for bug tracking. A detailed discussion of OneNote, TFS and Skydrive is outside the scope of this current paper. In terms of the DiCOT principles, most of the *mediating artefacts* to support collaboration were electronic (as described above). When artefacts were considered interesting for the whole team and they were not digital (e.g. whiteboards sketches in Seattle office), photos of the whiteboard were taken and shared through Skydrive or OneNote for giving access to dispersed members. Generally, team members shared all artefacts with the rest of the team, but few exceptions occurred: David and other team members had private OneNote tabs where they kept their own notes separate from the shared set, which were used as *scaffolding* to support their own activity. Other note-taking and sketching behaviour that was observed included making personal 'to do' lists (e.g. by Eliah in the Seattle team) and drawing initial diagram sketches (e.g. by David before committing a diagram to a drawing package). The management of *representations* and *resources* focused on OneNote and TFS.

3.3   Information Flow

Team members based in Seattle communicated through face-to-face conversations. The whole team communicated through email and Lync, mainly using one to one instant messaging chats, phone calls and screen sharing. Use of video and group text chat was very rare. Phone calls and screen sharing were only used when more detailed discussion was needed or for specific critical issues. Information was therefore *moved* around the team using each of these mechanisms, represented with dotted lines in Fig. 4. Team members were communicating together from few times per week to several times per day, depending on the role of each member and on the phase of the project.

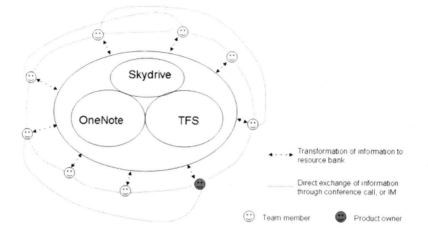

Fig. 4. Information flow within the partially dispersed team. OneNote, TFS and Skydrive were information hubs. Communication among team members occurred through face-to-face interactions, email and Lync. (note that all team members communicated freely with all others, and the communication lines are representative not exhaustive).

Since George was the product owner and Scrum master, he was regularly communicating with most of the team members as well as members of the other product groups and advisors and was managing the development of the project, therefore he was acting as an *information hub*. In addition, information was stored in OneNote, TFS and Skydrive and these were all significant *information hubs* and *information buffers*. Stand up meetings, triages and team conversations were also *information hubs* because key decisions were made at these times. The stand-up meeting was a co-ordination event but it was noticeable that during a stand-up, no documents were being shared. Individual team members took their turn to describe what they had been doing and what they will do next, as well as any blocking issues they had faced. During standups any additional discussion/brainstorming topics have been identified and scheduled promptly – often just after the standup. During the iteration planning meeting, screen and document sharing was more common, and for the sprint retrospectives an anonymized, shared note page was used for team members to write their thoughts and irritations anonymously before discussion; the page was later saved in OneNote. Team conversations, demonstrations, presentations, advisory board meetings and iteration planning meetings were recorded for later viewing by team members not present, or for re-viewing when documenting or testing stories. Recordings were stored through Skydrive and all retrospective comments were also stored in OneNote. These recordings were also *information buffers*.

When two team members are talking synchronously, then information is *transformed* the least. When information is entered into TFS, it has to conform to the specific fields and templates within the system. There was no evidence that this transformation caused any confusion or uncertainty, but nevertheless transformation was necessary. To capture information in OneNote also required some transformation – into a diagram or notes within the document structure.

Communication bandwidth varied from face-to-face groups meetings within the Seattle office or during the on-site meetings, to synchronous group conference calls, to recordings of conversations, instant messages, and one-to-one conversations. There were many different channels used for communication and there did not seem to be any concern or confusion over the type, frequency nor bandwidth of interactions.

Although there were regular team interactions, and a rhythm to the day and the sprint (as you would expect to find in any agile team), there was little communication that might be described as *'formal'*. Some demonstrations to the group of advisors were rehearsed and kept to strict time, and in that sense were 'formal' compared to the regular short interactions between the team members via Lync IM to ask for clarification or to ask for a synchronous conversation. However, the majority of the interactions were informal. Each member of the team knew when the stand-ups, iteration planning and other regular meetings were happening, and hence would be available through Lync on time for them. There was also an implicit agreement to block 2 hours after standup for team discussions. Apart from this, team members were self-organising and would attend to tasks and responsibilities as they arose. One factor which supported this way of working was that each person has their own and well-defined role (see Table 1). As such *behavioural trigger factors* were hard to spot.

4   Discussion

4.1   Agile Dispersed Development and Global Software Development Issues

In the introduction we discussed potential benefits [1] and main challenges facing distributed [27] teams, and agile distributed teams [9]. The team described in this paper is dispersed for including in the team the most talented developers and subject matter experts beneficial for the project. The case we reported here is a partially dispersed team following the XP@Scrum distributed development approach and our findings are in line with studies stating that agile practices can successfully be adopted in GSD [7]. Despite the fact that team members were distributed across different time zones and were geographically dispersed, the team collaborated using agile practices in order to complete the project.

GSD highlights the lack of informal communication in distributed settings due to geographical distance and time-zone differences [27]. In our partially dispersed team there were some overlapping working hours among team members, so *synchronous communication* and collaboration was possible, mainly through the use of Lync for IM and phone calls. When this was not possible, team members adapted their working hours to those of remote colleagues (e.g. European members attending evening meetings) or they were recording the meetings to share them asynchronously.

Communication was mainly *informal* and team members were easy accessible for impromptu conversations over Lync. Some team members reported that they were collaborating on a daily basis with some remote colleagues, even for several hours per day; no formal communication has been observed and documentation (e.g. shared digital artefacts, wiki pages, recording of the meetings) was limited to what is considered necessary for getting the work done, as in every agile project. This is in contrast with traditional GSD where detailed, comprehensive documentation as well as codified, explicit knowledge are considered necessary because communication is problematic and tacit knowledge is difficult to share [2]. *Pair programming* is a controversial practice that some authors consider very difficult to be performed in a dispersed settings [12] or even impossible [28] because pairs cannot sit side by side. In our team, pairing sessions were performed despite the geographical distance, using screen sharing and audio calls.

4.2   Co-located Agile versus Dispersed Agile

A previous distributed cognition analysis of a co-located agile team [14] identified three main observations:

1.   There are few mediating artefacts in the system and those that do exist are simple and lack detailed information, which encourages discussion.
2.   Information flows are simple and open, thus promoting situational awareness.
3.   The team works in an information-rich environment. Information is both easily accessible and immediately relevant and applicable.

Comparing these points to the team in this study, there are some parallels but also significant differences. Our partially dispersed team relied on several digital mediating artefacts (OneNote, TFS, recordings etc). Each of these contained very detailed information, and the software tools (particularly TFS) had sophisticated structures which require more effort to learn to use. This is not to say that the team members showed any indication of difficulties, but information was less accessible to newcomers or outsiders than in the co-located situation. The detailed information available to the team through these artefacts led to an information-rich environment, but significantly more transformation between representations was needed.

The simple, open flow of information in co-located agile teams makes use of physical space and relies on face-to-face communication and on physical artefacts [23]. A central role is played by the Wall and the Story Cards, and situational awareness is high (see Fig 5). In the dispersed team, information flows were open because anyone could contact anyone else on the team, but they were also restricted because information flow needed to be explicit – there was no equivalent to peripheral awareness among dispersed members. Communication among dispersed team members occurred through *ad hoc* computer mediated interactions and it was necessary to explicitly store the information in *information hubs* in order to share it. Comparing Figs 4 and 5 shows that the study reported here highlights very different patterns of interaction: the information flow of our dispersed agile team is focused on OneNote, TFS and artefacts shared through Skydrive (see Fig 4).

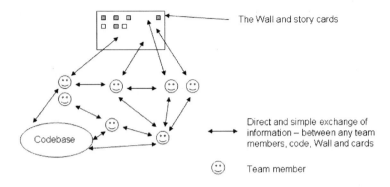

Fig. 5. Information flow within a co-located agile team

During the meetings among dispersed team members there was no clear equivalent to the Story Cards and the Wall: screen sharing was used to focus attention of the team but often team members were not sharing screens, but just in audio contact. Moreover, the walls in the Seattle office were used for listing topics and checklists, or for brainstorming and design sessions; walls were not used as in co-located agile for organizing story cards or focusing attention during stand-ups. Since team members were dispersed, awareness of each other's activity was not as straightforward as in co-located settings and it was the responsibility of individuals to share information and artefacts with other team members. While in co-located agile an important role is played by the social context [29], in our partially dispersed agile team we observed a much stronger role for individuals deciding what to share and with whom.

4.3   Limitations

In this paper we reported only one case study of a small partially dispersed agile team. Although elapsed time covered the majority of development effort, the team has been observed for a limited period. Not all locations were visited and only limited on-site observation was possible – this limitation is mitigated by one of the authors being a member of the team.

5   Conclusions and Future Work

Our distributed cognition analysis of one partially dispersed agile team shows that the information flow within the team is more complex than that in a co-located team in the following ways: our dispersed team relied on complex digital artefacts with sophisticated structures rather than on simple physical artefacts used in a sophisticated way. It was therefore important for team members to be familiar with the tools being used. Information sharing needed to be explicitly accomplished, and information needed to be transformed more often than in a co-located setting. In addition, the responsibility of what information to share when and through which medium lay with individual team members. These are important points for anyone wishing to set up a dispersed agile team.

The team members themselves did not refer to communication as problematic. There were no references to communication problems in the records of the retrospective sessions, and although technology sometimes caused difficulties in the meetings, team members were not distracted or deflected by them, but simply continued with their activities. We did not investigate why this was the case, nor any other challenges and problems they faced. This may be the subject of future work. Other future work will include the study of further dispersed teams and a more detailed analysis of the team studied here. For example, Social Network Analysis (SNA) has been used to identify the relationships between distributed team members, e.g. collaboration patterns and impact of distance on awareness [30]. This kind of analysis could be used to investigate the role of artefacts and on how information is shared between dispersed team members.

Acknowledgments. We'd like to thank the team members for their support.

References

1. Conchúir, E.Ó., Ågerfalk, P.J., Olsson, H.H., Fitzgerald, B.: Global Software Development: Where are the benefits? Communications of the ACM 52(8), 127–131 (2009)
2. Herbsleb, J.D., Moitra, D.: Global Software Development. IEEE Software 18(2), 16–20 (2001)
3. Carmel, E., Agarwal, R.: Tactical Approaches for Alleviating Distance in Global Software Development. IEEE Software 18(2), 22–29 (2001)
4. Cataldo, M., Bass, M., Herbsleb, J.D., Bass, L.: On Coordination Mechanism in Global Software Development. In: Second IEEE International Conference on Global Software Engineering, pp. 71–80. IEEE, Munich (2007)
5. Hossain, E., Babar, M.A., Paik, H.: Using scrum in global software development: a systematic literature review. In: Fourth IEEE International Conference on Global Software Engineering, pp. 175–184. IEEE, Limerick (2009)
6. Jalali, S.: Wohlin. C.: Agile practices in global software engineering-a systematic map. In: 5th IEEE International Conference on Global Software Engineering, pp. 45–54. IEEE, Princeton (2010)
7. Holmström, H., Fitzgerald, B., Ågerfalk, P.J., Conchúir, E.Ó.: Agile practices reduce distance in global software development. Information Systems Management 23(3), 7–18 (2006)
8. Layman, L., Williams, L., Damian, D., Bures, H.: Essential communication practices for extreme programming in a global software development team. Information and Software Technology 48(9), 781–794 (2006)
9. Paasivaara, M., Durasiewicz, S., Lassenius, C.: Distributed Agile Development: Using Scrum in a Large Project. In: 3rd IEEE International Conference on Global Software Engineering, pp. 87–95. IEEE, Bangalore (2008)
10. Lee, G., DeLone, W., Espinosa, J.A.: Ambidextrous coping strategies in globally distributed software development projects. Communications of the ACM 49(10), 35–40 (2006)

11. Kircher, M., Jain, P., Corsaro, A., Levine, D.: Distributed extreme programming. In: Extreme Programming and Flexible Processes in Software Engineering, Italy (2001)
12. Braithwaite, K., Joyce, T.: XP Expanded: Distributed Extreme Programming. In: Baumeister, H., Marchesi, M., Holcombe, M. (eds.) XP 2005. LNCS, vol. 3556, pp. 180–188. Springer, Heidelberg (2005)
13. Mockus, A., Fielding, R., Herbsleb, J.: Two case studies of open source software development: Apache and Mozilla. ACM Transactions on Software Engineering and Methodology 11(3), 309–346 (2002)
14. Sharp, H., Robinson, H., Segal, J., Furniss, D.: The Role of Story Cards and the Wall in XP teams: a distributed cognition perspective. In: Proceedings of the Conference on Agile 2006, pp. 65–75. IEEE Computer Society Press, Minneapolis (2006)
15. Vriens, C.: Certifying for CMM Level 2 and ISO9001 with XP@Scrum. In: Agile Development Conference, pp. 120–124. IEEE, Salt Lake City (2003)
16. Robinson, H., Segal, J., Sharp, H.: Ethnographically-informed Empirical Studies of Software Practice. Information and Software Technology 49(6), 540–551 (2007)
17. Hine, C.: Virtual ethnography. Sage Publications Ltd. (2000)
18. Marcus, G.E.: Ethnography through thick and thin. Princeton University Press (1998)
19. Hutchins, E.: Cognition in the Wild. MIT Press, Cambridge (1995)
20. Hollan, J., Hutchins, E., Kirsch, D.: Distributed Cognition: Toward a new foundation for human-computer interaction research. ACM Transactions on Computer-Human Interaction 7(2), 174–196 (2000)
21. Furniss, D.: Codifying Distributed Cognition: A Case Study of Emergency Medical Dispatch. MSc Thesis. UCLIC (2004)
22. Halverson, C.A.: Activity theory and distributed cognition: Or what does CSCW need to DO with theories? Computer Supported Cooperative Work 11, 243–267 (2002)
23. Sharp, H., Robinson, H.: Collaboration and Co-ordination in mature eXtreme Programming teams. International Journal of Human-Computer Studies 66, 506–518 (2008)
24. Flor, N.V., Hutchins, E.L.: Analyzing distributed cognition in software teams: a case study of team programming during perfective maintenance. In: Fourth Workshop on Empirical Studies of Programmers, pp. 36–64. Ablex, Norwood (1991)
25. Blandford, A., Furniss, D.: DiCoT: A Methodology for Applying Distributed Cognition to the Design of Teamworking Systems. In: Gilroy, S.W., Harrison, M.D. (eds.) DSV-IS 2005. LNCS, vol. 3941, pp. 26–38. Springer, Heidelberg (2006)
26. Beyer, H., Holtzblatt, K.: Contextual Design: Defining Customer-Centered Systems. Morgan Kauffman, San Francisco (1998)
27. Herbsleb, J.D.: Global software engineering: The future of socio-technical coordination. In: 2007 Future of Software Engineering, pp. 188–198. IEEE, Minneapolis (2007)
28. Shrivastava, S.V., Date, H.: Distributed Agile Software Development: A Review. Journal of Computer Science and Engineering 1(1), 10–17 (2010)
29. Sharp, H., Robinson, H.M., Petre, M.: The Role of Physical Artefacts in Agile Software Development: two complementary perspectives. Interacting with Computers 21(1-2), 108–116 (2009)
30. Damian, D., Marczak, S., Kwan, I.: Collaboration Patterns and the Impact of Distance on Awareness in Requirements-Centred Social Networks. In: 15th IEEE International Conference on Requirements Engineering, pp. 59–68. IEEE, New Delhi (2007)

Sensing High-Performing Software Teams: Proposal of an Instrument for Self-monitoring

Petri Kettunen and Simo Moilanen

University of Helsinki, Department of Computer Science
P.O. Box 68, FI-00014 University of Helsinki, Finland
{petri.kettunen,smoilane}@cs.helsinki.fi

Abstract. Agile/Lean software development teams are by definition striving for high performance. However, it is not straightforward to recognize and cultivate those high-performing teams. Sometimes the team members perceive their internal performance differently than their externally observed outcomes really are. This paper addresses those issues by proposing an instrument for self-monitoring and analyzing software development team performance. The key goal is that practicing teams can use it even on a daily basis to indicate and steer their own performance excellence. This is supported by certain principal performance analysis guidelines. A prototype implementation of the instrument is demonstrated with some empirical cases. The cases indicate that the instrument can indicate noticeable differences in the perceived performance of individual team members and the team external outcomes. It helps detecting potential performance problems and impediments as well as improving even high-performers, and explaining team performance differences.

Keywords: agile software teams, Lean product development, process improvement, organizational design, performance management.

1   Introduction

Teams and teamwork are central to Agile and Lean software development. Moreover, not just having teams but consciously concentrating on their performance is what brings the agility and leanness benefits. However, it is not yet thoroughly understood, how such high-performance teams are established and how they can be sustained.

High-performing teamwork has been investigated in many fields over the years. In particular, the success factors of new product development (NPD) teams are in general relatively well known [1]. However, the specific concerns and intrinsic properties of modern software development teams are essentially less understood in particular in larger scales.

In all, it is not clearly understood, what high performance means for software development in total, and how exactly such effects and outcomes are achievable in repeatable ways. The goal of this paper is to discover and address such areas and elements, focusing on the specific aspects of software development teams (with respect to work teams in general).

C. Wohlin (Ed.): XP 2012, LNBIP 111, pp. 77–92, 2012.

The approach in this paper is to address those problems by constructing a team survey and monitoring instrument. Such profiles can then be used to find potential commonalities and differences of the teams within and between different product development organizations. Software development organizations can gauge their teams with it for organizational improvement. Software teams themselves may utilize it for their own performance management.

The rest of this paper is organized as follows. Section 2 reviews the prior and related works of teamwork and performance. Based on that grounding, Section 3 proposes a survey instrument to profile software teams from the performance perspective. Section 4 presents actual profiling findings of real-life high-performing team cases, followed by consequent insights and implications in Section 5. Finally, Section 6 concludes with pointers to further research and development.

2   Background and Related Work

Successful R&D organizations rely more and more on teamwork (Sect. 2.1). However, in order to be able to form and develop such software teams (Sect. 2.3), appropriate performance measures and gauging must be set in the context (Sect. 2.2). That raises new research questions (Sect. 2.4).

2.1   High-Performing Teams

Industrial-strength software product development is almost always done in teams, even in globally virtual set-ups. However, although product development team performance has been investigated extensively in various industries, software development teams and their knowledge-intensive work are still open to even fundamental questions and gaps.

Furthermore, software teams do not exist in isolation in particular in larger product development organizations. The context of the team affects the team organization and their performance in several, sometimes subtle and even conflicting ways. There may considerable differences in different industries and competitive environments (e.g., automotive embedded software vs. mobile games).

Table 1 illustrates this broad perspective with the key research viewpoints. The reference points of our research agenda are thus in general work teams and new product development projects (e.g., [2], [3]). This is then specialized to software.

Table 1. High performing software teams research and development perspectives

Viewpoint	Key Questions
EXTERNAL	• *How does a high-performing team appear and manifest itself?*
INTERNAL	• *What happens inside a high-performing (software) team?*
DEVELOPMENT	• *How can we create and sustain such teams?*

The concept of value is central to high performance Agile/Lean software development. This line of thinking can be further extended beyond the direct product value towards its benefits to the customers and even their customers [2]. In principle, agile teams are sensitive to their environment, flexible, and responsive to changing customer needs [3]. Such teams understand the product value drivers as well as the role of the team in the overall value stream (process value). They are thus capable of sustaining high value delivery performance even under turbulent circumstances.

2.2 Software Team Performance

In general, there is no one universal measure of software team performance. With traditional project teams, the basic objectives of achieving the product goals (functionality, quality) within the constraints (resources, schedule, cost) are typical measures in product and process performance dimensions. With respect to the team context, it follows that the performance is relative to the organizational environment of the team. Consequently, we do not prescribe performance with fixed measures.

Prior literature has described many possible software team performance measures. Typical ones are in terms of meeting or exceeding all of the objectives of a software development project [4], stakeholder-rated performance (e.g., contribution to the firm performance) [5], post-release defect density [6], speed of delivery and timely delivery [7], and defect removal ability [8].

Since product/service value delivery is a principal performance driver for Agile/Lean software development teams, it should be imperative to measure it [9]. Software team performance in terms of value creation efficiency can be assessed with value stream mapping/analysis (VSM/A) and more generally value network analysis (VNA) methods [10]. High performance can then be defined in terms of optimal value creation (benefits vs. costs) [2], [11]. High-performing software teams excel in their value creation not only for the customers, but also for their organizations and for the team itself [12]. Conversely, while waste lowers performance it is relative to the defined value [13].

High-performing teams are proficient at tracking their performance. Although it is difficult to define general-purpose performance measures for specific software teams, the measurement systems can be developed based on existing general-purpose frameworks to begin with. In particular, the ISO/IEC 15939 standard provides such a platform [14]. Notably, teams may sometimes perceive their internal performance differently than the team externally measured outcomes exhibit. It is imperative to know systematically, who judges the success and when [15]. Finally, although financial performance measures are still the most obvious ones in industrial teamwork, recently additional dimensions have been proposed – such as 'triple-bottom-line' [16].

2.3 Developing High-Performing Teams

There is no universal recipe for creating and improving high-performing software teams [4]. Nevertheless, it is possible to find many generally applicable ways and measures to device and guide software teams towards high performance (e.g., TSP). All in all, high performance of software development teams is apprehended in multidisciplinary ways spanning many areas of modern business competence and R&D management. This paper focuses on software engineering (management) discipline.

However, it is fundamental to understand the connections to those related fields for instance with respect to knowledge workers in general. Table 2 aggregates typical performance factors presented in the existing literature. Notably agile software team models address most of those concerns.

Table 2. Software team performance influence factors

Factors	Ref
POSITIVE: exceptional designers, managing learning; negotiation and coordination processes; informal communication networks NEGATIVE: thin spread of application domain knowledge, fluctuating and conflicting requirements, communication and coordination breakdowns	[17]
NEGATIVE: software development risks	[18]
POSITIVE: "Healthy" levels of conflicts, resolved constructively NEGATIVE: unresolved conflicts (weak conflict management)	[5]
NEGATIVE: no standard evidence on previous or current projects, inappropriate software life-cycle models, missing concept of operations, lack of qualification testing, insufficient data modeling, poor system and software architecture designing, lack of competent software professionals	[19]
artifact reuse, team expertise, process maturity, functional requirement stability	[6]
POSITIVE: team knowledge sharing	[20]
POSITIVE: management support (e.g., resources, obstacle removal), team member characteristics (e.g., business process competence), communication quality, clear mission	[8]

Furthermore, those positive influences require typically certain supporting organizational enablers on the one hand, and removing possible hindrances and impediments on the other hand. Such typical enabling elements are selective hiring of new personnel (right people) [21], organizational constructs to facilitate longer-term process development and improvement [22], and team-member exchange [20].

2.4   Knowledge Gaps and Research Needs

Starting from Table 1 and following the line of thinking in Sect. 2.1-2.3, there are compelling and pressing needs to understand what high performance means in given software development domains and competitive environments. The objective of this investigation is to device aims for practicing software teams and their organizations to disentangle and thereby tackle those questions. We approach this set of interrelated research questions with a probing instrument coupled with performance analysis guidelines.

3   Instrument Design and Analysis Principles

In order to address the research problems summarized in Sect. 2.4, we propose a self-monitoring approach and instrument for software teams (Sect. 3.1). Moreover, this is coupled with performance analysis guidelines (Sect. 3.2).

3.1   Instrument for Self-monitoring

Traditionally, software organizations have collected large bodies of low-level basic measures such LOC, defect counts, and effort figures. However, much less is understood about their higher-level measures. That leads often to unclear linkages to the relevant performance indicators for example when leaning on the general-purpose measurement system ISO/IEC 15939 standard (c.f., Sect. 2.2).

For that, we have compiled a self-monitoring tool primarily for the software teams themselves to gauge their own performance measures. The premise of our instrumentation approach is by contrast to start the other way around top-down by looking for leading indicators of high (or conversely, lower) software team performance.

The provisional Instrument has been developed as follows. Starting from Table 1, the establishment is the literature review of different team performance factors described in Sect. 2, e.g., [23]. That groundwork is augmented with our empirical experiences with certain industrial software organizations. In addition, some earlier academic classroom studies of software teams have been incorporated [24]. The instrument has first been piloted in laboratory settings like presented in Sect. 4.1.

Table 3. Main structure of the Instrument

HIGH PERFORMING TEAM SURVEY
Performance
1. How do you score your team in general? {7 items}
2. How do you appraise the following team outcomes and impacts? {8}
3. How important are the following for your team? {18}
– ...
– *High software quality (e.g., reliability, usability)*
– ...
Team
1. How do you rate the following aspects from your point of view? {15}
2. How do you rate the following concerns? {8}
– ...
– *Our team is capable of quick round-trip software engineering cycles (design-build-test-learn).*
– ...
3. The best description of your team's level of development is: {4}
4. What are the modes of leadership in your team? {12}
5. What are the key roles in your team? {16}
– ...
– *Software engineers*
– ...
Organization
1. How do you rate the following organizational factors in your context? {20}
2. How important are the following aspects for you in your work? {12}
– *Solving software engineering problems (software design)*
– ...

A key design rationale for the present generic instrument has been to avoid using abstract conceptual vocabulary on the one hand, and vaguely-defined terms on the other hand. For instance, instead of asking whether the team is "innovative", we have formulated those question items in terms of newness of product (features), thereby looking for the lower-level constituting elements, which are usually closer to the daily work and talk of the practitioners. Situational factors may be tailored (Sect. 4.2).

Table 3 presents the current main organization of the Instrument with some software-specific sample question items[1]. There are three sections corresponding to the following prime questions:

1. How does the team perceive its (high) performance (drivers, goals)?
2. How does it function (means)?
3. Is the organization supportive – encouraging even higher performance (enablers/impediments)?

The current provisional answering scales are overall defined as qualitative 5-point Likert ratings as follows depending on the nature of the questions:

- Temporal: *Always / Usually / Occasionally / Seldom / Never*
- Weighing: *Key / Important / Relative / Some little* (= moderate) */ Little* (= low)
- Perceptional: *Strongly Agree / Agree / Neutral / Disagree / Strongly Disagree*
- Discretionary: *Very Important / Important / Somewhat / A little / Unimportant*

- In addition, there are open free-format text entry choices ('Other'), and the options to skip questions ('n/a', 'I don't know').

3.2   Analysis Guidelines

There is no prescribed process to use the Instrument, but the initial idea is to utilize it as follows. Ideally, all members should be respondents in order to see their common views or to discover potential differences in individual perceptions. Anonymous collection of the replies is thus recommended. The underlying philosophy is to discover the current state of the affairs of the particular team as perceived by the team members. Specifically, there is no fixed definition of 'high performance'. Individual, teams, and their contexts change over time. The replies should thus be analyzed with respect to the timeline. The overall design rationale has been to keep the Instrument lightweight. Ideally, it could then be used even daily at least partially.

It is important to understand that the given team responses must be analyzed in the specific organizational context. Moreover, the response profile should be evaluated in total rather than just as separate items like discussed in Sect. 5.1. Furthermore, it is important to see potential linkages and interdependencies with individual questions. While it is not possible to present detailed prescribed rules for all such interrelationships in general, the following are some basic ideas to begin with:

---

[1] A prototype implementation of the Instrument in its current form is available online.

- Is the team performing high? Does the team want to excel? (Performance section in Table 3)
- Do we have a proper team for the job? Does the team know its goals? (Team section in Table 3)
- Can the team perform high? Is it sustainable? (Organization section in Table 3).

4 Case Studies

The Instrument case studies were conducted in three different software teams in two different organizations. The first organization (Sect. 4.1) is in an academic set-up. The environment is however close to real work life. The second one (Sect. 4.2) is a global IT company. Sect. 4.3 compares and contrasts the cases, demonstrating how the Instrument results can assist in further performance analysis. Some analyses are provided to illustrate the conclusions and follow-up questions that could be made based on the results from the Instrument.

4.1 Student Case

The aim of the first case was to pilot the Instrument (Sect. 3.1) in a laboratory environment. The Software Factory at the University of Helsinki provides such research facilities.

Software Factory[2] conducts rapid software development experiments in collaboration with academia and industry. It takes real-life customer projects and produces working software product in fixed seven-week periods, typically using Agile/Lean software practices. The project team members are primarily students, but the industrial customers are closely involved and often on site. Researchers can use that as a platform to conduct empirical research on a variety of topics.

Table 4. Student case project descriptive information

ATTRIBUTE	Software Factory Project
Participants	6 persons (one academic staff member)
Interest groups	Customer (and their business customers), education organization, researchers
Customers	Start-up entrepreneur, frequently onsite and collaborating with their potential external customers (prototype demonstrations)
Team history	None together
Team expertise	Mostly experts, some novices; The academic member provided some prior knowledge.
Product start status	Previous customer prototype
Product end status	The customer was satisfied with the outcomes and knowledge gained during the project.
Team continuation	None

---

[2] www.softwarefactory.cc

Table 4 presents the main characteristics of the case project. The project team members were MSc-level students coming from different countries. In addition, there was one local staff member acting as a coach.

The Instrument test was conducted at a late phase of the project. Each team member (including the coach) was asked to fill in the survey online individually and anonymously. The result summary was published and discussed with the whole team in the project end debriefing session.

Table 5 shows the most striking survey results provided by the Instrument. Following the line of thinking in Sect. 3.2, Table 6 presents some plausible interpretations of the question items shown in Table 5. In particular, the varying distributions (level of agreement) of the responses are of interest here.

Table 5. Student case survey highlights (c.f., Table 3)

How do you score your team in general?	Always	Usually	Occasionally	Seldom	Never	I don't know
Does the team want to excel?						
Student Team	3	1	2	0	0	0
How important are the following for your team?	Always	Usually	Occasionally	Seldom	Never	n/a
Stable product specs						
Student Team	0	4	0	2	0	0
How do you rate the following aspects?	Strong Agree	Agree	Neutral	Disagree	Strong Disagr	I don't know
My team members have all the knowledge needed to perform at a high level.						
Student Team	0	2	3	0	0	0
What are the modes of leadership in your team?	Strong Agree	Agree	Neutral	Disagree	Strong Disagr	I don't know
Shared leadership						
Student Team	1	1	1	1	0	1
How do you rate the following organizational factors?	Strong Agree	Agree	Neutral	Disagree	Strong Disagr	I don't know
People set high standards of their work.						
Student Team	0	2	2	0	0	1
How important are the following aspects for you?	Very	Important	Somewhat	A little	Unimportant	n/a
Solving software engineering problems (software design)						
Student Team	2	1	1	1	0	0

Finally, by and large, the respondents (i.e., project team members) considered the Instrument to be illuminating. However, in addition, they pointed out the following issues: It took some 15 minutes to fill the full survey in. This is probably too much in daily use. The terminology (e.g., "organization") should first be clarified and agreed in the project context. Misinterpretations may cause threats to the reliability.

Table 6. Student case performance analysis

INSTRUMENT ITEMS (Table 5)	Expected Responses	Potential Explanations and Implications
Does the team want to excel?	Close to 'Always'	Not every team member has equal standard of their "excellence"; The team members are not really ambitious enough.
Shared leadership	Uniformity	The team has not agreed on the leader(s); Not every team member sees leadership in a similar way.
Solving software engineering problems (software design)	Close to 'Very Important'	Some team members are more interested in working in a higher-level of abstraction or closer to the customer space; Not everybody ranges software design activities equally (e.g., verification and validation).

4.2   Industrial Cases

The industrial cases were conducted at a large IT company, which in this paper will for confidentiality reasons be titled as 'ITCO'. ITCO is specialized in IT services, R&D and consulting. ITCO's headquarters is based in Europe and the company has functions in multiple countries around the world. The cases are described in detail below. Table 7 summarizes their demographic information (like in Table 4).

Industrial Case #1
The team studied in the first industrial case was expected to be a high-performance team due to previous good feedback, high-level professionalism of the team members, the long team composition time and the strict criteria for choosing the team members.

Both the project management and the customer were very satisfied with the team performance. The project manager responsible for the project's deliveries described the team as "professionals with good motivation and high output".

The team was handpicked by the customer and they worked at the customer's premises. All the team members were interviewed for the team and their performance was constantly monitored by the customer. If the customer wasn't satisfied with a team member's performance in the long run, the member was disassociated from the team and from the project altogether. The team had existed for about 18 months and at the time of the case study, and the team had stayed constant for about 12 months.

All the team members had at least 5 years, and some had over 10 years of software development experience. All the team members as well as all the teams in the project were working at the same site. The working method was applied Scrum. The case took place in Finland.

Industrial Case #2
The second industrial team studied was a young team that was struggling to meet its goals. The team had existed for about 2 months at the time of the study. The team was made up of new recruits who were experienced software developers, each team member having at least 5 years of software development experience.

The team was part of a project that had just started and was going on its ramp up phase. The project was distributed to two sites and the team studied here was the first team put together at the Indian offshore site.

At the time of the study, common ways of working or even a clear project organization were not yet established in the project. Despite the early stage of the project, the team was working on an actual *soon-to-be* production feature and had strong support from the on-site personnel. The project had upfront planning done and the software development was carried out using the Kanban method.

The project management was not satisfied with the team's output. Nevertheless, they tolerated it, because the team as well as the project was just starting out.

There was in addition the external management of the team involved. External, in this context, refers to the management that does not work within the team, and neither the managers nor the team members consider as part of the team. The management (two highly skilled persons) was responsible for recruitment, staffing and output of the offshore site. They served offsite project owners.

Table 7. Industrial case teams descriptive information

ATTRIBUTE	#1: Mature Industrial Team	#2: Young Industrial Team
Participants	6 persons	4 persons
Interest groups	Customer, firm	R&D management (home-office)
Customers	Onsite; professional IT-developers, IT-outsourcers and product managers	Offsite; IT-administration
Team history	18 months	2 months
Team expertise	High skill level	Medium-high skill level
Product start status	n/a	n/a
Product end status	n/a	n/a
Team continuation	Full	Discretionary

Like with the student case (Sect. 4.1), the teams were asked to fill in the Instrument web-pages anonymously. The basic version of the Instrument (Table 3) was slightly modified to the industrial context.

Both industrial teams answered nearly identically to the following questions: *The key performance influencing factors are under the team's own control; Our team is fully integrated with the surrounding organization; How often are there communication and coordination breakdowns? The team has full and immediate visibility and access to all necessary and useful information; The team is able to work in real time (smoothly, without unpredictable delays and glitches), i.e., the flow of work is steady; Our team is capable of short roundtrip software engineering cycles (design-build-test-learn); How often is the equipment needed by your team working and easily available?*

Given that Team #1 appears to be considerably more productive for ITCO than Team #2, it is interesting to notice how both of the teams answered to the previous questions. Basically both teams state that they are able to work rather smoothly in real time, together with the surrounding organization if needed, without major communication or coordination breakdowns, and they have all the equipment and information they need in place. This suggests that the productivity difference between the teams is not directly related to working methods or tools.

When probing the data to explain the performance difference between the industrial teams, the following turned out as obvious differences between the teams:

- Team maturity: Team #2 considered itself to be struggling with effective working methods and getting their tasks done where as Team #1 considered their team members to be clear on their responsibilities and that most of their time was spent on task accomplishing.
- The amount and appreciation of generalists in the team: When asked *What are the key roles in your team?* Team #1 seems to think generalist as a key role but Team #2 as a role of very low importance. The results of this for overall team performance would be interesting point of study and may very well explain some of the performance issues Team #2 is having.
- Resources spent on improving: As shown in Table 8, Team #2 considers itself to be continually improving where as the Team #1 considers itself much more stable on the improving aspect. The expected result was the opposite but this can be explained by Team #1 spending more of its resources on tasks at hand and less on performance improvement than Team #2.

The study also revealed an interesting issue with the potential of Team #1 to further improve the team performance. Both industrial teams get paid the same way, as a monthly salary. However, it is interesting to note in Table 8 that the newly formed Team #2 is much more satisfied in the way they are paid than the older Team #1. Also, as shown in Table 8, the members of Team #2 considered their setup considerably closer to entrepreneurial startup than did the members of Team #1, and for the question *People have time to think (no excessive stress, pressure)* Team #2 was far on the strongly agreeing side when Team #1 was at the neutral-disagree side.

The teams did answer similarly however when asked *Does the team want to excel?* Answers for both teams were at the tip of the positive end of the scale.

Those answers were somewhat as expected. The newly formed Team #2 can improve its results, since there is much that a new team can do to improve its performance via common working methods, tools and other group formation related matters. With Team #1, much of that "natural growth" and easy steps of improvement are already done and improving the team performance even further takes considerable effort.

Table 8. Industrial cases response highlights (c.f., Table 3)

How do you rate the following aspects?	Strong Agree	Agree	Neutral	Disag-ree	Strong Disagr	I don't know
The way we get paid encourages our team to perform at a high level.						
Team #1 (6 respondents / 6)	0	1	1	3	1	0
Team #2 (3 respondents / 4)	1	2	0	0	0	0
Our team is like a "startup" (entrepreneurial), i.e., continually improving.						
Team #1 (6 respondents / 6)	0	0	5	1	0	0
Team #2 (3 respondents / 4)	1	1	1	0	0	0

Team #1 seems to be busy at delivering products at its current velocity. Even though many team members would like to spend time on improving the team performance, it seems not to be feasible to do so. The surrounding organization is already satisfied with the team's performance, so resources are not allocated at improving the delivery performance even further and the team's performance is not related to personal incentives.

All this seems to add up to the fact, that the team doesn't have time to work on performance issues and none of the team members care to make the time as little personal gain is to be expected from introducing new ideas for delivery performance improvements. In other words, the team seems to be so busy with its day-to-day work, that there is no more room for the naturally occurring self-management that creates the "heroes" who take charge and push the change for the next rational thing to do.

If it is a conscious managerial decision to concentrate the efforts of Team #1 only towards the deliveries, it is a perfectly valid one. However, it may be a matter of circumstances that Team #1 has "drifted" to the state of no improvement. Then it is very important for the team as well as for the managers of the team to awake to the situation.

4.3   Comparisons

Based on the different cases described in Sect. 4.1 and 4.2, the following illustrates how the Instrument results can be used to compare team performances. Moreover, it is possible to contrast different teams for understanding their influence factors.

Table 9 presents the distributions of how the case team members perceived their level of maturity (as defined in [23]). In addition for the industrial team (#2), this is contrasted with how their home-office management sees the offshore team.

Table 9. Case teams' perceived maturity distributions (c.f., Table 3)

The best description of your team's level of development is:	Student Team	Team #1	Team #2	Team #2 by Mgmt
Team members are clear on their...	80%	67%	0%	50%
Effective working procedures have been ...	20%	33%	67%	50%
Currently struggling with how we can best ...	0%	0%	33%	0%
Just getting started	0%	0%	0%	0%

It was interesting to note how different teams approached the concept of team maturity. As shown in Table 9, the students were by far the most confident on their team's working methods even though they had been together for the least time of all the teams studied. This is an important point to notice as the Instrument is context-free in this aspect. Since the study was conducted at the very end of the project course, it is justifiable the students felt that their team was at its peak level of maturity.

The younger industrial team (#2) was filled with experienced developers used to projects lasting longer than the student project, so naturally their answers took place at the "less mature" end of the scale. The more mature industrial team's (#1) answers located at the higher end of the scale. Given that an average ITCO-project lasts for about 12 months, the answers of the industrial teams were as expected. It was also notable that no team considered themselves as a "*Just getting started*".

In Table 9, an interesting point to notice is that the home-office management of the Indian team (#2) considered the team much more mature than the team considered itself. This could very well be a source of trouble in the future. Overall this question illustrates clearly how the Instrument is context-free, i.e., it can be applied to different (organizational, cultural, team life-cycle) contexts. However, once the tool has been set up, the context becomes fixed and consideration must be taken when comparing different results gathered from different contexts. This is directly related to the difficulty of measuring productivity in the software development industry, as the productivity context for one team can be completely different from for another team.

5   Discussion

The aim of this investigation is to build holistic understanding of the key elements of high-performing software development teams (Sect. 5.1). The design rationale is to cover broadly all main areas (Sect. 5.2). They can then be analyzed further (Sect. 5.3).

5.1   Analysis and Evaluation

The aim of the Instrument is to be able to spot critical areas. Some initial validation of the coverage and strength are the case study insights (Sect. 4.1-4.2). However, more situational validation is needed (conclusion validity).

Self-monitoring has certain inherent risks (e.g., trust). A limitation of our approach is that the Instrument comprises a predefined set of general question items (construct validity). Some circumstantial performance-influencing factors may thus be missing (internal validity). Moreover, since team performance is relative to the context, the results may not be directly applicable in different organizations (external validity).

While software teams benefit from Agile practices in particular, longer-term organization-wide performance improvements require typically more, such as CMMI [22]. The underlying tenet of our Instrument approach is to highlight such key areas by taking a holistic view, not limiting to software engineering.

5.2   Implications

All things considered, our team self-monitoring approach with the Instrument serves the following overall organizational purposes and goals: The team becomes aware of its performance, the high performance influences can be understood systematically, and the organizational context elements surrounding "A-teams" become evident. Often there are noticeable gaps between how the software team perceived its performance and how the external management judges it. Such potential gaps should openly be recognized, and this is where the Instrument brings probes [13], [19].

The Instrument can be exercised for comparing different teams like shown in Table 9. Such indicative benchmarking could strive the teams for even higher performance [25]. However, care should be taken not to misuse such performance analysis (perceived vs. actual). In particular, cultural differences may affect the way team members feel free to analyze their performance objectively and openly like suggested by our international industrial cases (Sect. 4.2). However, it should be useful to identify such teams for organizational development and coaching purposes [26].

This leads to the question of what team performance measures are appropriate in different organizational contexts, and whether it is sensible to compare (benchmark) different teams between organizations [6]. By and large, software development lacks comparable market/industry standard levels of excellence, which could readily be used as yardsticks and objectives. Nevertheless, the Instrument survey profiles of the teams could possibly be compared and contrasted with respect to the following points: Do different high-performing teams feature equally? Do high-performing teams have compatible organizational surroundings (context)? Moreover, by repeating the surveys (even daily), timeline trends could be illuminated.

5.3   Future Work

In general, we aim for a systematized framework for instantiating and adjusting the generic instrument base designed here. The industrial case teams commented the full survey taking too long to complete and that some answer ranges were not in line with the questions. This brings up the idea of scaling it down making a lightweight version for rapid use. In addition, the terminology tailoring could be guided.

A further idea is to consider using the Instrument for team training purposes for example by Agile Coaches. A way to utilize the Instrument is to use it as an aid for depicting the desired future state of the *would-be* high-performing teams. This could be especially useful in the start-up phase of new software teams. Similar considerations may be applicable while transferring or reorganizing [27].

6   Conclusions

The insight here is that once the team members have at least once before experienced a truly high-performing team, they can recognize one although it may be hard to articulate it. Moreover, such perceptions can help in pointing out lower performance in practicing teams. This is the premise of our instrument for self-monitoring presented in this paper. It concentrates more on the social and organizational aspects of high-performing software teams.

In conclusion, like demonstrated by the case studies presented in Sect. 4, our approach offers the following prospects and possibilities:

- observing practicing high-performing software teams in action
- proposing practical guidelines for "creating" and improving such teams
- building emerging theory on high performance of software development teams
- expanding from single teams to high-performing software enterprises (scaling).

Acknowledgments. This work was supported by the Finnish National Technology Agency TEKES (SCABO project no. 40498/10).

References

1. Cooper, R.G., Edgett, S.J.: Lean, Rapid, and Profitable New Product Development. Book-Surge Publishing, North Charleston (2005)
2. Winter, M., Szczepanek, T.: Projects and programmes as value creation processes: A new perspective and some practical implications. International Journal of Project Management 26, 95–103 (2008)
3. Ancona, D., Bresman, H.: X-Teams: How to Build Teams that Lead, Innovate, and Succeed. Harvard Business School Press, Boston (2007)
4. Ginac, F.P.: Creating High Performance Software Development Teams. Prentice Hall, Upper Saddle River (2000)
5. Sawyer, S.: Effects of intra-group conflict on packaged software development team performance. Information Systems Journal 11, 155–178 (2001)
6. Kasunic, M.: A Data Specification for Software Project Performance Measures: Results of a Collaboration on Performance Measurement. Technical report TR-012, CMU/SEI (2008)
7. Symons, C.: Software Industry Performance: What You Measure Is What You Get. IEEE Software 27(6), 66–72 (2010)
8. Lu, Y., Xiang, C., Wang, B., Wang, X.: What affects information systems development team performance? An exploratory study from the perspective of combined socio-technical theory and coordination theory. Computers in Human Behavior 27, 811–822 (2011)
9. Laanti, M., Kettunen, P.: Cost Modeling Agile Software Development. International Transactions on Systems and Applications 1(2), 175–179 (2006)
10. Allee, V.: Value Network Analysis and value conversion of tangible and intangible assets. Journal of Intellectual Capital 9(1), 5–24 (2008)
11. Buschmann, F.: Value-Focused System Quality. IEEE Software 27(6), 84–86 (2010)
12. Patanakul, P., Shenhar, A.: Exploring the Concept of Value Creation in Program Planning and Systems Engineering Processes. Systems Engineering 13(4), 340–352 (2009)
13. Mossman, A.: Creating value: a sufficient way to eliminate waste in lean design and lean production. Lean Construction Journal, 13–23 (2009)
14. Staron, M., Meding, W., Karlsson, G.: Developing measurement systems: an industrial case study. J. Softw. Maint. Evol.: Res. Pract. 23, 89–107 (2010)
15. Agresti, W.W.: Lightweight Software Metrics: The P10 Framework. IT Pro., 12–16 (September-October 2006)
16. Osterwalder, A., Pigneur, Y.: Business Model Generation: A Handbook for Visionaries, Game Changers, and Challengers. John Wiley & Sons, New York (2010)
17. Curtis, B., Krasner, H., Iscoe, N.: A Field Study of the Software Design Process for Large Systems. Communications of the ACM 31(11), 1268–1287 (1988)
18. Ropponen, J., Lyytinen, K.: Components of Software Development Risk: How to Address Them? A Project Manager Survey. IEEE Trans. Software Engineering 26(2), 98–111 (2000)
19. Allen, M.: From Substandard to Successful Software. CrossTalk 22(4), 29–32 (2009)
20. Liu, Y., Keller, R.T., Shih, H.-A.: The impact of team-member exchange, differentiation, team commitment, and knowledge sharing on R&D project team performance. R&D Management 41(3), 274–287 (2011)
21. Pfeffer, J.: Seven Practices of Successful Organizations. California Management Review 40(2), 96–124 (1998)
22. Glazer, H.: Love and Marriage: CMMI and Agile Need Each Other. CrossTalk 23(1), 29–34 (2010)

23. Yeatts, D.E., Hyten, C.: High-performing self-managed work teams: a comparison of theory to practice. SAGE Publications, Thousand Oaks (1998)
24. Oza, V., Kettunen, P., Abrahamsson, P., Münch, J.: Attaining High-performing Software Teams with Agile and Lean Practices: An Empirical Case Study. In: 1st International Software Technology Exchange Workshop, Swedsoft (2011)
25. Höfner, G., Mani, V.S., Nambiar, R., Apte, M.: Fostering a high-performance culture in offshore software engineering teams using balanced scorecards and project scorecards. In: 6th IEEE International Conference on Global Software Engineering, pp. 35–39 (2011)
26. Sudhakar, G.P.: Understanding Software Development Team Performance. Scientific Annals of the "Alexandru Ioan Cuza" Univesity of Iasi, Economic Sciences Section (2010)
27. Smite, D., Wohlin, C.: Risk Identification in Software Product Transfers. In: 1st International Software Technology Exchange Workshop, Swedsoft (2011)

Release Readiness Indicator for Mature Agile and Lean Software Development Projects

Miroslaw Staron[1], Wilhelm Meding[2], and Klas Palm[2]

[1] Software Centre, Computer Science and Engineering
Chalmers / University of Gothenburg
SE-412 96 Gothenburg, Sweden
miroslaw.staron@ituniv.se
[2] Ericsson Metrics Team, Ericsson Product Development
Ericsson AB, Sweden
{wilhelm.meding,klas.palm}@ericsson.com

Abstract. Large companies like Ericsson increasingly often adopt the principles of Agile and Lean software development and develop large software products in iterative manner – in order to quickly respond to customer needs. In this paper we present the main indicator which is sufficient for a mature software development organization in order to predict the time in weeks to release the product. In our research project we collaborated closely with a large Agile+Lean software development project at Ericsson in Sweden. This large and mature software development project and organization has found this main indicator – *release readiness* – to be so important that it was used as a key performance indicator and is used in controlling the development of the product and improving organizational performance. The indicator was developed and validated in an action research project at one of the units of Ericsson AB in Sweden in one of its largest projects.

1   Introduction

Continuous delivery of customer value is crucial for software development companies operating in the market-driven context. This way of operating in the global market today is supported by the Agile and Lean ways-of-working with short feedback loops, empowered teams and customer involvement [1, 2]. Such concepts as customer value, customer pull and continuous quality assessment from Lean have taken the development organization to a mature stage with teams that are aware of the goals of the organization as well as the technical details of the products. The Agile software development methods are used for both small projects and for large development projects with over 100 designers [3-6] (and this trend increases). The methods are used also in the context of product maintenance, thus making the work of maintenance personnel more efficient [7].

As Agile methods are increasingly often used to address the challenges of continuous deployment, customer responsiveness and empowering teams for development of large software products, new challenges occur which relate to the

C. Wohlin (Ed.): XP 2012, LNBIP 111, pp. 93–107, 2012.
© Springer-Verlag Berlin Heidelberg 2012

parallel development of features of large software products. Multiple teams which develop code for distinct features on a single component might not be fully aware about the changes/development of the code which is done by other parallel teams working on the same component [8]. Since the teams are often independent (empowered, i.e. self-directed, self-selected, and self-managed), there is a need for automated support in maintaining the quality of the product [4, 9].

Due to the dynamics of multiple teams, parallel features and self-management/organization, the main area where the support is needed is *release readiness* – the area is important for project managers, product owners and for the release responsible that need predictions on when the product is going to be ready to be deployed to customer environments – also known as "definition of done". The release readiness is a concrete realization of the definition of done in the context of mature Agile and Lean organization.

However, metrics in this area cannot be done manually as the manual work significantly increases the costs of the metric and decreases its quality over time. Automation is the key aspect in the monitoring of these two areas as "measurement" is not an activity that contributed directly to the product development, but is very important for it. The efficiency of automated measurement outweighs costs of using the measures and makes the measures transparent for the whole development organization – from designers to unit managers.

Based on the above we addressed the following research question in this paper:

Which are the main indicators in the area of release readiness?

The research question was addressed through an action research project conducted collaboratively between University of Gothenburg and Ericsson AB in Sweden. The action research project took place in a product development organization which develops a mature core network telecommunication product handling mobile data traffic. The results of the project showed one single indicator which was introduced and validated in a large software development project at that unit and is under implementation at another large software development project.

The remaining of the paper is structured as follows: section 2 presents the most relevant related work. Section 3 describes the organizational context of our work and outlines the design and operation of our action research study. Section 4 presents the indicator and section 5 presents the results from the evaluation of the indicator in the organization. Finally section 6 contains the conclusions from our work.

2   Related Work

The work presented in this paper is the continuation of the work on monitoring bottlenecks in large software development organizations which was conducted in the same unit of Ericsson [4]. In the previous work we developed and introduced a method based on automated indicators for monitoring the capacity and bottlenecks in the work flow in the large software development project – i.e. the process/project view of software development in that organization. In our current work we addressed the product view by developing and introducing the quality readiness indicator – i.e. indicator showing when the product is ready to be released/deployed to the customers.

Measuring business value is one of the main measures which should be used by Agile teams and companies [10]. The awareness of how the team contributes to the value is an important driver for the success of Agile projects. What the authors of the cited article postulate is similar to what we intend to achieve – provide key information without introducing manual work overhead. The focus of the cited article is on the customer value, whereas the focus of this article is on quality risk monitoring and predicting delivery time – both articles complement each other.

Another important measure which is claimed to stimulate agility in software development teams is the RTF (Running Tested Features) measure, popular in XP [11]. The metric combines three important concepts – the feature (i.e. a piece of code useful for the end-user, not a small increment that is not visible to the end user), execution (i.e. adding the value to the product through shipping the features to the customer), and the testing process (i.e. the quality of the feature – not only should it be execute, but also be of sufficient quality). This measure stimulates smart continuous deployment strategies and is intended to capture similar aspects as our release readiness indicator although in smaller projects.

A set of other metrics useful in the context of continuous deployment can be found in the work of Fritz [12] in the context of market driven software development organization. The metrics presented by Fritz measure such aspects as continuous integration pace or the pace of delivery of features to the customers. These metrics complement the two indicators presented in this paper with a different perspective important for product management.

The delivery strategy which is an extension of the concept of continuous deployment has been found as one of the three key aspects important for Agile software development organizations in a survey of 109 companies by Chow and Cao [13]. The indicator presented in this paper is a means of supporting organizations in their transition towards achieving efficient delivery processes which are in line with the delivery strategy prioritized by practitioners in this survey.

3   Organizational Context

The indicator presented in this paper was based on a study of one unit of Ericsson with approximately 700 persons. The unit was located at multiple sites with over 30 development teams working in a software development project of ca. 150 persons. The unit was mature in both the software development paradigm (*streamline development*) and the measurement processes (adoption of ISO/IEC 15939, [14]). This ISO standard is one of the key aspects of our work since it defines one of the main concepts – *indicator* – used in the organization. The other key concepts are *information need* and *stakeholder*. The notion of indicators has shown itself to be one of the key aspects of the successful adoption of such "metrics" as quality readiness [14].

3.1   ISO/IEC 15939

The current measurement processes in the organization are based on ISO/IEC 15939:2007 standard, which is a normative specification for the processes used to define, collect, and analyze quantitative data in software projects or organizations. The central role in the standard is played by the information product which is a set of one or more indicators with their associated interpretations that address the information need [15]. The information need is an insight necessary for a stakeholder to manage objectives, goals, risks, and problems observed in the measured objects [15]. These measured objects can be entities like projects, organizations, software products, etc. characterized by a set of attributes. We use the following definitions from ISO/IEC 15939:2007 [16]:

- Base measure – measure defined in terms of an attribute and the method for quantifying it. This definition is based on the definition of base quantity from.
- Derived measure – measure that is defined as a function of two or more values of base measures. This definition is based on the definition of derived quantity from.
- Indicator – measure that provides an estimate or evaluation of specified attributes derived from a model with respect to defined information needs.
- Decision criteria – thresholds, targets, or patterns used to determine the need for action or further investigation, or to describe the level of confidence in a given result.
- Information product – one or more indicators and their associated interpretations that address an information need.
- Measurement method – logical sequence or operations, described generically, used in quantifying an attribute with respect to a specified scale.
- Measurement function – algorithm or calculation performed to combine two or more base measures.
- Attribute – property or characteristics of an entity that can be distinguished quantitatively or qualitatively by human or automated means.
- Entity – object that is to be characterized by measuring its attributes.
- Measurement process – process for establishing, planning, performing and evaluating measurement within an overall project, enterprise or organizational measurement structure.
- Measurement instrument – a procedure to assign a value to a base measure.

The view on measures presented in ISO/IEC 15939 is consistent with other engineering disciplines, the standard states that it is based on ISO/IEC 15288:2007 (Software and Systems engineering - Measurement Processes) [17], ISO/IEC 14598-1:1999 (Information technology - Software product evaluation) [18], ISO/IEC 9126-x [19], ISO/IEC 25000 series of standards, or International vocabulary of basic and general terms in metrology (VIM) [16]. Conceptually, the elements (different kinds of measures) which are used in the measurement process can be presented as in Figure 1.

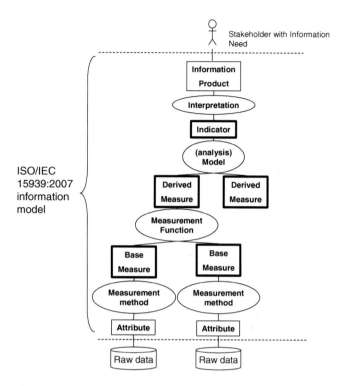

Fig. 1. Measurement system information model (from ISO/IEC 15939:2007)

One of the key factors for every measurement system is that it has to satisfy an information need of a stakeholder – i.e. there needs to be a person/organization who/which is dependent on the information that the measurement system provides. Typical stakeholders are project managers, organization managers, architects, product managers, customer representatives, and similar [20-23]. The indicator is intended to provide information along with interpretation, which implies the existence of an analysis model that eases the interpretation. The analysis model is a set of decision criteria used when assessing the value of an indicator – e.g. describing at which value of the indicator we e.g. set a red flag signaling problems in the measured object. The derived measures (based on the definition of the derived quantity) and base measures (based on the definition of the base quantity) are used to provide the information for calculating the value of the indicator.

3.2   Streamline Development, SD

The context of the case study was one of the software development organizations of Ericsson AB. The organization and the project within Ericsson, which we worked closely with, developed large products for the mobile telephony network. The size of the organization was several hundred engineers and the size of the projects can be up to 200 engineers. Projects were executed according to the principles of Agile software development and Lean production system referred to as Streamline development (SD) within Ericsson [24]. In short, the principles of Streamline development postulated that software development was organized as a series of activities centered around the product and executed mainly in cross-functional teams responsible for the design, implementation and partially testing of their part of the product (e.g. a feature) [25]. This was found to be rather typical process design that addressed market pull in Lean development [26].

A noteworthy fact observed in our study was that in SD the releases of new software versions to customers were frequent and that there was always a release-ready version of the system: referred to as Latest System Version, LSV [25]. It is the defects existing (and known) in that version of the system that were of interest for the project and product management. Ideally the number of known defects in that version of the system should be 0, however, during the development (i.e. between releases) this number might vary as there might be defects which are discovered during the process of integrating new features (parts of code) into the latest system version. In practice there are almost always defects being fixed as integration and testing is continuous. However, at release times the main branch was frozen with the purpose of removing all defects – this removal was the responsibility of the release project, which was a project aimed at packaging the product and preparing it for the market availability.

An overview of the development process with the list of metrics used by the relevant stakeholders is presented in Figure 2.

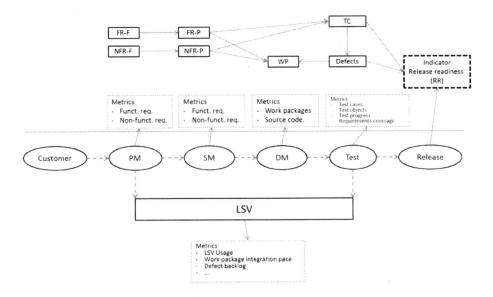

Fig. 2. Overview of the development process and measures collected

In Figure 2 the process started with the customer requirements being captured by Product Management (PM) who divided the requirements into functional and non-functional requirements for customer features (FR-F and NFR-F). These requirements were broken down into functional and non-functional requirements for product features (FR-P and NFR-P). These requirements were then packaged into work packages (WP) for design teams (DM). The requirements were also traced to test cases (TC) which verified that the requirements were implemented and that they were implemented with the appropriate quality (e.g. performance, security). All requirements were traced to test cases monitored by the quality manager at the organization (through automated measurement systems like [4, 27]). Defects could appear when the test cases were executed and these defects (Defect) were fed back to the design teams which had to remove them from the code before the product was released.

The main criterion for releasing the product was that all functionality was in place. This meant that all requirements were linked to test cases, all test cases were executed and all test cases were passed. This also meant that all defects were removed since discovering of a defect equals to failure of a test case which entails the need to re-execute the test case.

Because the above mechanisms were in place, including automated measurement systems for monitoring that all requirements were traced to test cases and that all defects are reported, only one indicator was needed and sufficient to check whether the product is ready to be released – RR (Release Readiness).

3.3   Research Method and Study Design

In this research we chose *action research* as the most appropriate approach [28]. We worked in close collaboration with product development projects at one of the units of Ericsson and provided measures (indicators) based on the requests from the organization. In this section we present in detail the design of cycles which focused on the development of the RR indicator and its evaluation. The summary of all action research cycles is as follows:

1. Initial cycle: elicitation of "theory" behind the measures. In this cycle we planned how understand/verify which factors are important for the measures – e.g. filtering criteria for test cases or types of changes. The whole research team was involved (the research team is described in the next paragraphs).
2. Initial development cycle: development of the measures and application of them on historical data. In this cycle we developed and validated the measures on the historical data available at the company. The university researcher was involved in development and the research team was involved in the feedback loop.
3. Deployment cycle: the developed indicators were deployed in the project with ca. 100 developers working on a large telecom network product. The university researcher was involved in data collection and monitoring of the quality of the data. The rest of the research team was involved in the monitoring of the situation in the project and checking whether the indicators reflect the current situation in the project.
4. Evaluation and Improvement cycle: the final cycle of the action research evaluated the empirical validity of the indicators. The evaluation was done by measuring the

correctness of the prediction. The whole research team was involved in the evaluation cycle whereas the measurement team leader was involved in the maintenance of the developed measurement system.

The sampling of the project was convenience sampling [29] – the research team was part of this project and the development of the indicator was needed for that particular development project.

Each cycle contained relevant roles, but the core research team consisted of:

- University researcher with background in software engineering and focus on software metrics
- Metric team leader with the responsibility to develop, deploy and maintain measurement systems in the company
- Quality manager with the responsibility for the quality in the project/product
- Test leader with the responsibility for test analysis and execution for the project/product where the measures were deployed.
- Deputy project manager with the responsibility to monitor delivery of features in the project/product where the measures were deployed.

The additional involved roles (in particular cycles) were team managers, line/section managers, and technical responsible for software components in the system.

Development of Indicators (cycle 2). For the development of the quality readiness indicator (QR) the research team started with an initial set of predictor variables per week, including:

- #[1] executed test cases
- # planned test cases (per priority and type)
- # failed test cases
- # passed test cases
- # defects discovered per test case
- # defects discovered
- # defects to be removed (defect backlog in Figure 2)
- # defects removed
- # defects verified
- # features integrated into the main code branch (work package integration pace in Figure 2)
- # empty integration spots (LSV usage Figure 2)

According to the ISO 15939 Measurement Information Model we characterized these predictor variables as base measures with precisely defined measurement methods for data collection. Statistical correlation analyses were performed and they were complemented with expert opinion on whether there exist causal relationships in the data (a method which was previously shown to be successful in that organization [5]). In particular the research team was interested in such aspects as for example *if more*

---

[1] Reads: "number of".

features are integrated, will that cause higher defect reporting rate after a number of weeks in a project? These aspects could be captured by statistical analyses of correlations or time series, but it was important for the team to capture the empirical properties of the development process together with the statistical dependencies in the data.

The goal of the research team was to find the minimal set of predictor variables that would not be correlated to each other and that would reflect the empirical properties of agile software development at Ericsson. This resulted in the set of 4 predictor variables (discussed in section 4).

Evaluation (Cycle 4). The evaluation cycle was planned to take place in a longer period of time after the measures were deployed into the organization. The evaluation was planned to be a number of meetings during a period of 6 months with the key stakeholders for the indicators – each meeting was a short interview. Two main questions were posed in the interviews:

- The indicator shows that the product will be ready to release in week <X>. Does it seem "right" according to your professional opinion and to your judgment of the situation in the project?
- In case you see any discrepancies, could you briefly describe why (according to you) this is the case?

The goal of these questions was to focus the stakeholder to reason about the empirical assessment of the same situation which was calculated by the indicators.

4   Release Readiness (RR) Indicator

In this section we present the release readiness indicator and its visualization at the company.

4.1   Time to Release

The product release-quality readiness indicator predicted when the product under development would have the sufficient quality for being released. The quality was measured in a number of open defect reports for the product – meaning that the right quality for releasing of the product was 0 defects. The 0-defect criterion was sufficient only when another criterion was fulfilled – all functionality was tested and all test cases were passed. This means that in practice the indicator of quality-release readiness had to take into account both.

In the case of the studied organization at Ericsson we introduced the following indicator (RR):

$$RR = (\frac{\#defects}{defect\_removal\_rate - (test\_execution\_rate - test\_pass\_rate)})$$

Where *#defects* was the number of open defects for the product[2], *defect_removal_rate* was the average number of removed defects during the last 4 weeks, *test_execution_rate* was the average number of test cases executed during the last 4 weaks and *test_pass_rate* was the average number of test cases passed during the last 4 weaks. The 4 weeks period was chosed based on statistical and empirical analyses. These analyses showed that based on the length of the test cycles and the defect removal activities the 4 week period was the most logical length for this prediction and provided the most accurate results.

The indicator predicted in which week the release would be possible given the number of known defects now, how many defects were removed on average in the last few (4) weeks, and how many defects were expected to be discovered given the number of test cases being executed[3].

The fact that the prediction formula contains only the test execution and pass rate instead of test planning was dictated by the fact that the organization was mature and its processes used continuous testing (i.e. running tests continuously and observing the number of passed test cases) rather than pre-planned testing sequences executed once in the project. The nature of the stakeholder for this indicator (project manager) and the auxiliary metrics of traceability of requirements to test cases made it possible to use this prediction formula with confidence that no vital information was omitted.

Figure 3 presents how the indicator was spread in the organization on a daily basis – in a form of MS Vista Sidebar gadget.

Fig. 3. MS Vista Gadget with predicted week of release

The content of the gadget shows 2 weeks for the project to obtain the release-quality *(weeks to release)*. The presentation is simple and succinct giving the stakeholder (the manager of the studied product development project) the necessary information. The gadget also contains information about the validity of the measure – Information Quality which abbreviates to *IQ*, [30].

---

[2] This measurement included all defects that need to be removed from the product before the release.

[3] One could notice that there is no measure like "#of test cases planned" in the formula. This is intentional as the rationale behind this indicator is that the test cases are to be executed until all defects are fixed – that in particular means that "failing" test cases are executed until they are passed.

5   Results from Evaluation

The results from the evaluation of our indicator were collected from the mentioned product development project at Ericsson. The introduction of the indicator showed that the organization effectively adopted it as a KPI – Key Performance Indicator and that the quality manager for the project used it to replace other activities in his work.

5.1   Evaluation Results

Figure 4 presents an excerpt from a chart where the release week is shown. Due to the confidentiality of the data we cannot provide accuracy metric like MRE (Mean Relative Error) as it would reveal the length of the development cycle for the product. However, we can show differences in the prediction in the absolute terms – shown in the diagram in Figure 4, alike the evaluation of other predictions in the same organization [31]. We followed up the indicator in a discussion with the stakeholder on a bi-weekly basis. The chart shows that the indicator predicted the release to be between week number 8 in 2011 and week number 14 in 2011. During the discussion with the stakeholder, the stakeholder was able to relate to the differences and pointed to particular events in the project which slowed the testing process, increased the pace of defect removal activities or reallocated resources. Each of the events caused the change of the indicator in the correct direction, for example: decreasing the pace of defect removal has increased the predicted release week when making the prediction in week 4, 5, and 6; increasing the test execution rate has decreased the time to release in week 9. The stakeholder perceived it to be normal that the indicator changes the prediction since the situation in the project changed during the evaluation period – in fact the stakeholder expected the indicator to show this trend.

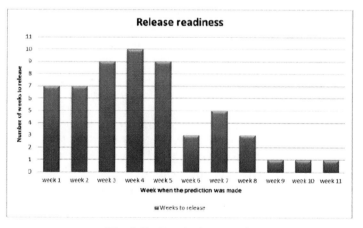

Fig. 4. Predicted release week

During the evaluation of the indicator with the quality manager, we obtained the following quote which summarizes his perception of the indicator:

"Thanks to this indicator I do not have to 'walk the floor' anymore and ask about the status. I have everything I need in one number and I can monitor that all necessary assumptions hold"

By saying *"monitor that all necessary assumptions hold"* the quality manager expressed his confidence in the indicator which was presented to him together with the associated statistics about such assumptions as:

- Traceability between test cases to requirements
- Traceability between test cases to work packages
- Traceability between work packages and requirements
- Code coverage by test cases

These assumptions reflect the ways of working in the project as presented earlier in Figure 2 in section 3.2. The measures which measured to what degree the assumptions hold for the indicator provided the complete picture for the quality manager and allowed him to assure the quality of information provided to the stakeholder – the project manager.

The release-readiness indicator and the metrics controlling the assumptions were fully automated – i.e. the process of collecting, analyzing and presenting information was executed entirely without the manual work. The data was collected from the defect database and the database containing log of executed, planned, passed and failed test cases. The full automation was appreciated and contributed to maintaining the high quality of the presented indicator [30] – and in this way making it trustworthy in the organization to such extent as being adopted as Key Performance Indicator (KPI). The stakeholder's evaluation of this indicator can be summarized in the following quote: *"This measurement combines all the information I want to know in order to understand the quality of the product as well as the status and progress of the development program, into one understandable and very clear KPI"*. The adoption of this indicator as one of the few KPI in the organization showed that the organization (with up to 200 engineers) perceived this indicator to be trustworthy enough to be used in observing organization's capability to continuously deliver the customer value.

5.2   Validity Evaluation

As every empirical study, our study has certain threats to validity, which are considered using the categories presented by Wohlin [32].

The main *external validity* threat was the fact that we evaluated the indicator at a single company. We minimized this threat by using the same indicator in another development project at Ericsson with similar results (although the evaluation was not as strict as the one presented in this paper). Based on the literature review and the presence of such metrics as feature backlog or RTF (Running Tested Features) in smaller Agile development projects, we believe that our results are applicable to other large software development projects where the assumptions described in section 3 are met. The main *conclusion validity* threat was the lack of statistical power in the evaluation of our indicator – we evaluated it in a single project and due to the confidentiality of the data we cannot reveal the accuracy of the indicator (as this would reveal the length of the development cycle in the organization). In order to minimize this threat we performed the empirical validation of the indicator in a series of meetings with the stakeholder. The main *construct validity* of our study is the fact that the organization's high maturity meant that the dependencies between metrics (such as traceability of requirements to test cases) were implicitly embedded into the formula. In order to minimize the threat we monitored these dependencies in supporting measurement systems in the organization.

6   Conclusions

In this paper we addressed the problem of supporting mature Agile and Lean software development organizations in effective and efficient prediction when the software product is ready to be released. The problem is evident in larger software development organizations with multiple parallel empowered teams contributing to the development of a single product. Before this indicator was introduced, the organization had worked in a release-planning matter with standard release planning. After the indicator was introduced the organization could stimulate its change towards a direction of being able to continuously release the current version of its large software product without the risk of jeopardizing the operations of the customer – i.e. at the high quality level.

The indicator presented in this paper was supported with a number of metrics that controlled the assumptions of the indicator. All measurement systems collecting the information were automated and therefore the metrics and the indicators were very much appreciated and spread throughout the company. Based on our experiences from the introduction of the presented indicator we could recommend companies interested in introducing this indicator to put special attention to deliver to the stakeholder the metrics for controlling the assumptions as part of the information quality evaluation.

Acknowledgements. This research has been carried out in the Software Centre, University of Gothenburg, and Ericsson AB.

References

[1] Poppendieck, M., Poppendieck, T.: Implementing Lean Software Development: From Concept to Cash. Addison-Wesley, Boston (2007)
[2] Salo, O., Abrahamsson, P.: Agile methods in European embedded software development organisations: a survey on the actual use and usefulness of Extreme Programming and Scrum. IET Software 2, 58–64 (2008)
[3] Korhonen, K.: Exploring Defect Data, Quality and Engagement during Agile Transformation at a Large Multisite Organization. In: Agile Processes in Software Engineering and Extreme Programming, pp. 88–102 (2010)
[4] Staron, M., Meding, W.: Monitoring Bottlenecks in Agile and Lean Software Development Projects – A Method and Its Industrial Use. In: Product-Focused Software Process Improvement, Tore Cane, Italy, pp. 3–16 (2011)

[5] Staron, M., Meding, W., Söderqvist, B.: A method for forecasting defect backlog in large streamline software development projects and its industrial evaluation. Information and Software Technology 52, 1069–1079 (2010)

[6] Gabrielle, B.: Rolling Out Agile in a Large Enterprise. In: Hawaii International Conference on System Sciences, pp. 462–462 (2008)

[7] Korhonen, K.: Adopting Agile Practices in Teams with No Direct Programming Responsibility – A Case Study. In: Product-Focused Software Process Improvement, pp. 30–43 (2011)

[8] Ball, T., Nagappan, N.: Use of relative code churn measures to predict system defect density. In: 27th International Conference on Software Engineering, St. Louis, MO, USA, pp. 284–292 (2005)

[9] Staron, M., Meding, W.: Defect Inflow Prediction in Large Software Projects. e-Informatica Software Engineering Journal 4, 1–23 (2010)

[10] Hartmann, D., Dymond, R.: Appropriate agile measurement: using metrics and diagnostics to deliver business value. In: Agile Conference, pp. 126–134 (2006)

[11] Jeffries, R.: A Metric Leading to Agility (2004), http://xprogramming.com/xpmag/jatRtsMetric

[12] Fitz, T.: Continuous Deployment at IMVU: Doing the impossible fifty times a day (2009), http://timothyfitz.wordpress.com/2009/02/10/continuous-deployment-at-imvu-doing-the-impossible-fifty-times-a-day/

[13] Chow, T., Cao, D.-B.: A survey study of critical success factors in agile software projects. Journal of Systems and Software 81, 961–971 (2008)

[14] Staron, M., Meding, W., Karlsson, G., Nilsson, C.: Developing measurement systems: an industrial case study. Journal of Software Maintenance and Evolution: Research and Practice, n/a–n/a (2010)

[15] International Standard Organization and International Electrotechnical Commission. Software engineering – Software measurement process. ISO/IEC, Geneva (2002)

[16] International Bureau of Weights and Measures. In: International vocabulary of basic and general terms in metrology = Vocabulaire international des termes fondamentaux et généraux de métrologie, 2nd edn., International Organization for Standardization, Genève (1993)

[17] International Standard Organization. Systems engineering – System life cycle processes 15288:2002 (2002)

[18] International Standard Organization. Information technology – Software product evaluation 14598-1:1999 (1999)

[19] International Standard Organization and International Electrotechnical Commission. ISO/IEC 9126 - Software engineering – Product quality Part: 1 Quality model. International Standard Organization / International Electrotechnical Commission, Geneva (2001)

[20] Umarji, M., Emurian, H.: Acceptance Issues in Metrics Program Implementation, pp. 20–20 (2005)

[21] Gopal, A., Mukhopadhyay, T., Krishnan, M.S.: The impact of institutional forces on software metrics programs. IEEE Transactions on Software Engineering 31, 679–694 (2005)

[22] Umarji, M., Emurian, H.: Acceptance issues in metrics program implementation, p. 10 (2005)

[23] Kilpi, T.: Implementing a Software Metrics Program at Nokia. IEEE Software 18, 72–77 (2001)

[24] Tomaszewski, P., Berander, P., Damm, L.-O.: From Traditional to Streamline Development - Opportunities and Challenges. Software Process Improvement and Practice, 1–20 (2007)

[25] Akg, A.E., Keskin, H., Byrne, J., Imamoglu, S.Z.: Antecedents and consequences of team potency in software development projects. Inf. Manage. 44, 646–656 (2007)
[26] Liker, J.K.: The Toyota way: 14 management principles from the world's greatest manufacturer. McGraw-Hill, New York (2004)
[27] Staron, M., Meding, W., Nilsson, C.: A Framework for Developing Measurement Systems and Its Industrial Evaluation. Information and Software Technology 51, 721–737 (2008)
[28] Susman, G.I., Evered, R.D.: An Assessment of the Scientific Merits of Action Research. Administrative Science Quarterly 23, 582–603 (1978)
[29] Yin, R.K.: Case Study Research: Design and Methods. SAGE Publications Inc. (2008)
[30] Staron, M., Meding, W.: Ensuring Reliability of Information Provided by Measurement Systems. In: Software Process and Product Measurement, pp. 1–16 (2009)
[31] Staron, M., Meding, W.: Short-term Defect Inflow Prediction in Large Software Project - An Initial Evaluation. In: International Conference on Empirical Assessment in Software Engineering (EASE), Keele, UK (2007)
[32] Wohlin, C., Runeson, P., Höst, M., Ohlsson, M.C., Regnell, B., Wesslèn, A.: Experimentation in Software Engineering: An Introduction. Kluwer Academic Publisher, Boston MA (2000)

A Palette of Lean Indicators to Detect Waste in Software Maintenance: A Case Study

Kai Petersen

Blekinge Institute of Technology, 37140 Karlskrona, Sweden
Ericsson AB, Box 518, SE-371 23, Karlskrona, Sweden
kai.petersen@bth.se, kai.petersen@ericsson.com

Abstract. Software maintenance is a key activity in software development requiring considerable effort and time. Hence, it is important to increase the efficiency and effectiveness of the maintenance process. The objective of this article is to introduce a palette of indicators to assess the maintenance process based on indicators lean indicators. Four indicators aiming at detecting waste have been proposed, namely the inflow of maintenance requests, the flow of maintenance requests through the maintenance process with regard to continuous value creation and high throughput, the analysis of lead-times, and the analysis of workload. The research method is case study in which the proposed indicators were applied on the maintenance process of one case company (Ericsson AB).

Keywords: Lean Measurement, Software Maintenance.

1 Introduction

Lean principles have revolutionized the way products are built by identifying waste and providing analysis tools for the production process to make it more efficient and effective [8]. Efficiency is defined as *"the degree of the economy with which the process consumes resources, especially time and money"* [14]. Effectiveness refers to *"how well the process actually accomplishes its intended purposes"* [14]. With respect to the seven wastes of software development [13] efficiency is strongly related to partially done work, handovers, motion and task switching, delays and defects, while effectiveness is related to extra features, extra processes, defects, and over-production. To leverage on the benefits achieved in lean product development (high quality, quick response to customer needs, just in time development with little work in progress) lean has become popular for software development as well [13]. To facilitate lean principles in product development and manufacturing indicators and measures were an important tool for continuous improvements. In particular, the indicators and measures provide the opportunity to detect whether or not a lean process has been achieved.

Development activities are distinguished into initial software development where the software product is specified, implemented and tested and thereafter delivered to the market, and software maintenance [1]. According to the IEEE Standard for Software Maintenance (IEEE 1219) the maintenance of software

C. Wohlin (Ed.): XP 2012, LNBIP 111, pp. 108–122, 2012.

is defined as *"the modification of a software product after delivery to correct faults, to improve performance or other attributes, or to adapt the product to a modified environment."* Software maintenance is a large part of the software development effort, with effort for maintenance being in the range of 50-80 % of all software development effort [17]. Given these observations software maintenance is an essential activity in software development and hence improvements in this activity have the potential to increase the efficiency and effectiveness of an overall software development organization. Therefore, the identification of information products focusing on software maintenance was considered an important effort in the investigated company. An information product consists of a palette of indicators and their associated interpretation. An indicator itself is a measure (or set of measures) associated with an analytical model. Without the analytical model, the measure is simply a variable with an assigned value (see ISO/IEC-15939/2002).

This paper proposes a palette of indicators for the maintenance process to support the identification of inefficiencies and effectiveness in software maintenance, and through that help to understand whether the organization adheres to lean principles. For that purpose, indicators and measures are mapped to lean principles to assess the process. A combined analysis of the indicators led to the identification of inefficiencies and ineffectiveness.

The remainder of the paper is structured as follows: Section 2 presents related work. Section 3 illustrates the indicators and how to conduct a combined analysis of them. Section 4 presents the research method, followed by the results (Section 5) and their discussion (Section 6). Section 7 concludes the paper.

2   Related Work

The related work focuses on indicators and measurements proposed in the maintenance context to assess maintenance performance.

Alam et al. [2] proposed measuring progress by recording code changes and studying the time dependencies between them. Progress tracking is done in analogy to construction where a building is continuously built based on dependent changes, and is an essential part of agile and lean methods [9]. This allows analyzing whether new MRs (Maintenance Requests) are built upon new changes done recently, or old changes, or whether they are independent. One limitation of the method is that it does not show the progress with regard to the backlog of changes to be implemented.

Schneidewind [16] proposed to measure mean time between failure when testing maintenance enhancements, defect density with regard to changed lines of code, and the overall test time needed.

Henry et al. [5] divided software maintenance into different abstraction levels (activities, tasks, and procedures), where procedures are a refinement of tasks, and tasks are a refinement of activities. At the different abstraction levels measures were proposed on process (effort, completion rate of tasks, defects corrected per week) and product level (number of upgrades implemented, impact of upgrade changes, number of Lines of Code (LOC) added). However, no ways of information visualization and analysis have been proposed.

Sneed and Brössler [18] proposed a set of measurements to evaluate software maintenance performance, namely productivity (size*change rate/maintenance effort), defect density (defects per lines of code), document degradation, and user perception.

Rombach and Ulery [15] used the Goal Question Metric paradigm (from hereon referred to as GQM) to identify goals, questions and metrics for analyzing the maintenance process. The GQM approach led collecting he number of changed module per maintenance task, effort (staff-hours) needed for isolating what to change (i.e. impact analysis), effort (staff-hours) for change implementation, and portion of reused documentation per maintenance task.

Stark [19] provided an experience report on the introduction of a measurement program for software maintenance. The measures were also derived based on the GQM paradigm. GQM led to three categories of measures, namely measures regarding customer satisfaction, costs of the maintenance program, and schedule.

Chan [3] raises the importance of addressing MRs quickly, i.e. with short lead-time. To capture the lead-time he distinguishes queuing/processing time (actual work is done) and service time (waiting).

A common indicator in lean is related to flow (cumulative flow diagrams), which allow to detect partially done work, bottlenecks, and discontinuous workflows as well as large hand-overs [12]. In connection to flow lean also stresses to limit work in process in relation to capacity by measuring inventory of work [11]. Furthermore, six sigma is used in lean to detect unstable situations (high variances) in process performance, e.g. with respect to built in quality [6].

The following observations regarding the related work can be made: Often the literature reported measures that are relevant for lean software development, but they are reported in isolation. For example, it is important to distinguish waiting time and service time (cf. [3]) as waiting time is often much easier to improve than actual work practices. In addition, the measures do not make explicit use of visualizations in form of indicators. These are addressed in this paper by combining different indicators used in the lean context for a holistic analysis.

3   Palette of Lean Indicators for Software Maintenance

Each of the indicators used in the palette is later on combined to conduct an analysis with respect to inefficiency and ineffectiveness. First, the indicators are presented, followed by a discussion of how a combined analysis is done.

– The number of maintenance requests provides an indication of built in quality, as with build in quality the effort of keeping software operational (preventive maintenance) or making it work again (corrective maintenance) would be lower. Expressing MRs with a process control chart [6] allows seeing the stability in the inflow with respect to the mean, e.g. increases of the number of critical requests should be investigated. Furthermore, the number of revisions indicates how many attempts are needed to implement the maintenance request.

- The cumulative number of work items in different phases over time are plotted in form of a cumulative flow diagram [12]. The diagram is capable of revealing bottlenecks, and large variances in the flow (e.g. large handovers of artifacts between phases). Removing the bottlenecks allows addressing delays and with that reduces the amount of partially done work in progress.

- The principle *"deliver as fast as possible"* is assessed through measuring the duration of how long work needs to be completed. The lead-times often have large variances. Some phases have longer lead-times than others and should be comparable with regard the distribution of lead-time. Hence, box-plots are proposed as an approach for visualization.

- Respect people is related to setting reasonable goals and expectations, which includes to avoid overload situations and keeping the workload below capacity as this supports a smooth workflow [11]. Hence, the workload should be plotted over time with control charts. The charts will reveal peaks in workload, and allow for a discussion about reasonable workload with developers.

The following sections describe the plaette indicators in further detail.

3.1   Maintenance Inflow (M1)

The maintenance inflow shows the incoming requests from customers for needed maintenance activities. As pointed out earlier, the MRs can be either corrective or preventive. The inflow should be measured as number of new MRs per time unit (e.g. week). The measure is visualized through a control chart, showing the time on the x-axis and the number of new MRs on the y-axis (also referred to as a time-series). Marking the mean value, and plotting upper and lower control limits to determine whether the process is under control could extend the control chart.

3.2   Visualization through Cumulative Flow Diagrams (M2)

A fictional example of the construction of a cumulative flow diagram is shown in Figure 1. The x-axis shows the time-line and the y-axis shows the cumulative number of of MRs. The top-line (marked as inflow by the arrow) is the total number of MRs in development. In week 9 this was around 160, while it increased to around 220 in week 20. Even though the flow is shown we propose to treat it as a separate indicator (M1) and with that analyze the stability of the process with regard to the mean value and the deviations from the mean through upper control and lower control limits, which is not possible within the flow diagram.

The second line from the top represents the handover from phase A to B, the following line from phase B to C, and so forth. The vertical distance between two lines shows the work in process for a phase at a specific point in time. For example, in week 15 there are about 50 MRs in Phase B.

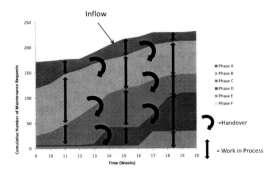

Fig. 1. Cumulative Flow Diagram

From the flow diagram a number of interpretations can be made with regard to continuous flow and throughput.

Continuous flow: Observing the figure it is visible that the flow of handovers from phase C to D is discontinuous. There is a long time of inactivity (week 9-13) and then suddenly a large handover occurs. That means, for example, that work done in week 9 and 10 can receive feedback from the following phase 5 weeks later. A long time of inactivity might lead to an overload situation when the work has to be done at once, and at the same time has potential of causing quality problems. For example, if phase D would be an integration testing phase with long times of inactivity a big-bang integration would become necessary.

Throughput: The throughput is characterized by the rate in which MRs are handed over from one phase to the other. As can be seen the handovers from phase A to B had less throughput from week 9 to 13 than the handovers from phase B to C, while the handovers became very similar after week 14. The throughput allows to make two observations: If the handover in a phase i is higher than in the phase $i+1$ this indicates a bottleneck as the work tasks come in with a higher pace than they go out. The other way around would indicate that the phase is running out of work, which in the case of maintenance could be good as it means free resources for other tasks in new software development.

The analysis can be done for single phases (e.g. analysis of MRs), or to get a picture of the overall performance of maintenance from start to finish, the incoming rate could be compared with the rate in which MRs are finalized.

3.3 Lead-Time (M3)

In order to measure the lead-times we propose to follow MRs through the maintenance flow by assigning states to them and using the measure time in state (TIS) [7] based on the transition date (TD) for checkpoint q and work-item i, or the current date (CD).

$$TIS_{qi} = \begin{cases} TD_{(q+1)i} - TD_{qi} & if\ TD_{(q+1)i}\ exists \\ CD - TD_{qi} & otherwise \end{cases}$$

When collecting the lead-time measures the mean values and variances should be analyzed and compared with each other. For example, one should compare the lead-time of critical and less critical MRs. Furthermore, distinguishing between processing time (value adding) and waiting time (non-value adding) allows to focus improvement efforts, e.g. when using value stream mapping to identify reasons and improvements for long waiting times. To visualize the differences we propose the use of box-plots showing the spread of the data.

3.4   Workload (M4)

The workload analysis is interesting with regard to the workload in value-adding activities over time. For that purpose the work in progress measured as the number of MRs (if possible, weighted by their effort) at a specific point in time should be plotted and analyzed using statistical process control. The control chart then should be used to have a dialog with the developers executing the activities to determine which work level is considered an overload situation. In order to be able to properly analyze the workload the effort for implementing MRs should be estimated based on their complexity, as a complex problem is likely to be causing more workload than an easy to fix problem. Categorizing requests in very complex, complex, and less complex, can for example, do this. Complexity means different things for different companies, and hence each company has to define its own thresholds for the categorization.

3.5   Combined Analysis

Looking at each individual measure only provides a limited view on the efficiency and effectiveness. For example, only looking at efficiency and identifying that the organization is highly efficient with respect to fixing maintenance requests might not be of use if primarily maintenance requests with low priority are fixed (lack of effectiveness). Hence, when conducting a combined analysis we recommend that observations from each of the indicators be captured in a matrix showing efficiency and effectiveness/ strengths and weaknesses.

4   Research Method

The research method used is an industrial case study [21], the study allowing to understand a specific situation (the use of lean software maintenance) in a given context. The goal of the study is to: Analyze *Lean Software Maintenance* for the purpose of *evaluation*, with respect to *the ability to show the presence/absence of inefficiencies/ ineffectiveness*, from the point of view of *the researcher*, in the context of *large scale software development dealing with maintenance*.

4.1   Case and Context

The case being studied is a development site of Ericsson AB, a Fortune 500 company working with large-scale software development producing telecommunication and multimedia applications that is ISO 9001:2000 certified. It is important to describe different dimensions of the context (e.g. product, market, process) in order to judge the outcome of a study and to be able to generalize the results [10]. The company is dealing with business critical applications with MRs on performance and reliability. The products are developed for a market, meaning that it is not developed for one specific customer (bespoke development). Instead, the product is offered to a market with many potential customers, not knowing exactly in advance who will actually buy the product. The studied product contains more than 850,000 lines of code. Testing on unit level is done with JUnit and for integration and regression testing with TTCN3 (Tree and Tabular Combined Notation, programming language for testing) [20].

4.2   Unit of Analysis

The unit of analysis is the maintenance process used for maintaining one large system developed at the case company. Figure 2 provides an overview of the maintenance process. The process starts with a customer raising a MR, which then is registered in the system by support. In the next step the MR is moved to the appropriate design organization. The next step is the analysis of the MR to understand it. In addition test cases are designed and executed to verify the MR. If the MR is understood and the test cases are clear it goes to the design, implementation, and test phase. If the MR is not clear, further analysis is necessary. In the analysis the design organization is working together with support receiving the information about the problem from the customer, and with experts knowing the system very well who serve as a consultant. When the MR is understood it is designed and implemented. The implementation of the MR needs to be verified, the verification being confirmed in a so-called technical answer, confirming that the solution is complete, coding standards are met, and that regression tests have been passed. If this is not the case the MR re-enters the analysis and/ or design and implementation stage. If the MR has passed it goes either to a correction package, which is further tested as a whole and then released with a number of correction, or in some cases it can go directly to the customer.

Based on the process it is tracked in which state/activity a MR resides. A loop is modeled in the tool for the situation where the technical answer does not accept the solution and thus the analysis and/ or implementation has to be redone. The number of iterations is numbered as revisions, revision A being through in first iteration, B being through in second iteration, and so forth.

4.3   Proposition

A proposition is similar to a hypotheses and states the expected outcome that is either supported or contradicted by the findings of the study [21]. The following proposition is stated for this study: *Indicators allow to capture the presence or absence of inefficiencies and ineffectiveness in a real world maintenance process.*

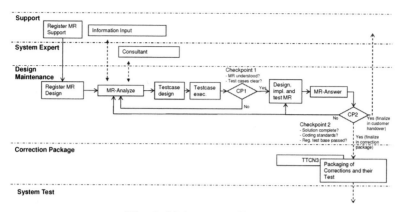

Fig. 2. Maintenance Process

4.4   Data Collection and Analysis

The data is collected through a company proprietary tool for keeping track of MRs that were internally or externally reported. That is, the incoming MRs are registered with their source and it is also visible which person entered them into the system. The time of entry is kept track of. In addition, the process steps are represented as states mirroring the process shown in Figure 2. This allows for the drawing of the cumulative flow diagrams and the measurement of the lead-times as defined by the lean software maintenance solution presented in this paper. Furthermore, the MRs are classified (weighted) based on their importance into as A, B, and C. The information about the classification has been obtained by a person having worked in testing and with experience in maintenance.

A: MRs that concern performance or stability of the system are mostly classified as A. They are important and most of the time they are not easy to fix. *B:* Problems in this category often concern the robustness of the system. In some cases robustness problems are also classified as A. *C:* These problems are less severe and more easy to fix, such as fixes in single functions. Depending on how intensively the function is used by the user, or how hard the functional MR is to correct the MR can in cases also be classified as B.

The analysis was done by applying the indicators and conduct an analysis to evaluate whether the solution is able to show the presence or absence of inefficiencies and ineffectiveness. The interpretation was done by the researcher who has good knowledge at the company's processes as he is embedded in the company. In addition, the results have been presented to a fellow practitioner to check whether the practitioner agrees with the observations made by the researcher to avoid bias.

4.5   Validity Threats

Correctness of data: One threat to validity when working with industrial data is the correctness and the completeness of the data. In the case of the company the tracking system for MRs has been used for almost 15 years and hence the practitioners are very familiar with using the system in their work, which reduces the threat of incorrect data. When changing the state of a MR the system automatically keeps track of the dates, which avoids that dates could be wrongly entered. Hence, the correctness and completeness of the data is given.

Company specific maintenance process: The maintenance process of the company is specific for the company. When applying the indicator in different companies the states would have to be changed depending on the steps in the maintenance process.

One company: When studying a company the results are true in the context of the company. In order to aid in the generalization of the results the context has been described. That is, the results were observed in a market-driven context working with large-scale software development.

Interpretation by the researcher: Another threat to validity is the correct interpretation of the data by the researcher. This threat was reduced (but not mitigated) as the researcher is embedded in the company and hence has knowledge about the processes. Presenting the results of the analysis to a practitioner working with testing and maintenance at the company reduced a bias in the analysis.

5   Results

5.1   Indicator for Maintenance Inflow (M1)

Figure 3 shows the inflow of A, B, and C MRs over time. It is clearly visible that B-MRs occur most often and continuously with a few peaks. A-MRs appear rather randomly and are spread around, which would be expected and desired as if many would be reported at once a disturbance of the regular development process could be expected. C-MRs are less frequent. Overall, the result shows that it would be worthwhile to investigate a reason for the peaks when many MRs are reported together. Otherwise, no significant inefficiencies or a particularly poor performance with regard to A-MRs can be observed.

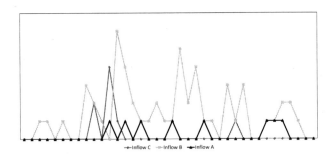

Fig. 3. MR Inflow for A, B, and C MRs (x-axis shows time and y-axis number of MRs)

5.2   Indicator for Flow of MRs (M2)

Figure 4 provides an overview of the indicators for MR flow.

Figure 4(a) shows the flow of A-MRs. It is apparent that the actual analysis and implementation appears to be a bottleneck in the beginning, leading to a high amount of the MRs being proposed as a solution at once. In addition the area of MRs waiting for finalization shows that improvements would be beneficial, as for a long time none of the accepted MRs are finalized and thus become available for the customer or for inclusion in a correction package.

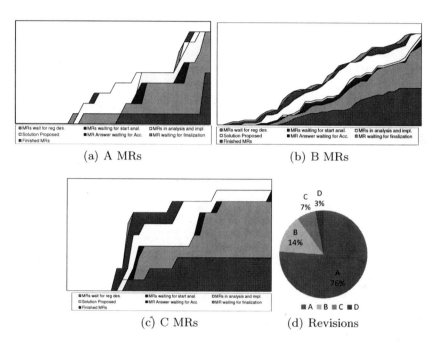

Fig. 4. Overview of Indicators for Constraint Identification - for Figures (a), (b), and (c) - x-axis shows time, y-axis number of items in different states

The maintenance flow for B-MRs (Figure 4(b)) shows that MRs are analyzed and implemented continuously. The same observation as for the A-MRs can be made here as well, with the difference that the B-MRs are finalized more continuously. However, it is apparent that the rate in which MRs (solution proposals) are accepted is much higher than the rate of finalization.

For the C-MRs a similar observation can be made, i.e. the MRs should be finalized in a more continuous manner.

With regard to differences between the A, B, and C MRs it should be noted that it is particularly important to avoid the queuing of MRs waiting for finalization in the A-case. The B-case appears to be more continuous, but still shows a bottleneck in this phase.

With regard to the iterations needed to successfully pass a MR through internal quality assurance Figure 4(d) illustrates that over 70 % of the MRs make it the first time (as A means when MR is implemented, then it passes the test immediately, without having to go through testing again). 14% have to go through testing twice to pass (B-revision), and only 7% have to go through test three times, and 3% four times. Overall, the analysis shows that no specific inefficiencies can be detected here. Of course, it would be worthwhile to investigate the reasons of why some MRs require several revisions (e.g. MRs related to revision C/ D).

5.3   Lead-Time Measurement (M3)

Figure 5 shows the lead-time of how long MRs reside in the different states, namely MR waiting for registration in design (S01), MR waiting for the analysis to start (S02), MR in analysis and implementation processing (S03), MR waiting for an answer acknowledging the solution (S04), and MR waiting for finalization (either as a direct delivery to the customer or the packaging into a maintenance request) (S05). The total lead-time is shown as well.

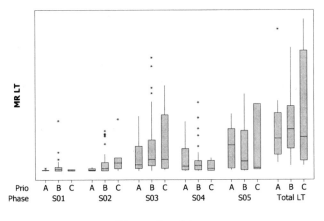

Fig. 5. Leadtime

Comparing A, B, and C MRs it is apparent that A and B MRs have a high overlap of the plots, and that the median values are similar. One could say that the lead-time should be the shortest for A-MRs. However, as noted before A-MRs are hard to fix and often rooted in performance problems, thus the similar lead-time in the analysis and design phase could be justified. However, at the same time it is striking that long lead-times are observed with regard to waiting times, the most significant waiting times being in waiting for finalization. In fact, the waiting times are very similar to the value adding time where the actual analysis and implementation takes place. As waiting time is often easier to improve in comparison to productive time the figures show an improvement potential.

The total lead-time shows that MRs classified as C have a similar median value as MRs classified as A, but the upper quartile for the lead-time is much higher. This is an indication for the lower priority of C MRs, and thus is an indication that the company focuses on effectiveness in concentrating more on getting A and B MRs to the market quickly.

5.4 Workload (M4)

The workload is illustrated as individual values and moving ranges in Figure 6. The continuous middle line shows the mean value, while the dashed lines show the upper and lower control limits being three standard deviations away from the mean. If values are outside of the control limits the situation is considered out of control. In this case a peak workload can be seen in the middle of the graph. For management to gain a better understanding of the workload situation we propose to use the chart and discuss the workload situation with the developers. This allows determining how much workload should be in the process at any given time to not overload the development organization.

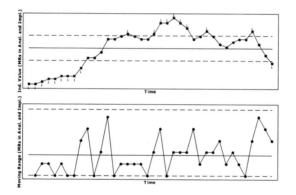

Fig. 6. Workload

5.5 Combined Analysis

In order to get a holistic picture it is important to bring the results together, as is done in Figure 7. The figure shows the presence of efficiencies and effectiveness on the top, and the discovery of inefficiencies and ineffectiveness on the bottom. Inefficiencies and Ineffectiveness are to be discovered as they show the improvement potential in the process. The efficiency generally refers to the performance that could be improved. The effectiveness shows strength and improvement potential with a focus on a comparative analysis between A, B, and C MRs.

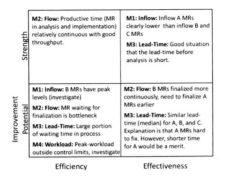

Fig. 7. Efficiency and Effectiveness Analysis

6   Discussion

The proposition of the study stated that *the proposed solution allows capturing the presence or absence of inefficiencies and ineffectiveness with regard to the questions raised and allow to discover the need for improvements.* Confirming the proposition indicates the usefulness of the method. In the results the method was used to show the presence or absence of inefficiencies and ineffectiveness. The following was identified:

With regard to the inflow of MRs into the development organization no striking quality issues have been identified with regard to A-MRs, they appeared randomly and did not occur in large batches. With regard to B-MRs we have shown that some peaks were visible, which should be investigated. Hence, the method showed some potential inefficiency here. One way of investigating corrective maintenance requests is to define a test strategy determining when a defect should have been found (known as fault-slip through [4]). This allows knowing how early the fault could have been detected.

The analysis of the flow showed that a bottleneck exists in finalizing the MRs across all types of MRs (i.e. A, B, and C). Hence, the reason for this waiting time should be identified with priority on the most critical MRs. It is interesting to observe that the bottleneck appeared in a phase, which is regarded as waiting time, which means that it could be more easily improved. No particular inefficiencies were identified with regard to iterations needed to pass through the internal quality control.

A comparison of the lead-times showed that more than 50 % of the lead-time appears to be waiting time. This is an interesting result as waiting time can more easily reduced than productive time, meaning that the measures show potential for the organization to significantly shorten their response time to MRs.

It was also demonstrated that peaks of workload could be identified.

Overall, this analysis that the proposition stated for this study holds, i.e. lean software maintenance is able to show the presence or absence of inefficiencies and ineffectiveness.

One important limitation of the indicators as implemented at the company is the classification of A, B, and C MRs, which should clearly distinguish between criticality (how important is the MR for the customer), but not size/complexity (how hard is it to fix the MR). This information would help analyzing which MRs should receive primary focus. For example, MRs with high priority that are easy to fix should be realized first. No information about complexity and effort of analysis and implementation was available. The information about complexity is also of importance to determine the workload, which in the case study was based on the number of MRs being in process at a specific point in time. The control chart for M4 can be displayed more accurately if each MR is weighted according to its estimated effort, effort correlating to size and complexity metrics.

7   Conclusion

In this paper a palette of indicators and their combined analysis has been presented. They support in the analysis of the software maintenance process with respect to inefficiencies and ineffectiveness. The indicators were the inflow of MRs, the visualization of the flow through the maintenance process with cumulative flow diagrams, lead-time measures based on state diagrams, and the analysis of workload peaks with process control charts.

The approach has been evaluated in an industrial case study at Ericsson AB. The study demonstrated that the approach was able to identify the presence or absence of inefficiencies and ineffectiveness in the maintenance process. We also have shown that lean software maintenance requires the company to keep track of few measurements, still allowing for a comprehensive analysis. In fact, the system implemented at the company allowed the immediate application. The prerequisites for implementing the approach are quite minimal, a company has only to keep track of registration of MRs with time-stamps, state-changes of the MRs in the process, and the criticality of the MRs have to be identified. Other companies can implement the process by defining specific states and keeping track of them. In the case of the studied company we were able to apply the measurements out of the box based on the tracking system already existing.

In future work lean software maintenance needs to be investigated in different industrial contexts.

References

1. April, A., Abran, A., Dumke, R.R.: Software maintenance productivity measurement: how to assess the readiness of your organization. In: Proceedings of the International Conference on Software Process and Product Measurement (IWSM/Metrikon 2004), pp. 1–12 (2004)
2. Alam, O., Adams, B., Hassan, A.E.: Measuring the progress of projects using the time dependence of code changes. In: Proceedings of the IEEE International Conference on Software Maintenance (ICSM 2009), pp. 329–338 (2009)

3. Chan, T.: Beyond productivity in software maintenance: Factors affecting lead time in servicing users' requests. In: Proceedings of the IEEE International Conference on Software Maintenance (ICSM 2000), pp. 228–235 (2000)
4. Damm, L.-O., Lundberg, L., Wohlin, C.: Faults-slip-through - a concept for measuring the efficiency of the test process. Software Process: Improvement and Practice 11(1), 47–59 (2006)
5. Henry, J., Blasewitz, R., Kettinger, D.: Defining and implementing a measurement-based software process. Software Maintenance: Research and Practice 8, 79–100 (1996)
6. Lunau, S., John, A.: Six Sigma Lean toolset: executing improvement projects successfully. Springer, Berlin (2008)
7. Miranda, E., Bourque, P.: Agile monitoring using the line of balance. Journal of Systems and Software 83(7), 1205–1215 (2010)
8. Morgan, J.M., Liker, J.K.: The Toyota product development system: integrating people, process, and technology. Productivity Press, New York (2006)
9. Petersen, K.: Is lean agile and agile lean? a comparison between two software development paradigms. In: Dogru, A.H., Bicer, V. (eds.) Modern Software Engineering Concepts and Practices: Advanced Approaches, pp. 19–46 (2010)
10. Petersen, K., Wohlin, C.: Context in industrial software engineering research. In: Proceedings of the 3rd International Symposium on Empirical Software Engineering and Measurement (ESEM 2009), pp. 401–404 (2009)
11. Petersen, K., Wohlin, C.: Software process improvement through the lean measurement (spi-leam) method. Journal of Systems and Software (2010) (in print)
12. Petersen, K., Wohlin, C.: Measuring the flow in lean software development. Softw., Pract. Exper. 41(9), 975–996 (2011)
13. Poppendieck, M., Poppendieck, T.: Lean software development: an agile toolkit. Addison-Wesley, Boston (2003)
14. Roberts, L.: Process reengineering: the key to achieving breakthrough success. ASQC Quality Press, Milwaukee (1994)
15. Rombach, H.D., Ulery, B.T.: Improving software maintenance through measurement. Proceedings of the IEEE 77(4), 581–595 (1989)
16. Schneidewind, N.F.: Measuring and evaluating maintenance process using reliability, risk, and test metrics. In: Proceedings of the IEEE International Conference on Software Maintenance (ICSM 1997), pp. 232–242 (1997)
17. Scott, T., Farley, D.: Slashing software maintenance costs. Business Software Review (1988)
18. Sneed, H.M.: Measuring the performance of a software maintenance department. In: Proceedings of the First Euromicro Conference on Software Maintenance and Reengineering (EUROMICRO 1997), pp. 119–127 (1997)
19. Stark, G.E.: Measurements for managing software maintenance. In: Proceedings of the IEEE International Conference on Software Maintenance (ICSM 1996), pp. 152–162 (1996)
20. Willcock, C.: An introduction to TTCN-3. Wiley, Chichester (2011)
21. Yin, R.K.: Case Study Research: Design and Methods, 3rd edn. Applied Social Research Methods Series, vol. 5. Prentice Hall (2002)

A Comparative Study of Scrum and Kanban Approaches on a Real Case Study Using Simulation

David J. Anderson[1], Giulio Concas[2], Maria Ilaria Lunesu[2],
Michele Marchesi[2], and Hongyu Zhang[3]

[1] David J. Anderson&Associates inc., Seattle, WA, USA
[2] DIEE - Department of Electrical and Electronic Engineering,
University of Cagliari, Piazza D'Armi, 09123 Cagliari, Italy
[3] School of Software, Tsinghua University, Beijing, China

Abstract. We present the application of software process modeling and simulation using an agent-based approach to a real case study of software maintenance. The original process used PSP/TSP; it spent a large amount of time estimating in advance maintenance requests, and needed to be greatly improved. To this purpose, a Kanban system was successfully implemented, that demonstrated to be able to substantially improve the process without giving up PSP/TSP. We customized the simulator and, using input data with the same characteristics of the real ones, we were able to obtain results very similar to that of the processes of the case study, in particular of the original process. We also simulated, using the same input data, the possible application of the Scrum process to the same data, showing results comparable to the Kanban process.

Keywords: Scrum, Kanban, Lean software development, software process simulation.

1 Introduction

A well-defined software process can help a software organization achieve good and consistent productivity, and is important for the organizations long-term success. However, an ill-defined process could overburden developers (e.g., with unnecessary meetings and report requests) and reduce productivity. It is thus very important to be able to understand if a software process is efficient and effective.

Many software processes have been adopted in industrial practices. For example, the Personal Software Process (PSP) [4] proposed by SEI shows software engineers how to plan, track and analyze their work. The Team Software Process (TSP) [5] is built on the PSP and extends it to a software project team. Scrum [13] is an iterative, incremental software process, which is by far the most popular Agile development process [15]. In recent years, the Lean-Kanban approach [1] advocates to minimize the Work-In-Process (WIP, which is the number of items that are worked on by the team at any given time) and to maximize the value produced by an organization.

C. Wohlin (Ed.): XP 2012, LNBIP 111, pp. 123–137, 2012.

Often the impact of a software process on software productivity is understood through actual practices. The evaluation of the effectiveness of agile practices, for instance, was performed by Maurer and Martel [6] and by Moser et al [9]. To be able to estimate the impact of processes before a project start, many software process simulation methods haven been proposed over the years. For example, Barghouti and Rosenblum [3] proposed methods for simulating and analyzing software maintenance process. Otero et al. [10] use simulation to optimize resource allocation and the training time required for engineers and other personnel. Melis et al. [8] [7] proposed an event-driven simulator for Extreme Programming practices such as test-driven programming and pair programming. In a previous work [2], some of the authors presented an event-driven simulator of the Kanban process and used it to study the dynamics of the process, and to optimize its parameters.

To help better understand and compare the software processes including the original PSP/TSP, Scrum, and Lean-Kanban processes, in this paper we propose a software process simulator, which can describe the details of a software project (e.g., features, activities, developers, etc.) and simulate how a process affects the project. Our simulator is an event-driven, agent-based simulator. We use it to simulate the PSP, the Scrum and the Lean-Kanban processes for software maintenance activities.

The simulations are performed over a Microsoft case study, which is based on four years of experiences of a Microsoft maintenance team in charge of developing minor upgrades and fixing production bugs. Our simulation results show that the Lean-Kanban approach can increase the efficiency of maintenance activities. These results are consistent with the actual experiences of the Microsoft team. After one year from the introduction of Lean-Kanban approach, this team was able to finish the outstanding work and to reduce the average time needed to complete a request. Our simulation work confirms that a WIP-limited approach such as Lean-Kanban can indeed improve maintenance throughput and improve work efficiency.

The paper is organized as follows: in Section 2, we introduce the case study and the related processes (PSP, Scrum, and Kanban). In Section 3, we describe our process simulator and its applications to the studied processes. We present the Microsoft case study and show the simulation results in Section 4. Section 5 concludes the paper.

2 The Case-Study and the Related Processes

This paper analyzes a real software development case study, where a transition was made from a traditional software engineering approach based on PSP to a WIP-limited Lean approach. We use real data from this case study to assess the software process simulator we developed, and as an input to a Scrum process simulation, to verify the possible results of the use of Scrum in the process.

The case study regards a maintenance team of Microsoft, based in India and in charge of developing minor upgrades and fixing production bugs for about 80

IT applications used by Microsoft staff throughout the world. It has already been described by one of the authors in the chapter 4 of [1], because it was one of the first applications of the WIP-limited approach described in that book, making use of a virtual kanban system. Note that there was no kanban board, because the board was not introduced until January 2007 in a different firm. The success of the new process in terms of reduced delivery time and customers' satisfaction has been one of the main factors that raised interest on such Kanban approach in software engineering.

The process is not about the development of a new software system, or about substantial extensions to existing systems, but it deals with maintenance, the last stage of the software life cycle. The importance of maintenance is well known, because it usually counts for the most part of the system's total cost – even more than 70% [16]. The typical maintenance process deals with a stream of requests that must be examined, estimated, accepted or rejected; the accepted requests are implemented updating the code, and then verified through tests to assess their effectiveness and the absence of unwanted side-effects.

In the following subsections we will briefly describe the original process used by the team, the new Kanban-based process, and a possible Scrum process applied to the same team.

2.1   The Original Process

The maintenance service subject of our case study is Microsoft's XIT Sustained Engineering, composed of eight people, including a Project Manager (PM) located in Seattle, and a local engineering manager with six engineers in India. The service was divided in two teams – development team and testing team, each composed of three members. The teams worked 12 months a year, with an average of 22 working days per month. The PM was actually a middle-man. The real business owners were in various Microsoft departments, and communicated with the PM through four product managers, who had responsibility for business cases, prioritization and budget control.

The maintenance requests arrived scattered in time, with a frequency of 20-25 per month. Each request passed through the following steps:

1. Initial estimate: this estimate was very accurate, and took about one day for one developer and one tester. The estimate had to sent back to its business-owner within 48 hours from its arrival.
2. Go-No go decision: the business owner had to decide whether to proceed with the request or not. About 12-13 requests per month remained to be processed, with an average effort of 11 man day of engineering.
3. Backlog: the accepted requests were put in a "backlog", a queue of prioritized requests, from which the developers extracted those they had to process. Once a month, the PM met with the product managers and other stakeholders to reprioritize the backlog.
4. Development phase (aka Coding): the development team worked on the request, making the needed changes to the system involved. This phase

accounted on average for 65% of the total engineering effort. Developers used TSP/PSP Software Engineering Institute processes, and were certified CMMI level 5.

5. Testing phase: the test team worked on the request to verify the changes made. This phase accounted on average for 35% of the total engineering effort. Most requests passed the verification. A small percentage was sent back to the development team for reworking. The test team had to work also on another kind of item to test, known as production text change (PTC), that required a formal test pass. PTCs tended to arrive in sporadic batches; they did not take a long time, but lowered the availability of testers.

Despite the qualification of the teams, this process did not work well. The throughput of completed requests was from 5 to 7 per month, averaging 6. This meant that the backlog was growing of about 6 request per month. When the team implemented the virtual kanban system in October 2004, the backlog had more than 80 requests, and was growing. Even worse, the typical lead times, from the arrival of a request to its completion, were of 125 to 155 days, a figure deemed not acceptable by stakeholders.

2.2   The Lean-Kanban Process

To fix the performance problem of the team, a typical Lean approach was used. First, the process policies were made explicit by mapping the sequence of activities through a value stream, in order to find where value was wasted. The main sources of waste was identified in the estimation effort, that alone was consuming around 33 percent of the total capacity, and sometimes even as much as 40 percent. Another source of waste was the fact that these continuous interruptions to make estimates, which were of higher priority, hindered development due to a continuous switching of focus by developers and testers.

Starting from this analysis, a new process was devised, able to eliminate the waste. The first change was to limit the work-in-progress and pull work from an input queue as current work was completed. WIP in development was limited to 8 requests, as well as WIP in testing. These figures includes an input queue to development and testing, and the requests actually under work. Then, the request estimation was completely dropped. The business owners had in exchange the possibility to meet every week and chose the requests to replenish the input queue of requests to develop. They were also offered a "guaranteed" delivery time of 25 days from acceptance into the input queue to delivery.

In short, the new process was the following:

1. All incoming requests were put into an input backlog, with no estimation.
2. Every week the business-owners decided what request to put into the input queue of development, respecting the limits.
3. The number of requests under work in both activities – development and testing – were limited. In each activity, requests can be in the input queue, under actual work, or be finished, waiting to be pulled to the next activity.

4. Developers pulled the request to work on from their input queue, and were able to be very focused on a single request, or on very few. Finished requests were put in "Done" status.
5. Testers pulled the "Done" requests into their input queue, respecting the limits, and started working on them, again being focused on one request, or on very few. Requests that finished testing were immediately delivered.

This approach was able to substantially increase the teams' ability to perform work, substantially lowering the lead time from commitment and meeting the promised SLA response of 25 days or less for 98% of requests. Commitments were not made until a request was pulled from the backlog into the input queue.

Further improvements were obtained by observing that most of the work was spent in development, with testers having a lot of slack capacity. So, one tester was moved to the development team, and the limit of development activity was raised to 9. This further incremented the productivity. The team was able to eliminate the backlog and to reduce to 14 days the average cycle time.

2.3   The Scrum Process

Scrum is by far the most popular Agile development methodology [15]. For this reason we decided to evaluate the introduction of Scrum for managing the maintenance process. A hypothetical introduction of Scrum would be similar to the Kanban approach, eliminating the estimation phase in exchange for a shortened cycle time. A typical Scrum process would be:

1. Incoming requests are put into a backlog. The Product Managers would act as the Product Owners, and the PM would act as the Scrum master (albeit) remote from the engineering team. The requests are prioritized by the Product Owners.
2. The development and testing proceeds through time-boxed iterations, called Sprints.
3. At the beginning of each Sprint, the Product Owners chose a given number of requests to implement in the Sprint. These requests are presented and estimated by developers and testers in a Sprint Planning Meeting.
4. Development and testing is performed on these requests during the Sprint, that is closed by a Sprint Review Meeting. The finished requests are delivered, while those still under work are passed to the next iteration.

Of course, we have no data about the adoption of Scrum for the maintenance process. However, we may make some observations about it. The first is that, even in the best case of a team able to self-organize giving more resources to coding with respect to testing, the cycle time cannot go below the iteration length. The meetings before and after each iteration would last at least one day, so it is better to have iteration lengths not too short – say at least two or three weeks – not to spend too much time in meetings. In general, we expect Scrum to produce relatively similar results – maybe just a little less effective.

An important point is that Scrum was not a viable choice for *"political"* reasons, because it was considered non-compatible with PSP or TSP, or both. Note that a recent work claims that Scrum and PSP can indeed be used together [12]. The Kanban system was not seen in this way, because PSP was not replaced but merely augmented with the Kanban system.

3   Agent-Based Process Modeling

To model the software maintenance process, we used an approach that can be described as event-driven and agent-based. It is event-driven because the operation of the system is represented as a chronological sequence of events. Each event occurs at an instant in time and marks a change of state in the system [11]. It is also agent-based because it involves the representation or modeling of many individuals who have autonomous behaviors (i.e., actions are not scripted but agents respond to the simulated environment) [14]. In our case the agents are the developers, but in a broad sense also the activities can be considered as entities that can change their behavior depending on the environment. For instance, the activities will not "accept" requests in excess of their limits, that can vary with time. The basic entities of the proposed model, common to all simulated processes, are the requests, the activities and the team members.

The maintenance request are atomic units of work. They are characterized by an arrival time, expressed in days after the starting day of the simulation, an effort that represents the man days needed to implement and test the request, a priority in a given range, and a state, representing the completion state of the request within each activity. The requests can be taken from real records, or can be randomly generated. In this case study they are randomly generated, using statistic parameters taken from the real data. All the requests have the same priority, because requests were prioritized by deciding on which of them the work had to be started, and not by assigning explicit priority values.

The activities represent the work to be done on the requests. They are ordered and are characterized by a name, a limit on the number of requests that can be handled in the activity at any given time, and the typical percentage of the total estimated cost of a request that pertains to the activity. In our model the activities are, in the order:

- **Planning:** it represents the choice of the maintenance requests on which to start the work. This activity implies no engineering effort, and puts the chosen issues in the "Input Queue" to the subsequent activity.
- **Development:** it studies the work to be done to the existing system (bug fixing or enhancement), and performs this work by changing the source code of the target system and producing a new executable. This activity accounts for 65 percent of the total work on a request.
- **Testing:** the last activity, where the work made is verified and accepted. If the request does not pass the verification, it is be sent back to the Development phase for reworking. The percentage of rejected requests was very low, also due to the high qualification of the development team (CMMI level 5). In this

study we will not consider this case. This activity accounts for 35 percent of the total work on a request.

The team members represent the engineers working on the requests in the various activities. Each member has a name, an availability state (available, non-available), and a "skill"in each of the relevant activities. If the skill is equal to one, it means that the team member will perform work in that activity according to the declared effort – for instance, if the effort is one man day, she will complete that effort in one man day. If the skill is lower than one, for instance 0.8, it means that a one-day effort will be completed in $1/0.8 = 1.25$ days. A skill lower than one can represent an actual impairment of the member, or the fact that she has also other duties, and is not able to work full-time on the requests. If the skill in an activity is zero, the member will not work in that activity.

In this case study the engineers can either be developers, with skill equal to one in Coding, and equal to zero in Testing, or testers, with skill equal to zero in Coding, and equal to 0.95 in Testing. This lower figure accounts for the time devoted by testers to test PTC requests (see the previous section), that are not considered as explicit requests in this study.

Each team member works on a single request (in a specific activity) until the end of each day, or until the work on the request in that activity is completed. When a new request is introduced, or work on a request ends, and in any case at the beginning of a new day, the system looks for idle engineers, and tries to assign them to requests available to be worked on in the activities they belong to. A request is handled by only one team member at any given time.

An important concept related to the work on requests is that of *penalty factor*, p. The penalty factor p is equal to one (no penalty) if the same team member, at the beginning of a day, works on the same request s/he worked the day before. If the member starts a new request, or changes request at the beginning of the day, it is assumed that s/he will have to devote extra time to understand how to work on the request. In this case, the value of p is greater than 1 (1.3 in our case study), and the actual time needed to perform the work is divided by p. For instance, if the effort needed to end work on a request in a given activity is t' (man days), and the skill of the member is s, the actual time, t, needed to end the work will be $t = \frac{t' s}{p}$. If the time extends over one day, it is truncated at the end of the day. If the day after the member will work on the same request of the day before, p will be set to one in the computation of the new residual time. The probability q that a member choses the same request of the day before depends on the number of available requests in the member's activity, n_r. In this case study we, set this probability equal to one for all considered processes.

A more detailed description of the specific events of the simulation, and of the general model can be found in [2], in the context of Kanban process simulation.

3.1   The Model of the Original Process

To model the original process, we introduced at the beginning of each day (event "StartDay") a check of the new requests. If one or more new requests arrived that day, one developer and one tester are randomly chosen, and their availability is set to "false" until the end of the day. In this way, we modeled the estimation work of accepted requests. We also modeled the estimation of not accepted requests by randomly blocking for a day a couple formed by a developer and a tester, with probability equal to the arrival rate of not accepted requests (about p = 0.45).

We set the maximum number of requests in the "Coding" phase at 50, not to flood this activity with too many requests.

3.2   The Model of the Scrum Process

To model the Scrum process, we had to introduce in the simulator the concept of iteration. To this purpose, we introduced the event "StartIteration", that takes place at the beginning of the day when the iteration starts. This event sets to "false" the availability of all developers and testers for a given time T_S, to model the time needed to hold the review meeting of the previous Sprint, and the Sprint planning meeting of the current one. T_S was set to one day in the considered case study.

Since the Scrum team is able to self-organize, and since the bottleneck of the work flow is coding, the Scrum team should self-organize to accommodate this situation. So, in the Scrum model we modeled all engineers both as developers and testers, in practice merging the two teams into one. In this way, coding is no longer the bottleneck, and the work is speeded up. This assumption gives a significant advantage to Scrum over other processes.

At the beginning of each Sprint, a set of request is taken from the Backlog and pulled into the Planning activity, to be further pulled to Coding. These request are chosen in such a way that the sum of their effort is equal to, or slightly lower than, a given amount of "Story points" to implement in each iteration. The requests that were still under work at the end of the previous Sprint are left inside their current activity, and their remaining effort is subtracted by the available Story points. The activities have no limit, being the flow of requests naturally limited by the Sprint planning.

4   Results and Discussion

We simulated the three presented models using data mimicking the maintenance requests made to the Microsoft team presented above. We generated two sets of requests, covering a time of four years each (1056 days, with 22 days per month). The average number of incoming requests is 22.5 per month, with 12.5 accepted for implementation, and 10 rejected. So, we have 600 accepted requests in total, randomly distributed. One of the sets had an initial backlog of 85 requests, as in the case study when the process was changed, while the other has no initial backlog.

The distribution of the efforts needed to complete the requests is Gaussian, with an average of 10 and a standard deviation of 2.5. In this way, most requests have an estimated effort between 5 and 15. Note that the empirical data show an average effort per request of about 11 man days. In fact, at least in the original process, the engineers were continuously interrupted by estimation duties, with a consequent overhead due to the application of the "penalty" for learning, or relearning the organization of the code to modify or to test. In practice, we found that the average effort to complete a request was about 11 in the simulation of the original process. This value is equal to the empirical evaluation of 11 "engineering man days" needed on average to complete a request.

For each of the three studied processes, we performed a set of simulations, with the same data in input. For each process, and each input dataset, the outputs tends to be fairly stable, performing several runs with different seeds of the random number generator. For each simulation, we report the cumulative flow diagram (CFD), that is the cumulative number of requests entering the various steps of the process, from "Backlog" to "Released", and statistics about the cycle time. The cycle time starts when work begins on the request – in our case when it is pulled to the "Coding" activity, and ends when it is released.

In the followings we report the results for the three processes.

4.1 The Original Process

Fig 1 shows a typical CFD for the data of the original process. This diagram was obtained using the dataset with no initial backlog, and then rescaling the initial time to the time when the backlog of pending requests reached the value of 85, that is at day 287 from the beginning of the simulation.

The figure makes evident the inability of the process to keep the pace of incoming requests. The throughput of the team is about 6 request per month, and the backlog of pending requests grows of about 6.5 per month. These figures exactly correspond to the empirical value measured on real data. The "Coding" line represents the cumulative number of requests entered into the Coding activity, while the "Testing" line represents the cumulative number entered into the Testing activity. Having limited to 50 the maximum number of requests in the Coding allow to have a relatively limited WIP. The cumulative number of released requests (dashed line) is very close to the Testing line, meaning that the time needed to test the requests is very short. The slope of the dashed line represent the throughput of the system.

Table 1. Statistics of cycle times in the Original Process

Time Interval	Mean	Median	St.Dev.	Min	Max
200-250	140.72	131.49	76.2777	35.02	371.53
251-300	150.18	151.03	79.72	12.61	364.89
301-350	170.34	168.65	89.89	9.96	363.23
351-400	162.65	120.16	88.58	64.51	334.69

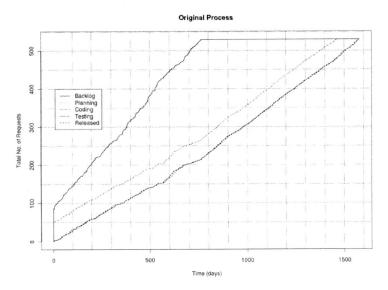

Fig. 1. The CFD of the original process

If we allow one tester to become also a developer, increasing the flexibility of the team, the throughput increases to 7.3 requests per month. Adding one developer and one tester to the teams, keeping the above flexibility, further increases the throughput to 8.1 requests per month, a figure still too low to keep the pace of incoming requests.

In Table 1 we report some statistics about cycle time in various time intervals of the simulation. In general, these statistics show very long and very variable cycle times. We remember that the backlog of pending requests reaches the value of 85, when the process was changed, at day 287. Around this time, the average and median cycle times are of the order of 150-160, values very similar to those reported for real data.

So, we can conclude that the simulator is able to reproduce very well the empirical data both in term of throughput and of average cycle time.

4.2   The Kanban Process

In the case of Kanban process, the input dataset includes an initial backlog of 85 requests, with no work yet performed on them. The process was simulated by moving a tester to the developer team after 6 months from the beginning of the simulation (day 132), as it happened in the real case. The activity limits were set to 8 (9 from day 132) and 8 for Coding and Testing, respectively, as in the real case.

The resulting CFD is reported in Fig. 2. Note the slight increase in the steepness of the Coding and Testing lines after day 132, with a consequent increase of the contribution made by Testing to the WIP. With the adoption of the

Kanban system, the throughput substantially increases with respect to the original process. Before day 132 the throughput is about 10 requests per month (30 per quarter); after day 132 it increases to about 12 requests per month (36 per quarter), almost able to keep the pace of incoming requests.

If we compare the throughput data with those measured in the real case (45 per quarter in the case of 3 + 3 teams, and 56 per quarter in the case of 4 + 2 teams), we notice that in the real case the productivity is 50 percent higher than in the simulated process. Our model already accounts for the elimination of estimations, and for not having penalties applied the day after the estimation. Note that the maximum theoretical throughput of 6 developers working on requests whose average is 10 man days is 13.2 per month, and thus 39.6 per quarter, not considering the penalties applied when a request is tackled for the first time both during coding and testing. In the real case, there were clearly other factors at work that further boosted the productivity of the engineers. It is well known that researchers have found 10-fold differences in productivity and quality between different programmers with the same levels of experience. So, it is likely that the same engineers, faced with a process change that made them much more focused on their jobs and gave them a chance to put an end to their "bad name" inside Microsoft, redoubled their efforts and acheved a big productivity improvement.

Regarding cycle times, their statistics are shown in Table 2, for time intervals of 100 days starting from the beginning of the simulation. These times dropped with respect to the original situation, tending to average values of 25.

We also simulated the Kanban process with an increase of both team sizes of one unit, after 8 months from its introduction, as in the real case. We obtained an increase of throughput to 14.7 requests per month, or 44 per quarter, with the average cycle time dropping to 14.3.

Table 2. Statistics of cycletime in the Kanban Process

Time Interval	Mean	Median	St.Dev.	Min	Max
1-100	25.18	22.74	14.06	6.98	146.72
101-200	28.99	27.97	12.92	11.69	87.53
201-300	24.41	22.05	8.15	11.62	49.18
301-400	26.39	24.13	10.37	11.23	78.34

4.3   The Scrum Process

We simulated the use of a Scrum process to manage the same input dataset of the Kanban case, that includes the initial backlog. In the presented case study, we choose iterations of 3 weeks (14 working days, accounting for the day spent in meetings) because it is the minimum time span accommodating requests whose average working time is more than 10 man days, and with about 15% of the requests longer than the average plus a standard deviation, so more than 12.5

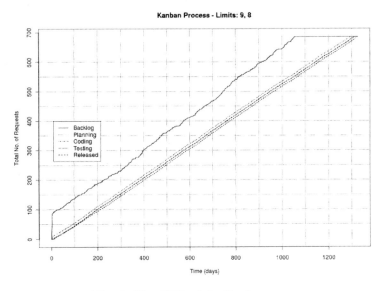

Fig. 2. The CFD of the Kanban process

engineering days. Remember the constraint that only one developer works on a request at a time – a constraint mimicking the way of work of the actual teams. With a two-week iteration the team should spend a lot of time to estimate the length of the requests, and in many cases it should split them into two smaller pieces to do them sequentially across two Sprints. Even with a 3 week Sprint some requests would need to be split, but we do not explicitly handle this case – simply, the remaining of the request is automatically moved to the next iteration.

The number of Story points to implement is set to 90. In fact, with 14 working days per team member during a Sprint, we have a total of 84 man days. We slighly increased this limit to 90, to accomodate variations. We found empirically that a further increase of this limit does not increment throughput. We remember that, in our model of Scrum, all 6 engineers are able to perform both coding and testing (the latter with 0.95 efficiency), thus modeling the self-organization of the team.

Fig. 3 shows the CFD diagram in the case of Scrum simulation. Note the characteristic "ladder" appearance of the Coding line, that represents the requests in input to each Sprint. This process is much better than the original one, and is almost able to keep the pace of incoming requests, with a throughput of about 11.5 requests per month. This should be compared with the throughputs of Kanban with both teams of 3 engineers (10) and with 4 developers and 2 testers (12). Had we not allowed the team to "self organize", the throughput would have been much lower.

The cycle time statistics are shown in Table 3. They are better than in the Kanban process, owing the highest team flexibility. Note that in our simulation, we do not wait for the end of the Sprint to release finished requests, but release them immediately. If we had waited until the end of the Sprint, as in a "true" Scrum implementation, all these average times should be increased of 3 days (50% of the difference between the Sprint length and the minimum cycle time, that is about 9). This is the average waiting time of a request between its completion and the end of the Sprint. Anyway, the Scrum results are very good, and comparable with the Kanban ones.

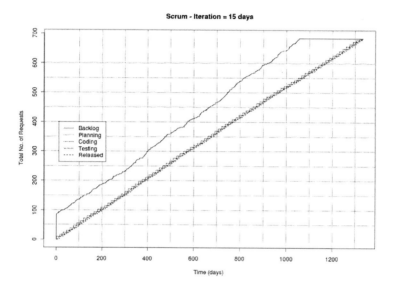

Fig. 3. The CFD of the Scrum process

Table 3. Statistics of cycle time in the Scrum Processes

Time Interval	Mean	Median	St.Dev.	Min	Max
1-100	16.69	15.74	4.65	8.62	28.00
101-200	16.68	15.79	5.90	9.03	34.51
201-300	16.41	15.71	4.72	9.72	30.50
301-400	16.79	16.41	4.92	8.91	28.02

5   Conclusions and Future Work

We presented the application of the process simulation model developed for assessing the effectiveness of agile and lean approaches described in [2] to a real case study, in which a maintenance team experimented the transition from a PSP/TSP, estimation-based approach to a Lean-Kanban process. We added also the modeling and simulation of a possible application of the Scrum process to the same case study, albeit Scrum was not really tried in the real case.

The proposed approach to model and simulate a software process, using an agent-based, fully object-oriented model, demonstrated very effective. It allowed us to model all three processes with minimal changes in the model and in the simulator. The use of a general-purpose OO language like Smalltalk eased this task, allowing a high flexibility in extending the simulator.

We used as input data a stream of maintenance requests synthetically generated, with the same statistical properties of real requests. We were able to fully reproduce the statistics of empirical results for the original process, both in terms of throughput and cycle times.

Regarding Kanban, the simulation results demonstrated a substantial improvement with respect to the original process, but in fact significantly lower than the improvement obtained in the real case, where the throughput was 50% higher than in the simulated results. This fact is worth further study, because in the real case it was reported a throughput that can be explained only with an increase in the productivity of the engineers of the team. Such an increase in individual productivity is a parameter difficult to introduce *a priori* in a simulation, without being accused of wishing to favour a process with respect to another.

The proposed simulation approach allowed us to easily model and apply to the case study also the Scrum process, despite its iterative nature, different from the "steady flow" nature of the two other processes. Since Scrum is based on self-organizing teams, we modeled this fact by eliminating the difference between developers and testers, a possibility suggested by the fact that in the real case a tester was actually moved to the development team. This self-organization gave Scrum an advantage in flexibility reflected in the lower average and maximum cycle time with respet to Kanban. On the contrary, the simulated Kanban process – when the teams are better balanced, with 4 developers and 2 testers – still overcomes Scrum in throughput.

Overall, we believe that the presented work demonstrated that our agent-based approach is very effective for modeling and simulation of agile and lean software development processes, that tend to be simple and well structured, and that operate on a backlog of "atomic" requirements. This is particularly true for maintenance processes, that naturally operate on an inflow of independent requests.

In the future, we plan to further evaluate our simulation method on a variety of software development and maintenance projects, including open source projects, with the aim to explore the optimal parameter settings that can maximize the overall development efficiency. We will devote a specific effort to analyze and model human factors that could affect the productivity of a development team, in relation with the specific process and practices used.

References

1. Anderson, D.J.: Kanban: Successful Evolutionary Change for Your Technology Business. Blue Hole Press (2010)
2. Anderson, D.J., Concas, G., Lunesu, M.I., Marchesi, M.: Studying Lean-Kanban Approach Using Software Process Simulation. In: Sillitti, A., Hazzan, O., Bache, E., Albaladejo, X. (eds.) XP 2011. LNBIP, vol. 77, pp. 12–26. Springer, Heidelberg (2011)
3. Barghouti, N.S., Rosenblum, D.S.: A Case Study in Modeling a Human-Intensive, Corporate Software Process. In: Proc. 3rd Int. Conf. On the Software Process (ICSP-3). IEEE CS Press (1994)
4. Humphrey, W.S.: Using a defined and measured Personal Software Process. IEEE Software, 77–88 (May 1996)
5. Humphrey, W.S.: Introduction to the Team Software Process. Addison Wesley (1999)
6. Maurer, F., Martel, S.: On the productivity of agile software practices: An industrial case study. Technical report, Univ. of Calgary, Alberta (March 2002)
7. Melis, M., Turnu, I., Cau, A., Concas, G.: Evaluating the Impact of Test-First Programming and Pair Programming through Software Process Simulation. Software Process Improvement and Practice 11, 345–360 (2006)
8. Melis, M., Turnu, I., Cau, A., Concas, G.: Modeling and simulation of open source development using an agile practice. Journal of Systems Architecture 52, 610–618 (2006)
9. Moser, R., Abrahamsson, P., Pedrycz, W., Sillitti, A., Succi, G.: A Case Study on the Impact of Refactoring on Quality and Productivity in an Agile Team. In: Meyer, B., Nawrocki, J.R., Walter, B. (eds.) CEE-SET 2007. LNCS, vol. 5082, pp. 252–266. Springer, Heidelberg (2008)
10. Otero, L.D., Centeno, G., Ruiz-Torres, A.J., Otero, C.E.: A systematic approach for resource allocation in software projects. Comput. Ind. Eng. 56(4), 1333–1339 (2009)
11. Robinson, S.: Simulation – The practice of model development and use. Wiley, Chichester (2004)
12. Rong, G., Shao, D., Zhang, H.: SCRUM-PSP: Embracing Process Agility and Discipline. In: Proc. 17th Asia-Pacific Conference on Software Engineering, APSEC 2010, pp. 316–325. IEEE Press (2010)
13. Schwaber, K., Beedle, M.: Agile software development with Scrum. Prentice Hall (2002)
14. Siebers, P.O., Macal, C.M., Garnett, J., Buxton, D., Pidd, M.: Discrete-event simulation is dead, long live agent-based simulation! Journal of Simulation 4, 204–210 (2010)
15. Version One.: State of Agile Survey (2010), http://www.versionone.com
16. Wolverton, R.W.: The Cost of Developing Large-Scale Software. IEEE Trans. on Computers 23, 615–636 (1975)

Impact of Test Design Technique Knowledge on Test Driven Development: A Controlled Experiment

Adnan Čaušević, Daniel Sundmark, and Sasikumar Punnekkat

Mälardalen University, Sweden
`firstname.lastname@mdh.se`

Abstract. Agile development approaches are increasingly being followed and favored by the industry. Test Driven Development (TDD) is a key agile practice and recent research results suggest that the successful adoption of TDD depends on different limiting factors, one of them being insufficient developer testing skills. The goal of this paper is to investigate if developers who are educated on general testing knowledge will be able to utilize TDD more effectively. We conducted a controlled experiment with master students during the course on Software Verification & Validation (V&V) where source code and test cases created by each participant during the labs as well as their answers on a survey questionnaire were collected and analyzed.

Descriptive statistics indicate improvements in statement coverage. However, no statistically significant differences could be established between the pre- and post-course groups of students. By qualitative analysis of students' tests, we noticed a lack of test cases for non-stated requirements ("negative"tests) resulting in a non-detection of bugs. Students did show preference towards TDD in surveys.

Although further research is required to fully establish this, we believe that identifying specific testing knowledge which is complementary to the testing skills of a new TDD developer would enable developers to perform their tasks in a more efficient manner.

Keywords: test driven development, controlled experiment, software testing.

1 Motivation

Test Driven Development (TDD), also known as test-first programming, is an essential part of eXtreme Programming (XP) [1]. TDD requires the developers to construct automated unit tests in the form of assertions to define code requirements before writing the code itself. In this process, developers evolve the systems through cycles of test, development and refactoring. In a recent industrial survey [2], we examined the difference between the preferred and the actual level of usage for several test-related practices. Among the 22 examined practices, surprisingly, TDD gained the highest score of 'dissatisfaction'. This means

C. Wohlin (Ed.): XP 2012, LNBIP 111, pp. 138–152, 2012.

that the accumulated absolute difference between the preferred and the actual levels of usage was highest in the case of TDD. The nature of this dissatisfaction could be stated as "Respondents would like to use TDD to a significantly higher extent than they actually do currently".

Subsequently we explored the current body of knowledge through an empirical systematic literature review [3] to identify the limiting factors which prevents the successful adoption of TDD. Insufficient developer testing skills was identified as one of the important limiting factors as part of the study. By developer testing skill, we refer to the developer's ability to write efficient and effective automated test cases.

1.1 Problem Statement

TDD in its essence teaches developers on how to perform software development providing some indirect basic testing skills, for example based on *positive testing* (i.e. testing to show that the software "works" using valid input). We are interested in identifying specific testing knowledge which is complementary to the already mentioned testing skills of a new TDD developer. We believe that such a strategy would enable developers to perform their tasks in a more efficient manner resulting in higher quality of software products.

1.2 Research Objective

In the form suggested by Wohlin et al. [4], the research objective of this study can be expressed as follows:

> To analyze *the effect of testing knowledge on TDD*
> for the purpose of *evaluation of factors affecting the outcome of TDD*
> with respect to the *factors' limiting effect on the usage of TDD*
> from the point of view of *the software developer*
> in the context of *eXtreme Programming software development*.

1.3 Context

To perform analysis with respect to the above objective, an experiment was organised as laboratory activities with master students enrolled in the Software Verification and Validation course at Mälardalen University during the autumn semester in 2010.

1.4 Paper Outline

This paper is structured according to the reporting guidelines provided in [5] (although some minor deviations from the reporting guidelines were made). In section 2 we present the related research works followed by the experimental design in section 3. Section 4 presents the details of execution of our experiment. The treatment and analysis of the collected data are given in section 5. In section 6, we present statistical inferences followed by conclusions and future research planned in section 7.

2   Related Work

Test-driven development is a practice derived from experience and without any ground theory it makes it very difficult to prove its efficiency in a formal way. This is one of the reasons why many experiments on TDD are conducted in order to provide empirical evidence of its claimed quality improvements.

In this section we present related work on empirical investigations of TDD identified in our recent systematic literature review [3], grouped w.r.t two aspects: (i) related to testing knowledge and (ii) general experiments on TDD.

2.1   TDD and Testing Knowledge

Sfetos et al. [6] performed an industrial survey on advantages and difficulties that software companies experienced when applying XP. Test-first was among the investigated practices. During interviews, developers identified difficulties in writing tests at the very beginning of the project.

Geras et al. [7] performed an experiment with professionals in academic environment providing subjects with two programs for development, one using test-last and one using test-first process. One of the conclusions made from the experiment is that without adequate training and having proper testing skills it is risky to adopt TDD.

Kollanus & Isomöttönen [8] analysed students perceptions and difficulties on TDD in an educational context experiment. As part of their conclusions they present different difficulties students had when designing tests. Generally, students find it difficult to design appropriate test cases and to design tests in small steps.

2.2   Experiments in TDD

In Table 1 we present experiments in TDD selected from [3] outlining experiment environment (industrial or academic) and type of subjects (students, professionals or mixed). A brief description of the aim and results of each TDD study is also presented.

3   Experimental Design

This section details the design of the experiment. Further practical experiment setup information, e.g., for replication purposes, can be found at the first author's webpage[1].

3.1   Goals, Hypotheses, Parameters, and Variables

The goal of the experiment was to test the effect of knowledge in software testing on *development speed, artefact quality* and *developer perception* when using TDD. In order to do so, the following null and alternative hypotheses were formulated:

---

[1] http://www.mrtc.mdh.se/~acc01/tddexperiment

Table 1. Research publications on experiments in TDD

AUTHORS	YEAR	EXPERIMENT SETTINGS	SUBJECTS
Müller & Hagner [9]	2002	Academic	Students

AIM: To evaluate benefits of test-first programming compared to traditional approach. RESULTS: Test-first does not accelerate programming, produced programs are not more reliable but test-first supports better understanding of program.

George & Williams [10]	2003	Industrial	Professionals

AIM: To evaluate quality improvements of test-driven development compared to a waterfall-like approach. RESULTS: Test-driven development produces higher quality code with the tendency of developers spending more time on coding.

Geras et al. [7]	2004	Academic	Professionals

AIM: To investigate developer productivity and software quality when comparing test-driven and traditional development approaches. RESULTS: There were little or no differences in developer productivity but frequency of unplanned test failure was lower for test-driven development.

Erdogmus et al. [11]	2005	Academic	Students

AIM: To evaluate functional tests in test-driven development when compared to traditional test-last approach. RESULTS: Test-first students created on an average more tests and tended to be more productive. There was no significant difference in quality of produced code between two groups.

Flohr & Schneider [12]	2006	Academic	Students

AIM: To investigate the impact of test-first compared to clasical-testing approach. RESULTS: No significant differences could be established, but students did show a preference towards test-first approach.

Janzen & Saiedian [13]	2006	Academic	Students

AIM: To examine the effects of TDD on internal quality of software design. RESULTS: Positive correlation between productivity and TDD, but no differences in internal quality. Perception on TDD was more positive after the experiment.

Müller & Höfer [14]	2007	Academic	Mixed

AIM: To investigate the conformance to TDD of professionals and novice TDD developers. RESULTS: Experts complied more to the rules of TDD and produced test with higher quality.

Janzen et al. [15]	2007	Academic	Professionals

AIM: To investigate effects of TDD on internal code quality. RESULTS: Programmers' opinions on TDD improved after the experiment but internal code quality had no significant difference between test-first and test-last approach.

Gupta & Jalote [16]	2007	Academic	Students

AIM: To evaluate the impact of TDD on designing, coding and testing when compared with traditional approach. RESULTS: TDD improves productivity and reduce overall development effort. Code quality is affected by test effort regardless of the development approach in use.

Kollanus & Isomöttönen [8]	2008	Academic	Students

AIM: To improve understanding on TDD in educational context. RESULTS: Students expressed difficulties with following TDD approach and designing proper tests. Regardless, they believed in the claimed benefits of TDD.

Höfer & Philipp [17]	2009	Academic	Mixed

AIM: To compare conformance to TDD of experts and novice programmers. RESULTS: Experts refactored their code more than novice programmers, but they were also significantly slower.

Huang & Holcombe [18]	2009	Academic	Students

AIM: To investigate the effectiveness of test-first approach compared to the traditional (test-last) development. RESULTS: Test-first teams spent more time on testing than coding compared to test-last teams. There was no linear correlation between effort spent on software testing and the software external quality.

Vu et al. [19]	2009	Academic	Students

AIM: To investigate how test-first and test-last methodologies affects internal and external quality of the software. RESULTS: Test-last team was more productive and created more tests. Students indicate preference towards test-first approach.

Madeyski [20]	2010	Academic	Students

AIM: To investigate how Test-first programming can impact branch coverage and mutation score indicator. RESULTS: The benefits of the Test-first practice can be considered minor in the specific context of this experiment.

- **Development Speed:**

  - **H^s_0.** When using TDD, there is no significant difference between the development speed of developers with or without knowledge in software testing.

- $\mathbf{H^s}_a$. When using TDD, developers with knowledge in software testing develop faster.

  – **Artefact Quality:**
    - $\mathbf{H^q}_0$. When using TDD, there is no significant difference between the quality of the artefacts produced by developers with or without knowledge in software testing.
    - $\mathbf{H^q}_a$. When using TDD, developers with knowledge in software testing produce artefacts of a higher quality.

  – **Developer Perception:**
    - $\mathbf{H^p}_0$. There is no significant difference in the perception of TDD between developers with or without knowledge in software testing.
    - $\mathbf{H^p}_a$. Developers with knowledge in software testing have higher preference towards TDD than those without knowledge in software testing.

The *development speed, artefact quality* and *developer perception* are operationalized in a list of response variables, provided in Table 2.

Table 2. Experiment Response Variables

Construct	Variable name	Description	Scale type
Development Speed	User Stories	Number of user stories finished within lab session.	Ratio
Artefact Quality	Defects	Number of defects found in code implementation by independent test suite.	Ratio
Artefact Quality	Coverage	Statement coverage of test suite when applied to code implementation.	Ratio
Artefact Quality	Complexity	Cyclomatic complexity of the code implementation.	Ratio
Developer Perception	Ease of use	The ease of use with which the steps of TDD could be followed.	Ordinal
Developer Perception	Preference	Subjects' perception of TDD.	Ordinal

In this experiment, the factor of *knowledge in software testing* is operationalized using a 10-weeks half-time advanced-level academic course in Software Verification and Validation. Some topics that are covered by course are: introduction to software testing and testing fundamentals, the test processes, how to practically write test cases, code inspection and security testing, test design techniques, static program analysis and real-time testing. The course content has been inspired partly by industrial certification courses (e.g., the International Software Testing Qualification Board (ISTQB) foundation- and advanced-level certification courses [21]), and partly by scientific courses and syllabi (e.g., the software testing course contents proposed by Ammann and Offutt [22]). For the purpose of this experiment, a subject is said to have knowledge in software testing if (s)he has taken part in the course lectures and exercises, and not to have knowledge in software testing if (s)he has not.

3.2   Experiment Design

The experiment design is detailed in Figure 1. Two groups of subjects (Group A and Group B) worked on two different problems (Problem 1 and Problem 2) as part of the labs, once before and once after the course (using TDD on both the occasions). During both the labs they used the Eclipse [23] integrated development environment (IDE) to create *working* software solutions in the Java programming language and the jUnit [24] testing framework for writing executable tests. Upon completion of each of the labs, the subjects answered a set of questions in an online survey system.

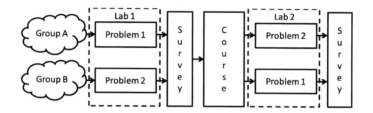

Fig. 1. Design of Experiment

3.3   Subjects

The subjects of the experiment were software engineering master students enrolled in the Software Verification and Validation course at Mälardalen University during the autumn semester of 2010. The experiment was part of the laboratory work within the V&V course, and the subjects earned credits for participation. Students were informed that the final grade for the course will be obtained from the written exam and their performance during labs would not affect their grades.

3.4   Objects

As stated above, the experiment used two specific software development problems for the experiment, namely: (i) Roman numeral conversion (Problem 1) and (ii) a bowling game score calculator (Problem 2). The specifications for Problem 1 were written by us (in the form of a list of user stories) for the purpose of this experiment, whereas the specifications for Problem 2 (also a list of user stories) were based on the Bowling Game Kata (i.e., the problem also used by Kollanus and Isomöttönen to explain TDD [8]). Detailed information about the problems and their user stories are provided on first author's webpage[2].

---

[2] http://www.mrtc.mdh.se/~acc01/tddexperiment

TDD Steps:

1. Write one single test-case
2. Run this test-case. If it fails continue with step 3. If the test-case succeeds, continue with step 1.
3. Implement the minimal code to make the test-case run
4. Run the test-case again. If it fails again, continue with step 3. If the test-case succeeds, continue with step 5.
5. Refactor the implementation to achieve the simplest design possible.
6. Run the test-case again, to verify that the refactored implementation still succeeds the test-case. If it fails, continue with step 5. If the test-case succeeds, continue with step 1, if there are still requirements left in the specification.

Fig. 2. TDD steps for development

3.5   Instrumentation

As one way of ensuring that subjects properly followed the steps of TDD, we provided the instructions for TDD prescribed by Flohr and Schneider [12] (see Figure 2). To avoid problems with subjects' unfamiliarity of jUnit testing framework and/or Eclipse IDE, subjects were given an Eclipse project code skeleton with one simple test case. Since this was all located in a subversion (SVN) repository, an instruction on how to obtain code from SVN and import it in Eclipse was also provided to students.

3.6   Data Collection Procedure

Teams were instructed to upload their source codes in a SVN repository. This way the lab instructor has a complete log of subjects' activities and the option to obtain code from a specific point in time.

Subjects answered survey questions using quiz assignments in the Blackboard learning management system for the course. Data from surveys is then exported in comma separated values (.csv) file format.

4   Execution

4.1   Sample

Twenty-eight students participated in the experiment. Students were informed that their work in computer laboratory would be used for the experiment, but they were not provided any details on the goal of the experiment itself. Also, we explicitly stated that their performance would not influence the final grade of the V&V course in any way. The final grade was determined by the written exam.

4.2   Preparation

Team numbers were assigned in sequential order based on the time of receipt of the e-mail requested by the lab instructor. Problems for the teams were assigned in an alternating manner between the two immediate teams (ex., if team i was assigned problem 1, one team i+1 was assigned problem 2 and team i+2 was assigned problem 1 again etc.).

Since the lab work was time-boxed to 3 hours, a Java code skeleton was created for students. It contained a program class with one empty method returning zero and a test class with one assert statement validating the previous mentioned method. This skeleton was made to be directly imported into Eclipse as an existing project.

For each team a corresponding subversion (SVN) repository was created with read/write permissions assigned only to students within the given team and to the lab instructor. To avoid difficulties in setting up SVN and importing project in Eclipse, an instruction on the usage of SVN and Eclipse was provided to the students.

4.3   Data Collection Performed

As explained to students in the lab instruction document, after creating a new test or after changing code in order to pass the existing tests, an SVN commit command had to be executed. This way the lab instructor had a complete log of activities during the lab and an ability to obtain source code of the team at any given point in time. The absence of some students from any of the lab sessions were clearly visible from their SVN repository since the date of source code was not the same as the date of the lab. Such data was excluded from the analysis.

5   Analysis

5.1   Descriptive Statistics

Based on initial experimental plan of response variables (see Table 2) a descriptive analysis was performed for each variable independently.

First, considering the development speed construct, Figure 3 presents the percentage of user stories finished during the experiment sessions as mean values with standard error deviation. As the figure shows, the development speed was relatively unaffected in both groups before and after the course.

Second, considering the artefact quality construct, Figures 4, 5, and 6 present percentage of statement coverage of students test suite, cyclomatic complexity of the code, and the number of defects detected by an independent test suite respectively. These measures are given as mean values with standard error deviations. In the case of code coverage, it can been seen that both post-test groups had better mean values than the pre-test groups. In the complexity and defects metrics, the differences between the experiment objects seem to obscure such visible results, if they exist.

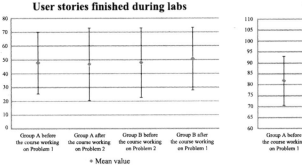

Fig. 3. Performance mean values

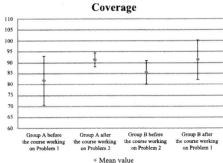

Fig. 4. Code coverage mean values

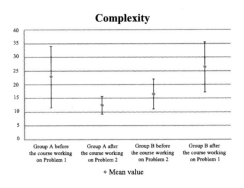

Fig. 5. Code complexity mean values

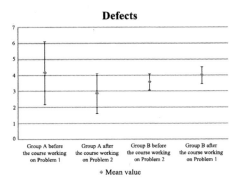

Fig. 6. Defects found mean values

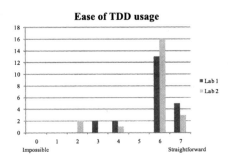

Fig. 7. How difficult was it to follow TDD

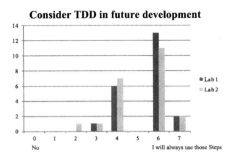

Fig. 8. Students perception of TDD

Finally, Figures 7 and 8 provide results related to the developer perception construct. The first of these figures presents the sum of student responses on the ease of use with which the steps of TDD are followed in labs. Possible responses vary from 1 to 8 where 1 means impossible to follow and 8 means it was straight-forward. Data is presented for both instances of labs. Figure 8 presents the sum of student responses on the perception of TDD. Possible responses varies from 1 to 8 where 1 means they will not consider using TDD in future developments and 8 means they will always use TDD. Data is presented for both instances of labs. Generally, students found TDD to be a preferable development method that is easy to use. However, there is no obvious difference between the pre-experiment and post-experiment perceptions on this matter.

5.2   Data Set Reduction

Source codes of 17 teams (9 from Group A and 8 from Group B) and 28 student responses in survey questionnaires were collected for analysis. The difference of 6 students were due to the fact that some students did not fill in the questionnaire but did perform the lab.

When the actual source code analysis was performed additional data points had to be removed. The projects of teams 4 and 13 were excluded due to several syntax errors which made the complete solution uncompilable and irrelevant for any of the analysis. During code coverage analysis a huge deviation occurred with Team 14. A detailed analysis revealed that students did not write any test cases during the lab but they subsequently submitted tests in SVN. Since this was opposite from the TDD practice stated in their lab instructions, data from this team was also excluded. After removing data from those three teams, finally we had data points from:

- 14 teams (7 from Group A and 7 from Group B) for source code analysis and
- 22 student responses for survey questionnaire analysis.

5.3   Hypothesis Testing

Hypothesis testing was performed in two steps: First, the **Mann-Whitney** non-parametric test was used to ensure that the differences in response variable data between the experiment groups and between the experiment objects were statistically nonsignificant. The α was set to 0.05, and consequently a resulting z score of more than 1.96 or less than -1.96 was required to show a significant difference between the objects or the groups.

The result of this analysis is shown in Table 3. As can be seen from the table, there were no significant differences between the experiment objects or groups, with the exception of a significant difference in object complexity. This parameter is consequently omitted from further analysis.

Second, on the basis of the nonsignificant differences between experiment objects and groups, the **Wilcoxon** signed rank test for paired nonparametric data was used in order to test the null hypotheses of the experiment. As in the Mann-Whitney case, the α was set to 0.05. The result of this analysis is shown in Table 4. For a null hypothesis to be rejected, it is required that $min(W_+, W_-) \leq \textbf{Critical } W$ holds. As shown in the table, none of the experiment's null hypotheses can be rejected based on the collected data.

Table 3. Mann-Whitney z scores for differences between experiment groups and objects. A significant difference in complexity between the experiment objects is found.

	Development speed	Artefact quality			Developer perception	
	User Stories	Defects	Coverage	Complexity	Ease of use	Preference
Group A vs. Group B	-0.16	-0.80	-0.34	-1.36	-0.30	1.34
Roman vs. Bowling	0.02	-1.91	0.05	**-2.64**	0.19	0.09

Table 4. Testing of null hypotheses of the experiment

Construct (Null hypothesis)	Parameter	W_+	W_-	$min(W_+, W_-)$	Critical W
Development speed ($\textbf{H}^s{}_0$)	User Stories	52.5	52.5	52.5	21 (14 non-zero differences)
Artefact quality ($\textbf{H}^q{}_0$)	Defects	22.5	13.5	13.5	4 (8 non-zero differences)
Artefact quality ($\textbf{H}^q{}_0$)	Coverage	25	80	25	21 (14 non-zero differences)
Artefact quality ($\textbf{H}^q{}_0$)	Complexity	Not tested			
Developer perception ($\textbf{H}^{pe}{}_0$)	Ease of use	30	25	25	8 (10 non-zero differences)
Developer perception ($\textbf{H}^{pp}{}_0$)	Preference	30	15	15	6 (9 non-zero differences)

6   Interpretation

6.1   Evaluation of Results and Implications

When looking at the descriptive statistics results of the code coverage variable we can notice a positive increase in performances of both the groups when comparing before and after the course results. Even though there were no statistically significant differences in code coverage values (null hypothesis could not be rejected), we think this was a borderline case. What we want to emphasise is that, on an average, the best performing group before the course was still worse than the worst group after the course:

$$\textbf{max}(A, B)_{precourse} < \textbf{min}(A, B)_{postcourse}$$

The level of complexity of the students program solutions changed for both groups from one lab to another, but this change had one direction for Group A and another for Group B. What we can only conclude from this data is that solutions for Problem 1 are of higher complexity than solutions for Problem 2.

We expected the number of defects variable to provide us with a direct way of evaluating the impact of testing knowledge. An independent suite of test cases for each problem was created but we could not use it to the full extent since different teams finished different numbers of user stories. Every team had on an average four bugs and in most cases those could have been found by test cases designed using a negative test design technique.

Students claimed they adhered to TDD practice during the experiment to a high extent (Figure 9). The ease of usage of TDD practice was also reported to a high extent (Figure 7) but interestingly students did not feel the same about their preference of using TDD in future development (Figure 8).

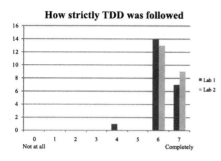

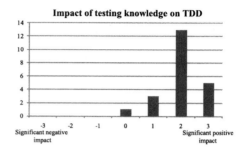

Fig. 9. How strictly TDD was followed   **Fig. 10.** Students opinion on the impact

6.2   Limitations of the Study

Typically, four types of validity are discussed in empirical research (i.e., *construct validity, internal validity, external validity* and *reliability*) [4].

Construct Validity refers to the correctness in the mapping between the theoretical constructs that are to be investigated, and the actual observations of the study. Some of the constructs investigated in this study are not trivially defined, and may be subject to debate (particularly in the case of *artefact quality* and *testing knowledge*). In order to mitigate this problem, we have used standard software engineering metrics (e.g., complexity and coverage), and provided detailed information on the operationalization of each construct involved in the experiment.

Internal Validity concerns the proper analysis of data. The statistical strategy used in this paper was to first eliminate the possibility of major confounding variables affecting the result (i.e., testing for differences between experiment objects or groups), and second, to test the null hypotheses. Furthermore, as the normality of the data could not be assumed, we used non-parametric tests to conduct these hypothesis tests. However, regardless of the strategy used, it is without question a fact that the sample size of the data was small, which is a major limitation for statistical analysis (and potentially also a cause for the inability for null hypothesis rejection). The only way to resolve this matter is through replications of the experiment.

External Validity relates to the possibility to generalize the study results outside its scope of investigation. As many of the previously published experiments on TDD (see Table 1), this experiment is performed in a course setting and suffers from the consequent threats to external validity (e.g., *student subjects, small scale objects, short experiment duration*). It is, however, uncertain to what extent this affects the results, as we are not examining a practice (TDD) directly, but rather assessing whether the practice improves given the acquisition of a certain knowledge.

Reliability concerns the degree of certainty with which a replication of this study, e.g., by a different set of researchers, would yield the same study outcome. Here, as the experiment package and guidelines are made available for replication purposes, the major reliability threat relates to the replicated execution of the V&V course. On the other hand, without having any deeper insight as to what specific testing knowledge would be beneficial for TDD, this needs to be considered future work.

7   Conclusions and Future Work

In this section a summary of the study results with directions for future work are presented.

7.1   Relation to Existing Evidence

In the related works section we mentioned three research papers where participants of their studies expressed difficulties with testing and/or constructing test cases. Opinions of the subjects of our study pointed out that testing knowledge had a relatively significant positive impact on how they performed TDD as can be seen in Figure 10. However, based on qualitative data from our experiment, we also inferred that our respondents had problems with creating negative test cases.

7.2   Impact

A growing number of research publications empirically evaluating TDD implicitly suggest that TDD will most likely provide benefit of higher code quality to the organisation which decide to implement this development process. However, to the best of our knowledge, there are no reports on failure of implementing or adopting TDD within a specific organisation. In this context a more relevant research question could be: where and why will TDD not work and how to overcome those factors?

Our experiment is a initial attempt to address this research question from an orthogonal perspective by evaluating specifically whether testing knowledge can support TDD in practice or it could be considered as a limiting factor (as stated in [3]). Though the present study is inconclusive, it opens up several interesting challenges for the research community. We believe that identifying specific testing knowledge, which is complementary to the testing skills of a new TDD developer, is essential. Such a knowledge would enable developers to achieve performance efficiency and higher quality of software products. Additionally, it will have a great impact on the industrial adoption of TDD.

7.3   Future Work

In this study we presented a detailed experiment with students as subjects, making it more accessible for other researchers to replicate or perform a similar experiment. Alongside of providing more evidence on how general testing knowledge supports TDD in practice, we think an evolving experiment should be created with more specific focus. This experiment would be a possibility to directly investigate the effect of knowledge of negative testing on TDD practice. It could be designed in a way to provide education to subjects specifically on how to design test cases for unspecified system behaviours and use that knowledge when performing TDD of software systems.

TDD per se provides an excellent opportunity for improving code quality by imbibing "test culture" in the development community. Adherence to TDD results in the generation of automated and executable test cases during the development phase itself, thus improving the testability of the system requirements. However, as indicated by our study, TDD needs to be supplemented with new process steps or test design techniques, which could potentially further enhance the robustness and the reliability of the system.

In a long term research perspective, we also intent to perform an industrial case study investigating how experienced developers could benefit from testing knowledge and what kind of specific testing knowledge they need in order to increase the quality of the code artefacts they produce.

Acknowledgments. This work was supported by SWELL (Swedish software Verification & Validation ExceLLence) research school and OPEN-SME research project.

References

1. Beck, K.: Extreme programming explained: embrace change. Addison-Wesley Longman Publishing Co., Inc., Boston (2000)
2. Causevic, A., Sundmark, D., Punnekkat, S.: An industrial survey on contemporary aspects of software testing. In: Proceedings of the 3rd IEEE International Conference on Software Testing, Verification and Validation, ICST, pp. 393–401 (2010)
3. Causevic, A., Sundmark, D., Punnekkat, S.: Factors limiting industrial adoption of test driven development: A systematic review. In: Proceedings of the 4th IEEE International Conference on Software Testing, Verification and Validation, ICST, pp. 337–346 (2011)
4. Wohlin, C., Runesson, P., Höst, M., Ohlsson, M.C., Regnell, B., Wesslén, A.: Experimentation in Software Engineering – An Introduction. Kluwer Academic Publishers (2000)
5. Jedlitschka, A., Pfahl, D.: Reporting guidelines for controlled experiments in software engineering. In: Jeffery, R., et al. (eds.) Proceedings of the 4th International Symposium on Empirical Software Engineering (ISESE 2005), pp. 94–104. IEEE Computer Society (2005)
6. Sfetsos, P., Angelis, L., Stamelos, I.: Investigating the extreme programming system - an empirical study. Empirical Software Engineering 11, 269–301 (2006)
7. Geras, A., Smith, M., Miller, J.: A prototype empirical evaluation of test driven development. In: Proceedings of the 10th International Symposium on Software Metrics, pp. 405–416. IEEE Computer Society, Washington, DC, USA (2004)

8. Kollanus, S., Isomöttönen, V.: Understanding tdd in academic environment: experiences from two experiments. In: Proceedings of the 8th International Conference on Computing Education Research, Koli 2008, pp. 25–31. ACM, New York (2008)
9. Muller, M., Hagner, O.: Experiment about test-first programming. IEE Proceedings Software 149, 131–136 (2002)
10. George, B., Williams, L.: A structured experiment of test-driven development. Information and Software Technology 46(5), 337–342 (2003)
11. Erdogmus, H., Morisio, M., Torchiano, M.: On the effectiveness of the test-first approach to programming. IEEE Transactions on Software Engineering 31, 226–237 (2005)
12. Flohr, T., Schneider, T.: Lessons Learned from an XP Experiment with Students: Test-First Needs More Teachings. In: Münch, J., Vierimaa, M. (eds.) PROFES 2006. LNCS, vol. 4034, pp. 305–318. Springer, Heidelberg (2006)
13. Janzen, D.S., Saiedian, H.: On the influence of test-driven development on software design. In: Conference on Software Engineering Education and Training, pp. 141–148 (2006)
14. Müller, M., Höfer, A.: The effect of experience on the test-driven development process. Empirical Software Engineering 12, 593–615 (2007)
15. Janzen, D.S., Turner, C.S., Saiedian, H.: Empirical software engineering in industry short courses. In: Conference on Software Engineering Education and Training, pp. 89–96 (2007)
16. Gupta, A., Jalote, P.: An experimental evaluation of the effectiveness and efficiency of the test driven development. In: Proceedings of the First International Symposium on Empirical Software Engineering and Measurement, ESEM 2007, pp. 285–294. IEEE Computer Society, Washington, DC, USA (2007)
17. Höfer, A., Philipp, M.: An Empirical Study on the TDD Conformance of Novice and Expert Pair Programmers. In: Abrahamsson, P., Marchesi, M., Maurer, F. (eds.) XP 2009. LNBIP, vol. 31, pp. 33–42. Springer, Heidelberg (2009)
18. Huang, L., Holcombe, M.: Empirical investigation towards the effectiveness of test first programming. Inf. Softw. Technol. 51, 182–194 (2009)
19. Vu, J.H., Frojd, N., Shenkel-Therolf, C., Janzen, D.S.: Evaluating test-driven development in an industry-sponsored capstone project. In: Proceedings of the 2009 Sixth International Conference on Information Technology: New Generations, pp. 229–234. IEEE Computer Society, Washington, DC, USA (2009)
20. Madeyski, L.: The impact of test-first programming on branch coverage and mutation score indicator of unit tests: An experiment. Inf. Softw. Technol. 52, 169–184 (2010)
21. The International Software Testing Qualifications Board (ISTQB), http://www.istqb.org
22. Ammann, P., Offutt, J.: Introduction to Software Testing. Cambridge University Press, Cambridge (2008) ISBN 0-52188-038-1
23. Eclipse, http://www.eclipse.org
24. jUnit Framework, http://www.junit.org

Escalation of Commitment:
A Longitudinal Case Study of Daily Meetings

Viktoria Gulliksen Stray[1], Nils Brede Moe[2], and Tore Dybå[2,1]

[1] University of Oslo, Gaustadalléen 23,
NO-0373 Oslo, Norway
stray@ifi.uio.no
[2] SINTEF, S.P. Andersens veg 15 B,
NO-7465 Trondheim, Norway
(nils.b.moe,tore.dyba)@sintef.no

Abstract. Escalating commitment is a common and costly phenomenon in software projects in which decision-makers continue to invest resources to a failing course of action. We conducted a longitudinal case study exploring the effect of daily meetings on escalating commitment. This was done in an agile project building software for the oil and gas industry. By analyzing data collected over a period of four years, and drawing on concepts from self-justification theory we found that daily meetings contributed to maintain a situation of escalating commitment. This especially occurs if the meeting becomes a place for reporting and defending decisions with team members feeling that they have to justify their choices towards the project management or fellow team members. Early signs of escalation such as rationalizing continuation of a chosen course of action must therefore be taken seriously.

Keywords: Escalating commitment, daily meetings, stand-up, Scrum, self-justification theory, agile software development.

1   Introduction

Escalation of commitment, which can be defined as an increasing commitment to a failing course of action [1], is a general phenomenon that is particularly common in software projects because of their complex and uncertain nature [2]. Keil et al. [3], for example, found that 30-40 % of all software projects experience escalation of commitment. Some of the most important and difficult decisions made in software projects involve escalating situations. In these situations decision-makers commit additional resources to a course of action with negative interim outcomes [4]. One of the most known escalating commitment projects is the baggage handling system at Denver International Airport [5]. The project delayed the opening of the airport by nearly two years and caused it to be $2 billion over budget [5].

Recently there is a trend in software development, through the introduction of agile software development (ASD), that the focus of decision-making has moved from the project manager to the software development team, and the decision-making process

C. Wohlin (Ed.): XP 2012, LNBIP 111, pp. 153–167, 2012.

has changed from individual and centralized to shared and decentralized [6]. Thus in agile software development leadership is shared, and important decisions on what to do and how to do it are made through an interactive process involving many people who influence each other, not just a single person [7].

Several studies have shown that decision-makers tend to invest additional resources in an attempt to justify their previous investments [1, 8, 9]. Because groups have the capacity of employing multiple perspectives when making decisions, one might believe that escalating commitment situations should occur less frequently in agile teams than in traditional teams. However, several studies show that when having group decision-making, escalating tendencies will occur more often and will be more severe than in individual decision-making due to group polarization and conformity pressures [10].

The most important forum for coordinating work and making decisions in ASD is through daily meetings, which are often called "stand-up meetings" or "Daily Scrum". The purpose of the daily meeting is to synchronize activities and improve communication among the entire team, and to create plans for the next 24 hours [11]. Accordingly, the daily meeting is the most important forum for exchanging information upon which decisions are based, in addition to being a decision-making forum itself.

Motivated by the importance of understanding escalating commitment in software development, and the daily meetings as an important place for group decisions and for exchanging information in agile software projects, we have identified the following research question:

What is the effect of daily meetings on escalating commitment in agile software projects?

To investigate this research question we conducted an in-depth longitudinal case study of escalating commitment in a multi-year new product development project. Over a 4-year period, the project suffered a number of setbacks and budget increases, as well as negative feedback on project progress.

The main contribution of this paper is an analysis of daily meetings in a project with escalating commitment, combined with a discussion of theoretical and practical implications. We interviewed 20 people in addition to observing teamwork and meetings. We used self-justification theory to analyze the interview transcripts and field notes. This theory suggests that individuals tend to escalate their commitment to a course of action in order to self-justify prior behavior, especially when they have been personally responsible for negative consequences [8].

The remainder of this paper is organized as follows: The next section outlines the background and relevant literature on daily meetings and escalating commitment. Section 3 describes the research methods used, Section 4 reports our results, Section 5 discusses the findings, and Section 6 concludes.

2   Background

In this section we first present background information on decision-making in an agile context. Then we explain why escalating commitment is important in the field of decision-making and software development before we introduce theories used to explain the phenomena of escalating commitment.

2.1   Decision Making in Agile Software Development

Product and project level decisions in a software company can be considered at the strategic, tactical, and operational levels [12]. In an ASD product company, strategic decisions are primarily related to product and release plans. Tactical decisions involve the project management view where the aim is to determine the best way to implement ASD strategic decisions. Finally, operational decisions are about implementation of product features and the process of assuring that specific tasks are carried out effectively and efficiently [6].

When explaining non-routine decisions, like in software projects where goals are constantly changing, the bounded rationality model [13] is often useful. This model assumes that decision-makers' rationality is restricted by the information they have, their cognitive limitations, and the types of problems they face. An uncertain task requires large amounts of information to be processed by decision-makers while performing the task [14]. The greater the uncertainty, the more difficult it is to program and routinize an activity by preplanning a response [15].

Another relevant theory on decision-making is naturalistic decision-making, which aids in understanding how people make decisions in real-world contexts that are meaningful and familiar to them [16, 17]. The advent of naturalistic decision-making shifted the concept of human decision-making from a domain independent general approach to a knowledge-based approach exemplified by decision-makers with substantial experience. The decision-making process was expanded to include the stage of perception and recognition of situations as well as generation of appropriate responses, not just a choice from given options [18]. Moving from plan-driven to agile development can be seen as moving from rational to naturalistic decision-making [6].

2.2   Escalating Commitment

One major source of error in decision-making is escalation of commitment [19]. The phenomenon has been widely studied in the Information Systems (IS) field [20-22]. Escalation is considered a costly and common problem in IT projects. Many software projects are over budget and have time overruns, and this is often caused by a situation of escalating commitment [23]. Escalating situations happen when decision-makers allocate resources in the hope of attaining a goal and then receive feedback that they have not yet reached that goal [24]. There will be an uncertainty surrounding goal attainment and the decision-maker must make a choice about whether to continue the previous course of action [24].

While any type of project is at risk of escalation of commitment, Montealegre and Keil [25] declared that IT projects are especially vulnerable to this phenomenon because software by nature is intangible, making it difficult to determine the amount of work left until completion.

Several theories have been used to explain the phenomenon of escalating commitment, and the most frequent theories have been prospect theory, self-justification theory, agency theory, and approach-avoidance theory [3]. Since self-justification theory has been shown to provide not only an important [24], but a primary explanation for escalating commitment [26] we chose to use this theory when studying the phenomenon in agile software projects. Additionally, in agile software projects the team members are given more personal responsibility than in traditional software projects, which is an important concept of this theory.

According to self-justification theory, individuals tend to continue to commit to a course of action in order to self-justify the correctness of an earlier decision to pursue a particular course of action [8]. "Individuals seek to rationalize their previous behavior or psychologically defend themselves against a perceived error in judgment", [8], p. 432, in other words: people do not like to admit to themselves or others that a previous decision was wrong [24].

Escalating behavior is seen as coming from a "retrospective rationality"; what has been invested in the past is considered relevant to the decision-making [3]. At a personal level this can be compared to a person who keeps standing in a long queue because he or she already has been standing there for a long time, even if the queue is moving slowly [27]. There are two constructs in the self-justification theory: *psychological justification*, where an individual seeks to justify his actions in order to prove to himself that he is competent and rational, and *social self-justification* where he seeks to justify the same to others [3].

Psychological justification cannot be assessed directly since it happens in the subconscious mind of the decision-maker, factors which can indicate that a person engages in psychological justification is; being extensively involved in a project, repeatedly expressing support for it, feeling personally responsible or being emotionally attached to the project [3].

Social self-justification often leads to behaviors to save face, and one indicator of social self-justification is when a decision-maker does not want to admit mistakes [3]. In the case that a decision-maker is very closely identified with the project or would look bad if the project was terminated, this may suggest a high need for self-justification [3].

Additionally, the level of personal responsibility influences the need to self-justify: a person who has a high level of personal responsibility for a previously chosen course of action is more likely to commit more resources to this course than individuals with a low level of personal responsibility [1].

3   Research Method

Since the goal of this research is to explore and provide insight into the phenomenon of escalating commitment and the decision-making processes in agile software development, it is important to study software development teams in practice. Therefore, we chose a case study since case studies are especially useful for such exploratory research where an in-depth understanding of a phenomenon in its context is desired [28].

3.1   Case Study Design

We designed a single-case longitudinal study [28] of escalating commitment in a Scrum project to understand the role of daily meetings in such projects. The particular case was initially part of a multiple case study involving two companies on understanding shared decision-making in agile software development [6]. While the multiple case study [6] identified challenges of shared decision-making in four projects, this study focuses on the phenomena of escalating commitment in one of the projects. The two first authors extended the data, which was the base in the study of shared decision-making, by collecting additional data over a period of one year. A single case study was chosen since it shows a critical case for testing a well-formulated theory. We relied on interviews and participant observations when collecting data.

Most case studies on escalation of commitment rely on data collected in retrospect, after the project has been recognized as a case of escalating commitment. By including data from before the project experienced escalation, this longitudinal study gave us a unique opportunity of understanding escalation of commitment. In this study we chose to focus on daily meetings, as this is the main place for decision-making and coordination of work in agile teams.

3.2   Study Context

This study was conducted in the context of a larger action research program, in which the company introduced elements of agile development in response to identified problems. The Company is a medium-sized software company with approximately 150 employees in four organizational units. Each developer was usually fully allocated to one project, and when there was a need for additional competence, for example on user interface or modeling, additional internal resources were used.

The goal of the project was to develop an engineering software product for the oil and gas industry. Today several clients are interested in buying the software product, and at the time of the study a few contracts had been signed. The project involved developing a new system while at the same time trying to obtain input from the marketing department and potential clients.

Eight months into the project Scrum was introduced and from then on the team followed Scrum rules and was given significant authority and responsibility for many aspects of their work, such as planning, scheduling, assigning tasks to members, and making decisions. They usually relied on three-week sprints, however, the length of the sprint sometimes changed during vacations, and before and after deliveries. They conducted Scrum meetings in each sprint, such as sprint planning meeting, sprint review, and retrospective.

The project had two different Scrum Masters during the four years. The first one was an experienced developer who had worked in the company for several years. He stayed on the project for the three first years. The second Scrum Master was an experienced project manager and architect.

3.3   Data Collection and Analysis

The two first authors conducted 20 semi-structured interviews with developers, Scrum Masters, and Product Owners. Each interview lasted from 20 to 50 minutes and covered the five main topics; meetings, teamwork, decision-making, agile practices, and the project. Examples of questions are: How is work coordinated? How do you perceive the daily meeting? How is feedback given? How are decisions made? How are problems solved?

Everyone involved in the project was interviewed, including Product Owner and line manager, one or several times. All interviews were recorded and fully transcribed. The interview guide was based on the teamwork model proposed by Dickinson and McIntyre [29], which includes the most common elements that are considered in research on teamwork processes and that can be used on decision-making and self-managing teams [30]. The two first authors also observed retrospectives and daily meetings.

Participant observation was selected as a research technique to investigate the phenomenon of escalating commitment. It is a particularly relevant approach when 'the phenomenon is obscured from the view of outsiders' [31]. During coffee and lunch breaks the two first authors also discussed status, progress, and how issues were perceived by team participants. Telephone and e–mail were also used for such discussions. Notes were taken during dialogues, interactions, and activities. A short summary was written after each observation. We asked some team members to explain and comment on our observations.

All the transcribed data from the interviews, observations, and documents was imported into a software tool for analyzing qualitative data, NVivo (www.qsrinternational.com). The two first authors read all interviews and observations, and coded interesting expressions of opinions, problems, events, happenings, or actions/interactions in the text by assigning the piece of text to a category ("node" in NVivo). A category represents a phenomenon, that is, a problem, an issue or an event that is defined as being significant. When categories were found to be conceptually similar in nature they were grouped under more abstract, higher-order categories. Finally, NVivo was used to create connections between categories and their subcategories.

4   Results

The phenomenon of escalating commitment was observed in the following two distinct phases. In the first phase of our study we found the team to justify their decisions to the Product Owner. In the second part of the study we found the team members justifying their decisions to each other. We will now describe our findings in these two phases.

4.1   The Team Justifying Their Decisions to the Product Owner

The project started in 2006. After 8 months, Scrum was introduced by the second and third authors in close collaboration with the company. The main motivation was the urgent need for delivering features more often. So far, the management who funded the product development project perceived the progress as too slow and threatened to cancel the project. Also three potential customers (three of the world's biggest oil companies) felt that the product development was going too slow, and therefore they did not sign contracts. Delivering software every month and better responding to potential customers was seen as necessary for continuing to get funding, therefore the project decided to start using Scrum and to rely on iterative development. The Scrum Master, Product Owner, and the team were given Scrum training over two days. In addition the Scrum Master got coaching from an experienced Scrum trainer the first year.

After introducing Scrum, the team and the management had to make an important decision regarding which technology the product should be based on. There were two choices:

1) Base the project on an existing framework for data processing that already existed within the company, or
2) Build their own framework from scratch independently of what already existed, and use third part components when needed.

The Product Owner (PO) and the project management let the team decide themselves. The team chose 2) because:

- The existing framework was seen as too immature at the time of the decision
- The people that had developed the framework were very busy, and were not part of the project team. The team felt they needed help from the experts of the framework to implement it in the project
- The team needed to show progress. If they chose 1) it would require several months adjusting the existing framework before new features could be implemented. Choosing 2) made it possible to develop the framework in an iterative way and to start delivering features without the framework being complete.

The PO, who also was a project manager, frequently communicated with the customers and he participated in the daily meetings. His goal of participating in the daily meetings was to frequently inform the team what the potential customers were interested in, and to better understand the challenges the team faced. It soon became evident that there were challenges when the team planned their work based on the product backlog. Some of the features identified by the various customers were conflicting and some were too vaguely defined. The Scrum Master said:

"We are now dealing with three potential customers, and they ask for three different solutions. We need to urgently figure out how to satisfy them all."

Decisions on how to prioritize and how to understand the requirements needed a constant dialogue between the PO and the team, therefore it was perceived as very useful to have him in the daily meetings. By observing the daily meetings it was clear that the PO gave a lot of feedback, and important discussions arose on how to understand what was supposed to be delivered.

Estimates were given by the team on the various features, however it soon became evident that the team had overcommitted and had a much lower progress than expected by the team itself and by the PO. Because of the slow progress, the PO started to question the decisions and work done by the team members while in the daily meetings. The PO felt that the team members did not take real responsibility when they did not complete the tasks on time. Also the PO felt that the team was missing a good strategy for developing the architectural framework for the product. Both from the interviews and from observing daily meetings it was evident that the PO and the team did not fully trust each other. The effect was team members ending up defending their decisions and their work, especially if they were running late on a task. One developer explained:

"I experienced the daily meeting like an oral exam. If you had estimated two days on the task, and you had used three days and still not finished, you knew you had to explain why you were running late. You always prepared for the daily meeting; I wrote down in detail what I had done on a small piece of paper."

While everyone agreed that the daily meeting was about informing each other, it was obvious that this meeting became the place for the developers to give detailed progress reports to the PO and to give detailed explanations for why things did not turn out as expected. It was about defending their decisions and their progress against what they felt the management expected, and less about informing each other.

The Scrum Master initiated several improvement actions to make the situation better. He introduced; pre-planning meetings so he and the Product Owner could prepare the product backlog for the planning meeting, pair programming to create shared ownership, and a dedicated meeting room for the team to visualize and track all tasks.

In this period the team members had frequent meetings regarding how to solve problems, how to develop the architectural framework and how to implement features. The team members felt they based their decisions on consensus, and when they prepared for the daily meetings it was all about defending their decisions to the PO, who often questioned them. This was also the case if the team had identified e.g. a need for upgrading the development tools, the hardware or their competence.

For two more years this pattern of behaviour continued. Project progress was still perceived as slow by the ones paying for the project, and the pressure on the team and the PO increased. Because of this, the PO felt he had to make the team commit to deliver more features. The team tried to protest, but that did not help and the team usually ended up with an unrealistic backlog for each sprint. At the same time it became more and more difficult to estimate how much time it would require to implement new features. It was obvious that there were problems with the architectural framework, because adding a feature always ended up with the need to change previous code. Additionally, the team was not able to estimate what needed to be changed and how long this would take. The situation gradually deteriorated and the solution was to work harder; resulting in a lot of overtime work. The daily meeting continued to be a place for the PO to question the team and for the team to defend their actions. There was never a discussion on whether they had previously made the right decisions, or if the project was heading in the right direction. The focus was on continuing to do what they were doing, and to defend their decisions. After a while the team stopped conducting daily meetings on a regular basis. The reason for this was that they thought it did not add any value to meet every day.

4.2   Team Members Justifying Their Decisions to Each Other

Three years after Scrum was introduced the former Scrum Master quit the company. The project got a new Scrum Master, who also became the new project manager, and four new developers joined the project. Additionally, it was decided that the PO should not participate in the daily meetings anymore to better protect the team against the continuous input from the market. Daily meetings were again held five days a week.

While the project was revitalized, it still had severe problems with progression. The Scrum Master and the management identified part of the newly developed framework and code developed by the old team members as a major problem. It was written in such a way that it became more and more difficult to change. It was time-consuming to add new features, and the new architectural framework could not be extended to support features that were essential to enter a new market. The old team members did not share the view on the source of the problems, and wanted to continue to use the self-developed framework and code. They also wanted to commit additional resources to this course of action. The management perceived this course of action as a failing one.

For a period conflicts arose between the new and the old team members. The new developers felt the code and architectural framework developed had poor quality, while some of the old team members felt disregarded when their previous work was questioned and the new team members started cleaning up in "their" code.

The daily meetings changed from a place the team defended itself to the Product Owner, to a place were the old team members defended themselves to the new Scrum Master and the new developers. The old team members felt it was important to prove to the new team members that they did good work. This seemed like a defence mechanism that was activated when their previous work and decisions were questioned. Daily meetings were experienced by some as a means for showing each other that they were working between the meetings. One developer said:

"Yes, it is ok to have a formal rallying point just to say that "I am here, and I am actually working on something."

Another developer explained how he perceived the daily meeting:

"You can feel the pulse go up, because you are supposed to talk about the things you have done and show progress."

Some team members defended themselves by telling a lot of details about what they had done since the last meeting. One developer explained the effect of this detailed reporting:

"There are often too many details in the daily meetings so people fall off. Because you don't know what the others are doing, you have no idea what they are talking about when they start to talk about their own stuff."

The Scrum Master tried to change the daily meetings from being a place where detailed reports were given to him to a forum where the team members could talk to each other and have less focus on details. However, we still observed that some team members continued to give detailed technical reports during the daily meetings. One reason for this was that the team members worked on separate parts of the code and therefore they did not know what the others in the team were doing. The specialization caused them to feel responsible for their own modules and defend their "own" code in these modules.

In spring 2011 a plan was made to exchange their new self-developed framework with the existing company-based framework that the project had decided not to use three years earlier. The old team members were frustrated about this decision because they had invested several years in the new code, which was now to be removed. The old team members were given the opportunity to work out a solution to keep the their code, but they did not come up with one.

When the code rewriting started, the old team members did not fully support the decision, and some team members continued to defend their previous actions. The team was in a crisis for several months because the whole team was not working in the same direction. Some developers even considered leaving the team.

Replacing bigger parts of the code caused the system to become even more unstable, even worse than before. Progress was slow and task estimation was still very difficult. Doing one change to the system could take from hours to days, and the developers could never tell. Some of the old team members became furious about this and the atmosphere in the team went from bad to worse. In the interviews it was revealed that there was a lot of blaming going on in the team. The new team members blamed problems on the old developers that in their mind had written code with poor quality. The old team members blamed the replacement of their code to be the reason for the new problems emerging. From observing a full day retrospective, we noticed that none of the conflicts between the team members or problems related to the old code were discussed.

It took more than five months before the team members that had been on the project from the beginning accepted the decision of exchanging the framework. They were committed to their previous work and did not want to admit that exchanging it was a good solution. The daily meetings were the place for defending previous decisions and showing others that they did a good job. After the old developers started accepting the changes needed to be done, the daily meetings started to improve, however there was still an uncertainty related to the delivery of the next big release.

5   Discussion

We have described a project with escalating commitment and how the project members perceived the daily meetings. In the beginning of the project the daily meetings became a meeting where the team members felt they had to defend their decisions and work to the PO. Both parties used the daily meetings to justify their own work. Later in the project the daily meetings became a forum where some of the team members felt they had to defend their decision and their work to each other and to the Scrum Master.

In this section we will discuss our research question and elaborate on how the daily meeting became a meeting for psychological and social self-justification and how this contributed to maintain the escalating situation.

5.1   Psychological Self-justification

There are three common reasons for psychological self-justification [3]: (1) Being extensively involved in a project, (2) being emotionally attached to the project, and (3) feeling personally responsible for the project. In the observed project, the team members had been a part of the project for many years, which led them to be emotionally attached and extensively involved. Also because the project coordinated work by relying on specialization and corresponding division of work they felt personally responsible for the modules they worked on. Feeling such personal responsibility and being emotionally attached are both usually positive qualities of a team. However, as we found, they can also maintain an escalating situation. The main reason for this was that the daily meetings were used as a forum for defending decisions.

We saw team members seeking to justify their choices on a regular basis in the daily meetings. In the first phase of the project the team members all agreed on their choice being a good one, however they believed they needed to use the daily meetings to justify it to the PO. The team members felt personally responsible for the choice that was made, and they became emotionally attached to the code they had written. The daily meetings were perceived as an oral exam where team members gave detailed and technical descriptions on what they had been doing since the previous meeting.

Three years into the project it was decided that they had to replace the self-developed framework with an existing framework, the team members who had developed the framework became very frustrated. They had worked on this for three years, and replacing the code was equal to saying that their work was wasted. Some of the old developers felt their position was threatened, and for several months many of them resisted this change. They used a lot of energy complaining about the new framework and the work carried out by the new developers. The daily meeting became a place for telling the others that they were adding value to the project.

Our findings are in line with the results of Staw et al. [1], who found that individuals with a high level of responsibility are more likely to find a greater need to justify previous decisions. Because the team had developed their own framework over several years they continued to justify why this framework was the right one, and the daily meeting became the most important forum for doing so.

When it was decided to replace the framework, the old developers became very frustrated, and subsequently they used the daily meetings to defend their work and position in the team. Also, Pan et al [23] found that there might be a sense of anxiety in a project when a team is told to give up their commitment to a failing course of action.

Agile software projects rely on feedback sessions such as review and retrospective meetings. These meetings might make it easier to overcome commitment to a prior, failing course of action and agree on a turnaround strategy. However, people need to feel secure to be willing to give up a prior course of action [22], which means that for retrospective meetings being able to facilitate de-escalation of commitment the team members must feel secure. In this project the conflicts in the team were never discussed in retrospective meetings, which might indicate that they did not feel secure.

In the study by Pan et al. [22] of de-escalation the team managed to work towards a project turnaround because of open communication and they found that psychological safety was crucial. The communication in the team that we studied was not open, and the team members did not seem secure, which might contribute to explaining why the escalation continued for such a long time.

5.2   Social Self-justification

Social self-justification is another important construct for self-justification, which can be indicated by: (1) Behaviors to save face, (2) not wanting to admit mistakes, and (3) being very closely identified with the project. From the interviews and from observing the daily meetings we found that the team members and the PO did not fully trust each other. This led to a behavior of not wanting to admit mistakes and trying to save face in the daily meetings. When new team members were added to the project, the old team members started to defend their previous decisions because they did not want to admit mistakes to the new developers. In addition, the old team members closely identified themselves with the software being developed.

The project received negative feedback on their progress, and continued for many years without changing the course of action. In other studies on escalating commitment it has also been found that decision-makers often tend to allocate more resources if they receive negative feedback about the chosen course of action, than if they receive positive feedback [32].

We also found that the project members and the PO relied on placing blame as a way of justifying decisions. They both blamed the technology, other circumstances beyond control (e.g. the customer) and the work done by others. The Product Owner blamed the developers for writing code of low quality, and the developers blamed the PO for overselling to the customers and giving them ambiguous and conflicting requirements. The new developers blamed the code written by the existing developers, while the existing developers started to blame the new code when the system had a lot of errors during the exchange of the framework. This is in line with the findings of Heng et al. on blaming as a means of justifying decisions [33].

The result of this blaming was that the daily meetings became the place to prove that the work they were doing was good and important. Studies on escalating commitment have found that if people are motivated to justify their decisions, the situation of escalating commitment continues, while if this motivation is reduced the situation can be de-escalated [33]. The daily meeting was a forum where the team members constantly had to justify their decisions and therefore contributed to maintaining the escalation.

5.3   Implications for Practice

To avoid situations of escalating commitment it is important to make sure that the daily meeting is not a place for defending decisions. Not only do the team need to watch their internal process, they also need to consider which non-team members are allowed to participate or observe the meeting. If team members start to defend their decisions or give detailed reports of what they have done because people outside the team are present in the daily meetings, we advise that these people outside the team do not participate on a regular basis.

Early signs of escalation such as rationalizing continuation of a chosen course of action, and when team members start giving detailed and technical descriptions of what they have done since last meeting, must be taken seriously. Further when the team becomes aware of the signs of escalating commitment, this needs to be addressed on the retrospective meetings. Finally, team members should get, and also give, feedback on how they communicate about their work in the daily meeting.

6   Conclusions and Further Work

There are many reasons why a software project can fail, and escalating commitment, in which a project continues to absorb resources to a failing course of action, is one of them. Over a period of four years we were able to see how daily meetings affected the situation of escalating commitment. We found that the self-justification theory, with the two factors psychological and social self-justification, helped to explain how the daily meetings contributed to maintain the escalating situation. Our results show that the daily meeting became a forum for self-justification where team members defended their decisions and actions to the Product Owner and to each other, and that the daily meeting, therefore, instead of initiating de-escalation became the most important mechanism for maintaining the escalating situation.

The project under study followed Scrum practices, but still experienced a situation of escalating commitment. One might think that agile software projects do not suffer from such escalating commitment because the agile development process emphasizes that the project should embrace change and rely on iterative development and frequent communication, but our study shows that it also happens in agile software projects.

This study focused only on the effect of daily meetings on escalating commitment. Other factors such as knowledge and experience of the team members may also have had an effect on the escalating situation and these should be assessed in future studies. Future work should also investigate how the escalation process emerges in agile software projects, for instance by using the process model given by Mähring and Keil [21, 34]. More research is needed to understand which mechanisms are needed for agile projects to discover a situation of escalating commitment and to enter a phase of de-escalation. In addition there is a need for better understanding of daily meetings in agile software projects, their usefulness (or lack of) in agile software projects, and what can be done to improve daily meetings. Research should also study techniques for daily meetings to make sure they do not maintain a situation of escalating commitment.

Acknowledgments. This work was supported by the Research Council of Norway through grant 193236/I40. We appreciate the input received from managers and project participants of the investigated company, and we are grateful to the reviewers of this paper who gave us valuable feedback.

References

1. Staw, B.: Knee-Deep in the Big Muddy: A Study of Escalating Commitment to a Chosen Course of Action. Organizational Behavior and Human Performance 16(1), 27–44 (1976)
2. Robey, D., Keil, M.: Blowing the Whistle on Troubled Software Projects. Communications of the ACM 44(4), 87–93 (2001)
3. Keil, M., Mann, J., Rai, A.: Why Software Projects Escalate: An Empirical Analysis and Test of Four Theoretical Models. MIS Quarterly 24(4), 631–664 (2000)
4. Keil, M.: Pulling the Plug: Software Project Management and the Problem of Project Escalation. MIS Quarterly 19(4), 421–447 (1995)
5. Keil, M., Montealegre, R.: Cutting Your Losses: Extricating Your Organization When a Big Project Goes Awry. Sloan Management Review 41(3), 55–68 (2000)
6. Moe, N.B., Aurum, A., Dybå, T.: Challenges of Shared Decision-Making: A Multiple Case Study of Agile Software Development. Information and Software Technology, 1–38 (in press, 2012)
7. Moe, N.B., Dingsøyr, T., Dybå, T.: Overcoming Barriers to Self-Management in Software Teams. IEEE Software 26(6), 20–26 (2009)
8. Staw, B.M., Fox, F.V.: Escalation: The Determinants of Commitment to a Chosen Course of Action. Human Relations 30(5), 431–450 (1977)
9. Bazerman, M.H., Giuliano, T., Appelman, A.: Escalation of Commitment in Individual and Group Decision Making. Organizational Behavior and Human Performance 33(2), 141–152 (1984)
10. Whyte, G.: Escalating Commitment in Individual and Group Decision Making: A Prospect Theory Approach. Organizational Behavior and Human Decision Processes 54(3), 430–455 (1993)
11. Schwaber, K., Sutherland, J.: The Scrum Guide. Scrum Alliance (2011)
12. Aurum, A., Wohlin, C., Porter, A.: Aligning Software Project Decisions: A Case Study. International Journal of Software Engineering and Knowledge Engineering 16(6), 795–818 (2006)
13. Simon, H.A.: A Behavioral Model of Rational Choice. The Quarterly Journal of Economics 69(1), 99–118 (1955)
14. Morgan, G.: Images of Organizations. SAGE Publications, Thousand Oaks (2006)
15. Dybå, T.: Improvisation in Small Software Organizations. IEEE Software 17(5), 82–87 (2000)
16. Lipshitz, R., Klein, G., Orasanu, J., Salas, E.: Taking Stock of Naturalistic Decision Making. Journal of Behavioral Decision Making 14(5), 331–352 (2001)
17. Fjellman, S.M.: Natural and Unnatural Decision-Making. Ethos 4(1), 73–94 (1976)
18. Klein, G.: Naturalistic Decision Making. Human Factors: The Journal of the Human Factors and Ergonomics Society 50(3), 456–460 (2008)
19. Lunenburg, F.C.: Escalation of Commitment: Patterns of Retrospective Rationality. International Journal of Management, Business, and Administration 13(1), 1–5 (2010)
20. Keil, M., Rai, A., Cheney Mann, J., Zhang, G.: Why Software Projects Escalate: The Importance of Project Management Constructs. IEEE Transactions on Engineering Management 50(3), 251–261 (2003)
21. Mähring, M., Keil, M.: Information Technology Project Escalation: A Process Model*. Decision Sciences 39(2), 239–272 (2008)
22. Pan, G., Pan, S., Flynn, D.: De-Escalation of Commitment to Information Systems Projects: A Process Perspective. The Journal of Strategic Information Systems 13(3), 247–270 (2004)

23. Pan, G., Pan, S., Newman, M., Flynn, D.: Escalation and De-Escalation of Commitment to Information Technology Projects: A Commitment Transformation Analysis of an E-Government Project. Information Systems Journal 16, 3–21 (2006)
24. Brockner, J.: The Escalation of Commitment to a Failing Course of Action: Toward Theoretical Progress. Academy of Management Review 17(1), 39–61 (1992)
25. Montealegre, R., Keil, M.: De-Escalating Information Technology Projects: Lessons from the Denver International Airport. MIS Quarterly 24(3), 417–447 (2000)
26. Mayur, S., Desai, D.V.C.: Escalation of Commitment in Mis Projects: A Meta-Analysis. International Journal of Management & Information Systems 13(2), 29–38 (2009)
27. Newman, M., Sabherwal, R.: Determinants of Commitment to Information Systems Development: A Longitudinal Investigation. MIS Quarterly 20(1), 23–54 (1996)
28. Yin, R.K.: Case Study Research: Design and Methods. Sage, Thousand Oaks (2008)
29. Dickinson, T.L., McIntyre, R.M.: A Conceptual Framework of Teamwork Measurement. In: Brannick, M.T., Salas, E., Prince, C. (eds.) Team Performance Assessment and Measurement: Theory, Methods, and Applications, pp. 19–43. Psychology Press, NJ (1997)
30. Moe, N.B., Dingsøyr, T., Dybå, T.: A Teamwork Model for Understanding an Agile Team: A Case Study of a Scrum Project. Information and Software Technology 52(5), 480–491 (2010)
31. Jorgensen, D.L.: Participant Observation: A Methodology for Human Studies. Sage publications, Thousands Oak (1989)
32. Bowen, M.G.: The Escalation Phenomenon Reconsidered: Decision Dilemmas or Decision Errors? Academy of Management Review 12(1), 52–66 (1987)
33. Heng, C.S., Tan, B.C.Y., Wei, K.K.: De-Escalation of Commitment in Software Projects: Who Matters? What Matters? Information & Management 41(1), 99–110 (2003)
34. Keil, M., Mähring, M.: Is Your Project Turning into a Black Hole? California Management Review 53(1), 6–31 (2010)

Agile User Stories Enriched with Usability

Ana M. Moreno and Agustín Yagüe

Universidad Politecnica de Madrid
Madrid, Spain
ammoreno@fi.upm.es, agustin.yague@upm.es

Abstract. Usability is a critical quality factor. Therefore, like traditional software teams, agile teams have to address usability to properly catch their users experience. There exists an interesting debate in the agile and usability communities about how to achieve this integration. Our aim is to contribute to this debate by discussing the incorporation of particular usability recommendations into user stories, one of the most popular artifacts for communicating agile requirements. In this paper, we explore the implications of usability for both the structure of and the process for defining user stories. We discuss what changes the incorporation of particular usability issues may introduce in a user story. Although our findings require more empirical validation, we think that they are a good starting point for further research on this line.

Keywords: Agile development, usability patterns, user stories, HCI.

1 Introduction

ISO 9241-11 [1] defines usability as "the extent to which a product can be used by specified users to achieve specified goals with effectiveness, efficiency and satisfaction in a specific context of use". In short, usability is also generally referred to as "quality in use" [2].

The integration and cross pollination between usability and agile practices have been a rapidly expanding area of work and research in the last few years. The increasing number of publications concerning the field or the active Yahoo discussion group called Agile Usability are two signs of change. One of the premises of this line of work is that usability is a critical quality factor and needs to be dealt with during agile development in order to provide a quality user experience. Both the HCI and agile communities agree on this point. On the HCI side, for example, Nielsen [3] states that an agile development team must recognize interaction design and usability methods as explicit methodology development components, whereas, on the agile side, Ambler [4] claims that an end product's good usability can be ensured only by systematic usability engineering activities during development iterations.

This is not, however, a straightforward process. Different authors have highlighted challenges that need to be overcome if both fields want to work together. Differences in terminology (Ferreira et al.[5]), goals (Lee[6]) and approaches to software construction (Desilets[7]) are some of the most often cited obstacles to this integration.

C. Wohlin (Ed.): XP 2012, LNBIP 111, pp. 168–176, 2012.

Nonetheless, several topics dealing with this road to integration are under debate. At the organizational level, there is an interesting discussion about how the UX team should work with the agile team (Ferreira et al.[8]). Another interesting line of work addresses when UX design should take place in an agile process (Constantine[9]), [10,11,12,13].

Some time ago, the HCI literature provided very specific usability recommendations with a clear positive impact on the final quality of use of software systems. Examples are give the user the option to cancel an ongoing process [11,12,13,14], to undo a task [15,16], provide the user feedback on what is going on in the system [15,17,18], adapt software functionalities to the user profile [19] or provide clear and marked exits for the application [17]. Such usability recommendations are in line with what Nielsen lately referred to as fast and cheap usability techniques [20], as quick usability actions that help to significantly increase user satisfaction.

Such recommendations represent specific functionalities to be incorporated into a software system. Therefore, as discussed in [21], they can be considered as functional usability requirements that complement traditional requirements.

Advancing along the above road to usability and agile integration, we address how to deal with the above functional usability requirements in an agile context. We explore how to represent such functional usability requirements in user stories, one of the most popular artifacts for conveying agile requirements.

To do this, we have structured the paper as follows. Section 2 describes the usability recommendations that we will deal with and discusses the need for full specification. Then Section 3 discusses an approach for documenting this type of usability information into user stories. Section 4 introduces a software tool set up to support the inclusion of usability mechanisms in user stories. Section 5 describes how the approach is validated. Finally, Section 6 outlines some conclusions and future work.

2   Specifying Functional Usability Features

This section describes the usability recommendations that we will deal with and discusses the need for full specification. We have worked on the functional usability recommendations proposed in [21], that is, usability heuristics with key benefits (according to the usability literature) and with strong design implications, according to the software engineering literature. Table 1 provides an overview.

One question that arises is whether such features need to be explicitly specified and, if so, exactly what information should be listed. For example, would it be enough to state in the user story that a particular functionality should include status feedback? From a usability perspective, many details have to be taken into account for a system to provide satisfactory *system status feedback*, including what states to report, what information to display for each state, how prominent the information should be in each case (for example, should the application keep control of the system or should users be able to do something else while system status is being reported)... Therefore, much more information than just a description of the usability feature must be considered in order to properly build such feedback recommendations into a software system.

Table 1. Usability mechanisms addressed

Usability Mechanism	Goal
System Status	To inform users about the internal status of the system
Warning	To inform users of any action with important consequences
Long Action Feedback	To inform users that the system is processing an action that will take some time to complete
Global Undo	To undo system actions at several levels
Abort Operation	To cancel the execution of an action or the whole application
Abort Command	To cancel the execution of a task in progress
Go Back	To go back to a particular state in a command execution sequence
Structured Text Entry	To help prevent the user from making data input errors
Step-by-Step Execution	To help users to do tasks that require different steps with user input and correct such input
Preferences	To record each user's options for using system functions
Favorites	To record certain places of interest for the user
Multilevel Help	To provide different help levels for different users

Notice that neither customers/users, nor, as Chamberlain et al. [13] claim, agile developers are generally usability experts. So, unless this type of usability information is documented in some way, good usability would, as Jokela and Abrahamsson [22] mentioned, be more or less a fluke resulting from customer and/or developer intuition. Whether the sources of this information are customers/users, developers, usability experts or usability elicitation guidelines [21], such information may, from an agile perspective, require new user stories and/or modifications to the original functional stories (new acceptance criteria, new tasks…). Therefore, they will have an impact on the workload associated with the respective user stories and, consequently, on the sprint plan. It is our understanding that this type of usability information should be somehow represented or documented as part of user stories, so it can be properly estimated and implemented. The next section discusses an approach for documenting usability information in user stories.

3   Documenting Usability in User Stories

Bearing in mind recommendations on how to write good user stories [23] and documentation on usability mechanisms [24], we have identified three ways in which the incorporation of usability influences user stories:

1. Addition of new stories to represent requirements directly derived from usability. We call these new stories "usability stories" to distinguish them from traditional user stories, as they represent usability features to be provided by the system.
2. Addition or modification of tasks in existing user stories. This means that some actions derived from usability constraints should be performed in an existing user story. This task could be as simple or detailed as needed.
3. Addition or modification of acceptance criteria. These acceptance criteria appear because the user story functionality needs to include some specific actions that modify the operating environment.

At least one, if not all three, of these three actions has to be taken when writing user stories with usability. Table 2 shows the implications of each analyzed usability mechanism when it is included in a user story. Table columns represent the above actions and rows contain the usability mechanisms . Cells marked with an "X" signal that the incorporation of the usability mechanism requires the respective action. For example, the implementation of the warning mechanism affects the user story by modifying acceptance criteria, adding new acceptance criteria, adding new tasks and adding a new usability story to the product backlog. Table 2 was built empirically as a result of two case studies and is being further validated, as discussed later.

Table 2. Mapping between usability mechanisms and actions

	New Task	Modify Task	New Acceptance Criteria	Modify Acceptance Criteria	New Usability Story	New User Story
System Status		X	X	X	X	
Warning	X		X	X	X	
Long Action		X	X		X	
Abort command	X	X	X		X	
Abort operation		X	X			
Go Back	X	X	X			
Text entry		X	X			
Step by Step	X		X	X		
Preferences						X
Favorites		X	X		X	
Help		X	X		X	

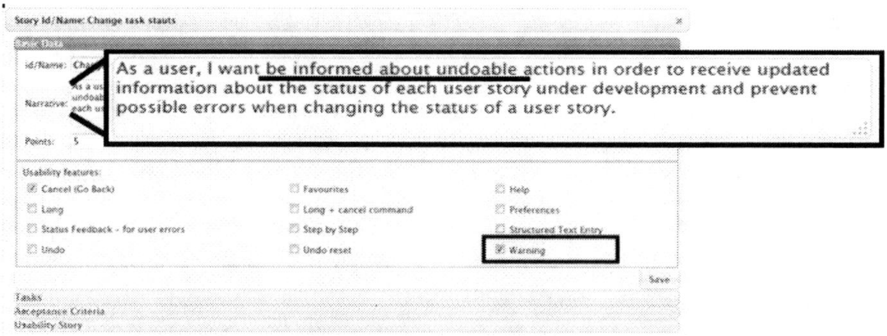

Fig. 1. User story description with usability features

Based on [23,25], the term usability story could be defined as "an artifact that is used to represent usability features that a system/software should support because they are needed by a user to use in a more easy and trusty way and that gives value to the user/acquirer. Usability stories are documented as user stories because both are similar. The next section shows an example of a usability story for implementing warning messages. User stories and usability stories are referred to differently to highlight that usability stories are created to address usability requirements related to a particular user story. Usability stories will be elicited not from product owners but from usability mechanisms designed to improve the use of a particular functionality represented in a user story. The next section gives an example of a user story including the warning usability mechanism.

4   Tool and Process

To support the inclusion of usability mechanisms into user stories, we have modified an open source tool for managing user stories (ScrumTime http://www.scrumtime.org/). The main features added to ScumTime are:

- A list of usability mechanisms available as checkbox items to be associated with each user story.
- A list of usability affected tasks: when a usability mechanism has been selected for a user story, recommendations about new tasks to be added (or the modifications to existing tasks) as a result of including this mechanism are displayed in the task panel.
- A list of usability affected acceptance criteria: when a usability mechanism has been selected for a user story, the new criteria (or changes to existing criteria) to be taken into account to check that the implementation covers the usability features are displayed in the acceptance criteria panel.
- Usability story: when a usability mechanism has been selected for a user story and this mechanism requires the creation of a usability story, the usability story is automatically added to the product backlog.
- Help functionality: examples on how to add usability tasks and acceptance criteria for each usability feature are provided through a new help functionality.

Let us look at an example to illustrate how the tool works. Consider an application managing user stories in agile projects. One of the features of this application might be *"graphically change the status (created, in progress, stopped, done) of a user story"*. A user story description that does not consider usability features might read **"As a user, I want to change the status of a user story and receive updated information about the status of each user story under development"**.

This user story description does not include any information about usability. Suppose, for example, that customers want to be warned about undoable actions (*warning feature*). Following the process described by authors in [26], this feature should be added to the user story because some technical actions have to be taken to inform customers. Fig. 1shows how the tool does this. The description has been zoomed-in and the words related to the warning pattern have been highlighted.

Basic tasks and acceptance criteria are fixed later, when the user story is detailed during sprint planning. A new task has to be added to account for the usability feature.

As Fig. 2 shows, a new task, highlighted by a zoomed-in black box, is added to describe the warning task. All the tasks that are required because of the usability features are listed on the right side of the screen. They are also boxed in black.

Finally, new acceptance criteria should also be considered (see Fig. 3.), plus a new usability story to represent the warning window.

If different usability mechanisms are associated with a user story, the implications for the tasks and acceptance criteria will appear in a compressed folder which users can expand at their convenience (Figs. 2 and 3 show the go back and warning mechanisms, for example).

The main objective of the tool is to capture the usability meta-knowledge related to the inclusion of particular usability mechanisms in a software system. Consequently, a developer without too much usability knowledge can contribute to the development of usable systems. Notice that, as already discussed; neither users nor developers are ordinarily usability experts. Therefore, an automated tool storing this usability meta-knowledge can be helpful if there are no usability experts on hand.

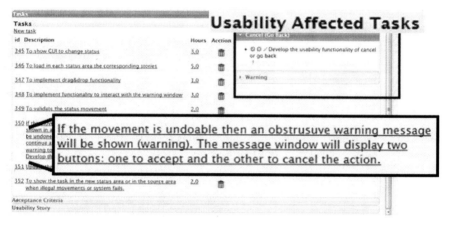

Fig. 2. User story tasks that support the warning feature

5   Proof of Concept

At the time of writing this paper, the validation process was still in progress. It is, however, a two-part process. First, we have worked on validating the usability knowledge summarized in Table 2. To do this, UPM software engineering graduate students developed a small agile project (a tool for managing user stories) as part of their degree project. The tool implemented 24 usability stories incorporating the described usability mechanisms. Using the results we were able to test the usability implications for tasks, acceptance criteria and new usability stories derived from each usability mechanism.

Second, we are validating the tool described in Section 4. It has been tested by UPM software engineering master students, all of whom have 2 to 4 years' experience as software practitioners. As part of their master's thesis, they developed a real application using our tool for creating and documenting user stories. In particular, we worked with three agile teams composed of 3 to 4 developers. The final results are still under evaluation, but early feedback suggests that usability features were easy to add to the user stories and not much usability knowledge was required to do so. The main identified problems were management issues concerning the removal of usability features after their tasks or acceptance criteria were defined.

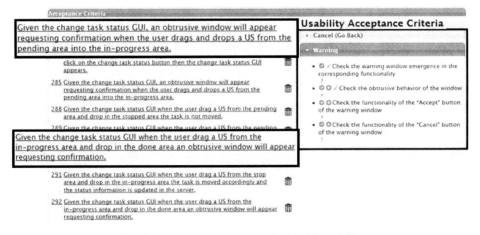

Fig. 3. User story acceptance criteria with usability

Finally, from the preliminary experience using the tool, we can conclude that it is easy to check the usability features of each user story, but it takes some practice to incorporate the usability discussion into the regular user story creation flow. The tool is available at *http://scrumtime.eui.upm.es*.

6   Conclusion

Our hypothesis is that usability constraints may have a major impact on the system to be built. They should, therefore, be dealt with in the development process. This paper aims to present preliminary results on incorporating particular usability mechanisms into agile user stories.

We map the main usability mechanisms and their implications for user stories and also introduce a tool that captures the usability knowledge related to such implications. The approach is still undergoing validation, but preliminary results suggest that the workload for incorporating particular usability mechanisms using the stored usability knowledge leads is reasonably acceptable.

The concept of usability story has been defined to represent the stories needed to implement the required usability mechanisms.

This research raises several issues, like, for example, when to deal with usability functionalities in an agile process or how to manage the size of user stories containing quite a few of usability mechanisms.

The next steps are related to further validating our solution and a detailed analysis of the open issues.

Acknowledgments. The work reported here has been partially sponsored by the Spanish Ministry of Industry, Tourism and Trade INNOSEP: INcorporating inNOvation in Software Engineering Processes project. (TIN2009-13849). We would like to thanks to Diego Yucra for his efforts adapting Scrumtime.

References

1. ISO 9241-11, 98: Ergonomic Requirements for office work with Visual Display Terminals. Part 11: Guidance on Usability. ISO (1998)
2. ISO/IEC. 1999, ISO14598-1, 99: Software Product Evaluation: General Overview. ISO/IEC (1999)
3. Nielsen, J.: Agile Development Projects and Usability. Jakob Nielsen's Alertbox, November 17 (2008),
   http://www.useit.com/alertbox/agile-methods.html
   (visited December 2010)
4. Ambler, S.W.: Tailoring Usability into Agile Software Development Projects. In: Law, E., Hvannberg, E., Cockton, G. (eds.) Maturing Usability. Quality in Software, Interaction and Value. Springer, Heidelberg (2008)
5. Ferreira, J., Noble, J., Biddle, R.: Agile development iterations and UI design. In: AGILE 2007: Proc. of the AGILE 2007, pp. 50–58. IEEE Computer Society, Washington, DC (2007)
6. Lee, J.C.: Embracing Agile Development of Usable Software Systems. In: CHI (2006)
7. Desilets, A.: Are Agile Usability and Methodologies Comparable (2005),
   http://www.carleton.ca/hotlab/hottopics/Articles/June2005-AreAgileandUxMet.html (visited on December 2010)
8. Ferreira, J., Sharp, H., Robinson, H.: Values and Assumptions Shaping Agile Development and User Experience Design in Practice. In: Sillitti, A., Martin, A., Wang, X., Whitworth, E. (eds.) XP 2010. LNBIP, vol. 48, pp. 178–183. Springer, Heidelberg (2010)
9. Constantine L.L.: Process agility and software usability: Toward lightweight usage-centered design. Constantine & Lockwood, Ltd., Tech. Rep. 110 (2001),
   http://citeseer.ist.psu.edu/465732.html
10. Miller, L.: Case study of customer input for a successful product. In: ADC 2005: Proceedings of the Agile Development Conference, pp. 225–234. IEEE Computer Society, Washington, DC, USA (2005)
11. Patton, J.: Hitting the Target: Adding Interaction Design to Agile Software Development. In: Proceedings of OPSLA 2004 (2004)
12. Haikara, J.: Usability in Agile Software Development: Extending the Interaction Design Process with Personas Approach. In: Concas, G., Damiani, E., Scotto, M., Succi, G. (eds.) XP 2007. LNCS, vol. 4536, pp. 153–156. Springer, Heidelberg (2007)
13. Maiden, N., Chamberlain, S., Sharp, H.: Towards a Framework for Integrating Agile Development and User-Centred Design. Springer, Heidelberg (2006)
14. Usability Pattern Collection (December 2010),
   http://www.cmis.brighton.ac.uk/research/patterns/
15. Shneiderman, B.: Designing the User Interface: Strategies for Effective Human-Computer Interaction. Addison-Wesley (1998)
16. Tidwell, J.: Designing Interfaces. In: Patterns for Effective Interaction Design. O'Reilly (2005)
17. Nielsen, J.: Usability Engineering. John Wiley & Sons (1993)
18. van Welie, M.: Patterns in Interaction Design, http://www.welie.com (accessed November 2008)
19. Rubinstein, R., Hersh, H.: The Human Factor. Digital Press, Bedford (1984)
20. Nielsen, J.: Fast, Cheap, and Good: Yes, You Can Have It All (January 2007), http://www.useit.com/alertbox/fast-methods.html (visited December 2010)

21. Juristo, N., Moreno, A., Sanchez-Segura, M.-I.: Guidelines for eliciting usability functionalities. IEEE Trans. Softw. Eng. 33(11), 744–758 (2007)
22. Jokela, T., Abrahamsson, P.: Usability Assessment of an Extreme Programming Project: Close Co-operation with the Customer Does Not Equal to Good Usability. In: Bomarius, F., Iida, H. (eds.) PROFES 2004. LNCS, vol. 3009, pp. 393–407. Springer, Heidelberg (2004)
23. Cohn, M.: User Stories Applied: For Agile Software Development. The Addison-Wesley Signature Series. Addison-Wesley Professional (March 2004),
    `http://www.amazon.ca/exec/obidos/redirect?tag=citeulike09-`
    `20n&path=ASIN/0321205685`
24. Juristo, N., Moreno, A.M., Sanchez-Segura, M.-I.: Analysing the impact of usability on software design. J. Syst. Softw. 80(9), 1506–1516 (2007)
25. Beck, K.: Extreme Programming Explained: Embrace Change. Addison Wesley (1999)
26. Moreno, A.M., Yague, A.: Adding usability recommendations into Agile user stories. In: Proc. 1st Workshop Dealing with Usability in an Agile Domain at XP 2010 (2010)

Evidence-Based Timelines for Agile Project Retrospectives – A Method Proposal

Elizabeth Bjarnason and Björn Regnell

Department of Computer Science, Lund University, Lund, Sweden
{elizabeth.bjarnason,bjorn.regnell}@cs.lth.se

Abstract. Retrospective analysis of agile projects can support identification of issues through team reflection and may enable learning and process improvements. Basing retrospectives primarily on experiences poses a risk of memory bias as people may remember events differently, which can lead to incorrect conclusions. This bias is enhanced in project retrospectives which cover a longer period compared to iteration retrospectives. To support teams in recalling accurate and joint views of projects, we propose using an evidence-based timeline with historical data as input to project retrospectives. The proposed method was developed together with a large software development company in the telecommunications domain. This paper outlines a method for visualizing an evidence-based project timeline by illustrating aspects such as business priority, iterations and test activities. Our method complements an experience-based approach by providing objective data as a starting point for reflection and aims to support objective analysis of issues and root causes.

Keywords: agile, software process, retrospective, software visualization.

1 Introduction

Continuously improving through introspection is a recognized part of agile methods and is applied in, e.g. pairing, use of automated testing and in retrospectives [2, 5, 12]. Retrospectives are commonly performed after each sprint or iterations when the development team gathers to reflect on their way of working, to identify improvements and agree on modifications for the next iteration [5, 6]. This approach aims at enabling self-governing teams to respond quickly to changes, which may require modifying how they work [6]. In addition, retrospectives may have a therapeutic effect that can further support communication and interaction within the team [3], a highly-valued aspect of agile software development.

However, there are also challenges when applying retrospectives in an agile context. Self-governing development teams tend to focus primarily on short-term issues that directly concern their team. Drury et al. found that teams that only perform iteration retrospectives, not reflecting beyond each individual cycle, tend to focus on tactical decisions rather than long-term strategic issues with the risk of losing sight of the goals of the organization [6]. In addition, it has been found that efficient coordination and communication outside of the development team, e.g. with other

C. Wohlin (Ed.): XP 2012, LNBIP 111, pp. 177–184, 2012.

dependent teams, is a challenge in particular for large-scale agile software development [9, 15]. Once projects are completed project members may be re-assigned and may quickly forget the details since accurate memory recall of project events tend to decrease with elapsed time [1, 7]. Another issue is that project-level retrospectives often require multiple viewpoints to obtain a full picture of the project since many people with different roles and focuses are involved over time.

In this paper, we propose to use evidence-based timelines to address the above challenges. The proposed method is aimed at supporting fact-based memory recall by providing a project timeline based on time-stamped data mined from various systems and databases. This method was developed together with and is planned to be evaluated at a large software development company that operates in the telecommunications domain.

The rest of this paper is organized as follows. Section 2 describes previous work on retrospectives. The research approach is described in 3, while section 4 describes our proposed method. The method is discussed in the light of related work in Section 5. Finally, we conclude and describe future research in Section 6.

2   Retrospectives

Retrospectives are prepared to enable productive face-to-face meetings, where the whole team is encouraged to share experiences and then reflect on and analyse those experiences in order to identify important issues and agree on an action plan for improvements [1, 3, 5, 13]. Retrospectives often rely primarily on the participants' experiences of what has taken place. This focus on subjective opinions may turn retrospectives into emotional venting sessions rather than being constructive fact-based discussions [3, 6]. This relates to *memory bias,* one of the barriers to learning from post-mortem reviews identified by Zedwith et al.. Memory bias is caused by the fact that what we remember is selective, and that repression of memories can override potentially important and valuable information that could have been used to learn and improve future situations [20].

Collection of both subjective experiences and objective information is included to some extent in the post-mortem process described by Collier et al.. Presenting objective data to the project team was found to enable focusing on actual problems of a sizeable magnitude, rather than merely subjective opinions [3]. In addition, objective data was found to be useful, in combination with subjective information, in supporting group analysis and identification of root causes and suitable actions [3].

Furthermore, Baird et al. observed that accurate recall of events becomes harder as time elapses [1]. The timing aspect has been reported as the main reason why project retrospectives rarely take place [7]. While 3 to 12 months after project delivery is suggested as the best time for such a retrospective, by then people tend to be tied up in new projects and a lot of the details of the previous project have been forgotten [7]. Jorgensen et al. discuss similar issues and state that project retrospectives based on subjective opinions are very likely to be biased, which in combination with simplified analysis leads to a high risk of drawing incorrect conclusions [8]. To combat this, the advice is to combine experience with knowledge (i.e. actual facts) and to use statistical techniques, in combination with being aware of the biases [8].

3   Research Approach

Our proposed method has been developed in collaboration with one of our partner companies which operates in the telecommunications domain. The company has around 4,000 employees and is faced with the challenge of developing software for a market that rapidly changes. This requires an ability to quickly adapt to change and to ensure a short time to market in order to keep up with competitors. The company wanted to evaluate their agile software development process with the goal of further improving the lead time and development efficiency. The current process assessments are performed per organizational unit and conducted on individual development teams, and not on the entire project life cycle, which includes several handovers between different teams and units. A new method was needed to assess the full development cycle from initial feature request through development in self-governing cross-functional teams to system integration and testing, and customer acceptance testing. A typical software release project contains around 200-250 new features. The total lead time from feature request until customer acceptance ranges from 9 weeks to 2 years. The feature development teams consist of 1 to 40 developers and testers. The company had three high-level goals for the new method:

i. The people involved in the full development cycle should be encouraged and motivated to learn and improve from the findings of the assessment.
ii. The assessment should take place after project completion (to get a full picture) and the effort required from participants (who have moved on to other assignments) must be reasonable to the individuals.
iii. Comparison analysis of several features needs to be facilitated, in order to identify common patterns, good practices etc., and enable organization-wide improvements.

To meet these high-level goals the concept of project longitudinal retrospectives for individual features was selected. This allows for collaborate reflection and learning for all the roles involved in the full life cycle of a feature, i.e. the main development team, and the maintenance team(s) and system-level functions (e.g. system architecture and system verification) with which the main development team interacts. In order to support comparison of multiple features, a structured and common format for the retrospectives, both in how they are prepared, performed and reported was required. For this reason, and to support memory recall and minimal preparation time for the participants, we selected to prepare a timeline with relevant time-stamped data from the available systems. These pre-prepared feature timelines *visualize* the *evidence* gathered from various systems and, thus, provide memory prompts and enable reflecting on past events without requiring much preparation of the participants. The timelines are intended to be used as the starting point for project retrospectives.

A number of meetings were held with representatives from the different units, i.e. business, software development and system verification, to discuss and review the method as it was developed. The researchers designed the proposed method, which was produced iteratively over a period of 1-2 months with regular feedback from the company. A feature timeline was produced for an example feature by extracting time-stamped data from systems used for project- and scope- management, and for software development. Over several iterations with intermediate reviews, the *aspects* to include, the data (or *evidence*) to extract for each aspect, and how they are to be *visualized* was agreed with the company representatives. This initial desktop validation [19] was considered successful by the company representatives, and the method is at the time of writing planned to be evaluated at the company.

4   Creating Evidence-Base Timelines

Method Outline. The proposed method includes four parts as input to a retrospective: goals, aspects, evidence, and visualization. *Goals* are defined for the retrospectives in order to focus on strategic improvement areas. Based on these goals, the *aspects* that are to be covered at the retrospective meetings and visualized in the timelines are then defined. The aspects are preferably selected with an eye to what data can be extracted. Both goals and aspects can be defined for continuous reflection (and, thus allow long-term comparison) or to assess issues specific for a certain project. Individual retrospectives can be aligned by defining common goals and aspects.

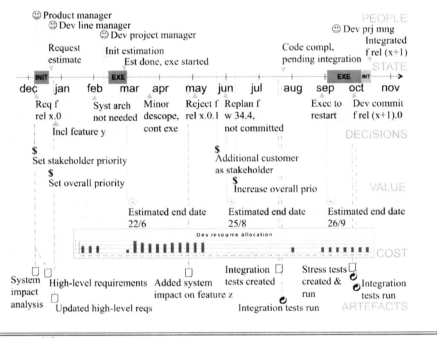

Fig. 1. An example of an evidence-based timeline for a feature

When the set of aspects to include are agreed with relevant parties, *evidence* is collected in the form of time-stamped data extracted from various available systems. The project life cycle is then *visualized* by displaying the collected evidence along a timeline. The timeline is distributed in advance to the retrospective participants together with a set of selected issue reports which form a basis for discussions at the retrospective meeting.

At the retrospective, the project history is *visualized* by posting the prepared timeline on the wall and using this as a basis for discussion and analysis. The overall timeline and the included *aspects* are first presented to orient the participants before going into detailed analysis per time period. The different aspects and relationships between them are investigated and discussed from the perspective of how they affect the issues covered by the *goals* defined for the retrospective. Missing or incorrectly shown events are elicited from participants. In addition, the participants contribute with explanations and underlying root causes for phenomena observed in the timeline. Clarifications, corrections and additional information are added to the timeline at the meeting, thus producing an updated and jointly agreed picture of the feature history as an outcome of the retrospective meeting. Over time, multiple timelines are produced using the same template, thus simplifying comparison analysis.

Timelines in Context. The main retrospective *goal* for our partner company was to assess lead time with focus on communication and decisions throughout the development process. The following six *aspects* were selected to be covered by the retrospective: (1) project state (e.g. development iteration, integration, system testing), (2) decision points, (3) business value, (4) development cost (estimated and actual) and planning (e.g. estimated and actual delivery time), (5) creation and modification of specific artefacts (e.g. requirements, test cases), and (6) role assignments. *Evidence* for these aspects were gathered from various systems available at the company, e.g. databases for scope management, project planning and tracking, requirements and test cases, wiki pages, document management systems, code repository etc.. The time-stamped data was then *visualized* per aspect along a timeline, see Figure 1. For the aspects (3) – (5), namely business value, development cost and planning, and artefacts, the different events are represented by icons that illustrate the type of event, e.g. role assigned, business value or development time estimated. The evidence is grouped according to aspect, each of which is visualized in a swim lane. The aspects of project state and decision points are placed in direct proximity to the timeline axis, while the events of all other aspects are related to the timeline axis by dashed lines. This is to simplify identification of simultaneously or sequentially occurring events by displaying them in proximity to each other. For example, Figure 1 reveals that the decision taken in May to reject the feature for one release was preceded by discovery of impact on another feature (Artefacts), and followed by removing the development resources (Cost). Thereafter, an additional stakeholder was identified, the priority of the feature was increased (Value) and the execution was restarted (Decision & Cost).

For the retrospective meetings at our partner company, a similar approach to involving key roles for project history day [3] has been selected. In our case, we decided to include roles responsible for managing the development team (product manager, project manager, software line manager, architect), and representatives from system verification and system architects. These roles may also invite other persons with specific technical competence and relevant experience, e.g. developers or testers. In all, we expect around 6-8 participants per feature excluding the moderator(s).

5   Discussion

Visualization of timelines can support more efficient processing of information and aid in identifying patterns and changes over time, and may thus stimulate memory and aid in creating a joint picture from many different perspectives [5]. All of these aspects are important objectives of retrospectives, thus making visualization of project history and evolution an interesting avenue for improving retrospective analysis and learning. Visualization of timelines has been suggested as a technique also in the field of computer forensic to enable analysis of large amounts of time-stamped data from confiscated computers [14]. In that context, the use of an interactive tool for visualizing timelines has been found to support criminal investigators in finding patterns and evidence, and to complete the task more efficiently and accurately [14]. In addition, visualization of the evolution of project data from multiple sources has been shown to be promising in understanding the relationship between multiple concerns or aspects [18], which is also part of the analysis performed at a retrospective. A different approach to visualizing the evolution of a project is investigated by Ripley et al. with the dual purpose of providing awareness of current and post-mortem events, as well as, the evolution of a project and, thus, allowing both steering a running project and learning from a completed one [16].

The purpose of our method is to stimulate a deep common understanding of issues and decisions including the underlying factors and motivations for a project. This is similar to the motivation for the project history day advocated by Collier et al. [3]. The timeline technique has been found to be beneficial in providing a joint common background and understanding of a whole project, and in supporting reflection on and observations of patterns at the project level [12]. The usage of experience-based timelines has been reported as supporting teams in reflecting on a project's process and in revealing discrepancies in interpretations of events [11]. In addition, Collier et al. found that simple timeline data gathered from three points in time supported reflecting and analysing issues concerning over- and underestimation of project cost [3]. Evidence-based timelines may act as *integrators* at the retrospective meetings and thereby, similarly to the usage of whiteboards and post-its, support creating an environment productive to constructive reflection and sharing [4].

Furthermore, using historical data has been found to support prompting memory and aiding in reflecting on project processes [10], as well as, motivating participation in deeper analysis also for team members without previous information about the full development cycle [17]. Timelines can also be useful for eliciting events with an objective approach, focusing on facts rather than opinions and have been reported to enable people to grasp different perspectives and resolve conflicts more easily [1].

However, using large amounts of data as input to retrospectives requires both filtering to avoid information overload [12], and structuring to provide focus [10]. By preparing the data beforehand saves time at the actual retrospective meeting [12], which is the case with the proposed use of evidence-based timelines.

6   Conclusions

We propose the usage of evidence-based timelines as input to agile project retrospectives. Visualization of time-stamped project data may enhance identification of patterns and problems and thereby support in-depth analysis of the project process. A deep and joint understanding of a full process can be stimulated by applying a timeline technique [5], and thus enable joint identification of problems and root causes [3, 12]. However, producing timelines requires time and effort of the participants [3]. This cost can be reduced for the participants, by, e.g. a process manager preparing the evidence-based timeline before the retrospective, and further reduced by tool support for extracting and displaying data. Examples of data that could be visualized in timelines include project schedules, problem reports, change requests, requirement and test case entities, frequency and size of source code changes. The amount of available and version controlled documentation and data limits the extent of what can be visualized in the timelines.

The project data prepared in a timeline before the meeting is complemented by gathering subjective data at the retrospective. This approach may thus enable providing a more complete and richer in-depth view of the project process by combining objective and subjective data. Furthermore, a structured collection of retrospective reports may enable organizations to more easily analyze and identify patterns between retrospectives and support improvements and learning within the whole organization [3, 4].

Finally, future work includes evaluating and further refining the proposed method in a pilot case study and investigating how to perform meta-analysis of multiple retrospectives. In addition, tool support and visualization techniques for time-stamped data are also interesting areas to pursue.

Acknowledgements. We would like to thank the practitioners involved in discussing and provided valuable input to the design of this method. The work is partially funded by the Swedish Foundation for Strategic Research.

References

1. Baird, L., Holland, P., Deacon, S.: Learning from Action: Imbedding More Learning into the Performance Fast Enough to Make a Difference. Organizational Dynamics 27(4), 19–32 (1999)
2. Beck, K.: Extreme Programming Explained. Addison-Wesley (2000)
3. Collier, B., DeMarco, T., Fearey, P.: A Defined Process for Project Postmortem Review. IEEE Software 13(4), 65–72 (1996)

4. Desouza, K.C., Dingsoyr, T., Awazu, Y.: Experiences with Conducting Project Postmortems: Reports versus Stories. Softw. Process Improve. and Pract. 10, 203–215 (2005)
5. Derby, E., Larsen, D.: Agile Retrospectives: Making Good Teams Great! Pragmatic Bookshelf (2006)
6. Drury, M., Conboy, K., Power, K.: Decision Making in Agile Development: A Focus Group Study of Decisions and Obstacles. In: Agile Conference 2011, pp. 39–47 (2011)
7. Glass, R.L.: Project Retrospectives, and Why They Never Happen. IEEE Software 19(5), 112–113 (2002)
8. Jorgensen, M., Sjoberg, D.: The Importance of NOT Learning from Experience. In: Proc. of European Software Process Improvement, Copenhagen, Denmark (2000)
9. Karlstrom, D., Runeson, P.: Combining Agile Methods with Stage-Gate Project Management. IEEE Software 22(3), 43–49 (2005)
10. Krogstie, B.: Using Project Wiki History to Reflect on the Project Process. In: Proc. of 42nd Hawaii International Conference on System Science (2009)
11. Krogstie, B., Divitini, M.: Shared Timeline and Individual Experience: Supporting Retrospective Reflection in Student Software Engineering Teams. In: 22nd Conf. on Softw. Engineering Education and Training (2009)
12. Maham, M.: Planning and Facilitating Release Retrospectives. In: Agile Conference 2008, pp. 176–180 (2008)
13. Nolan, A.J.: Learning from Success. IEEE Software 16(1), 97–105 (1999)
14. Olsson, J., Boldt, M.: Computer Forensic Timeline Visualization Tool. Digital Investigation 6, 78–87 (2009)
15. Pikkarainen, M., Haikara, J., Salo, et al.: The Impact of Agile Practices on Communication in Software Development. Empir. Softw. Eng. 13, 303–337 (2008)
16. Ripley, R.M., Sarma, A., van der Hoek, A.: A Visualization for Software Project Awareness and Evolution. In: VISSOFT 2007, pp. 137–144 (2007)
17. Sertic, H., Marzic, K., Kalafatic, Z.: A Project Retrospective Method in Telecom Software Development. In: ConTEL 2007, pp. 109–114 (2007)
18. Treude, C., Storey, M.: CONCERNLINE: A Timeline View of Co-Occurring Concerns. In: ICSE 2009, Vancouver, Canada, pp. 575–578 (2009)
19. Wohlin, C., Gustavsson, A., Höst, et al.: A Framework for Technology Introduction in Software Organizations. In: Proc. Softw. Process Improve. Conf., pp. 167–176 (1996)
20. von Zedtwitz, M.: Organizational Learning Through Post-Project Reviews in R&D. R&D Management, 21(3), 255–268 (2002)

Who Is Stronger in Your Agile Deployment –
The Id or the Superego?

Stavros Stavru and Sylvia Ilieva

Sofia University "St. Kliment Ohridski"
5, James Bouchier Str., P.B. 48
1164 Sofia, Bulgaria
{stavross,sylvia}@fmi.uni-sofia.bg

Abstract. Many studies and industrial reports have demonstrated the tendency towards the increasing number of organizations, interested in agile software development. With the transition from intentions to actions, the question that naturally arises is how the deployment process should be approached. In this paper we argue that shared organizational values, which we call organizational *Superego*, should be the main drivers for the deployment and post-deployment assessment of agile methods and techniques. Along with that we propose a new organizational classification technique, which assesses the power of the Superego to shape organizational behavior, together with an organizational value framework to be used for strengthening it. We further discuss how a strong Superego would approach the deployment of agile methods and techniques, and outline a future agile deployment framework, based on organizational values.

Keywords: Agile Adoption, Deployment and Post-Deployment Assessment of Agile Methods and Techniques, Organizational Values, Organizational Culture.

1 Introduction

Recent industrial reports have confirmed the tendency from previous years that the number of organizations, interested in or already deploying agile methods and techniques, is continuously increasing [1, 2]. In their transition to agile software development, these organizations are faced with many challenges, including the deployment process and how it should be approached [3]. In this paper we address this particular challenge, taking the perspective of organizational values.

By organizational values we mean the "...*latent constructs that refer to the way in which people evaluate activities or outcomes*", and which drive and "*regulate both means and ends*" of the organization [4]. Many authors have emphasized the importance of organizational values in (1) regulating different spheres of organizational life – from organizational goals and objectives to concrete behavior and character of organizational members [4]; (2) guiding and securing commitment for organizational change [4, 5]; (3) ensuring depth, stability, and consistency to management practices [5]; and many more [4, 5]. Even a new management paradigm

C. Wohlin (Ed.): XP 2012, LNBIP 111, pp. 185–192, 2012.

has been proposed, known as *management by values*, which is argued to have a tremendous potential to overcome the shortcomings of its predecessors, including the management by instructions and management by objectives [5]. Taking into account the arguments of these organizational studies and the increasing evidence in respect to organizational values [4, 5], we were convinced that *organizational values would have the potential to successfully drive the deployment of agile methods and techniques.*

Organizational values, as a core cognitive element of the organizational culture [4], have been studied in the context of agile software development. A brief overview of these studies could be found in [6], where the importance of organizational culture to agile deployment is also argued. While most of these studies are focused on *cultural compatibility* and define the *ideal organizational context for agile deployment*, the organizational values have been overlooked. The same is valid in regards to the many agile deployment paradigms, frameworks and approaches, currently existing in the literature. QIP, the paradigm proposed by Pikkarainen et al. and other paradigms, briefly summarized in [7], have emphasized the importance of *setting goals and objectives for the deployment process*, but they are isolated from organizational objectives and values. The Strategically Balanced Process Adoption makes a step further by aligning the deployment process to *organizational strategic objectives* [8], but the linkage to organizational values is still missing. Some other deployment frameworks, including the Agile Adoption Framework (AAF), Agile Adoption and Improvement Model (AAIM), Objectives, Principles and Practices Framework (OPPF), briefly presented in [9], are focused on the strict adherence to agile methods and techniques for achieving *organizational agility* (and their expected organizational benefits), taking into account organizational values only to assess the appropriateness of the deployment (AAIM, OPPF) or the readiness of the organization (AAF, AAIM). Other approaches [10], suggest that agile methods and techniques should be *adapted and tailored to best fit organizational and project context*, but they also lack sufficient attention on organizational values.

This paper briefly presents the current state of our research work and is organized as follows: Section 2 discusses the organizational context suitable for the deployment of agile techniques based on organizational values; Section 3 outlines how organizational values could be determined and secured; Section 4 briefly describes how the deployment will be approached from organizational values perspective; and Section 5 summarizes contributions and presents plans for future work.

2   Who Is Stronger – The Id or the Superego?

Being interested in the deployment of agile techniques in respect to organizational values, we were concerned with the kind of *organizational context*, where such deployment would be applicable at all. It was obvious that (1) there should be organizational values, explicitly defined by the organization; (2) these organizational values should have the power to influence organizational decisions (incl. the selection of agile techniques) and shape organizational behavior (incl. the deployment of these techniques); and (3) they should be applicable in terms of organizational justification and assessment (incl. the post-deployment monitoring and assessment of agile techniques). In order to formally specify this organizational context, we studied many of the existing organizational assessment and classification techniques, thoroughly reviewed in the excellent work of Jung et al. [11]. Although some of these techniques as Organizational Culture Assessment Tool (based on Competing Values Framework), Denison Organizational Culture Scale, van der Post Questionnaire, Interactive Projective Test and Organizational and Team Culture Indicator [11], take into consideration the clarity, variety and impact of organizational values, there was no technique in the literature (to the extent of our knowledge), which assesses and classifies organizations in terms of organizational values and their power to drive and justify organizational behavior. To fill this gap and provide a formal specification for the organizational context, suitable for the deployment of agile techniques, based on organizational values, we have proposed a new organizational assessment and classification technique. This technique was initially inspired by the concept of strong culture [14] and further refined through reviewing of existing industrial surveys (as the Aspen Institute's survey [13]), exploring how deeply organizational values are embedded in organizations, what best practices for managing organizational values do exist, etc. It adapts the concepts of *Id, Ego* and *Superego*, as defined in the Sigmund Freud's structural model of psyche [12] and provides a new organizational metaphor [15], which we called the "*organization as psyche*". The proposed mapping between these concepts in a personal and an organizational context is briefly described in Table 1.

Table 1. The concepts of Id, Ego and Superego in personal and organizational context

Personal Id	Organizational Id
The Personal Id comprises the unorganized part of the personality structure and is responsible for the uncoordinated *instinctual* trends [12].	The Organizational Id pursues the *individual or group interests* of stakeholders (named *organizational instincts*), resulting in inconsistent, conflicting and irrational organizational behavior.
Personal Superego	**Organizational Superego**
The Personal Superego is the organized part of the personality structure, which strives for perfection, *defines and pursuits personal values* and is responsible for the consciousness [12].	The Organizational Superego defines *shared organizational values* and continuously monitors controls and evaluates the behavior of the organization in regards to these values.
Personal Ego	**Organizational Ego**
The Personal Ego is the realistic part, which tries to balance between the Id and the Superego and shapes the actual behavior [12].	The Organizational Ego is responsible for the actual behavior of the organization, where individual interests and organizational values are constantly confronting.

The proposed technique is a one dimensional assessment and classification technique [11], which aims at answering the question of "*Who is stronger in your organization – the Id or the Superego?*" It does so by using a self-reporting questionnaire, currently consisting of 30 items with 7-point Likert response. These items, partially influenced by Kotter and Heskett's questionnaire [14] and further developed based on an extensive literature review, assess organizational values in terms of their *determination* (the degree to which they are explicitly and clearly defined), *enactment* (the degree to which they are taken into consideration and woven within the organizational life) and *commitment* (the degree to which they are accepted and supported by organizational stakeholders). The self-reporting questionnaire, together with the questionnaire design, its reliability and validity will be thoroughly presented in a future paper.

Using the proposed technique, the organization is further classified into one of the following categories: *Dominant Id*, *Conflicting Ego* and *Dominant Superego*. This categorization reflects the level of determination, enactment and commitment of organizational values in a given organization, and is briefly presented in Table 2.

Table 2. The Dominant Id, Conflicting Ego and Dominant Superego types of organizations

Assessed aspect	Dominant Id	Conflicting Ego	Dominant Superego
Determination of organizational values			
Organizational values are explicitly defined and consistent, are understandable and familiar to organizational members, are frequently communicated and revised, are associated with concrete measures and indicators, etc.	Low	Medium to High	High
Enactment to organizational values			
Organizational values have influence on and are incorporated in organizational decisions and behavior, organizational members are continuously monitored, controlled and evaluated in respect to these values, etc.	Low	Low to Medium	High
Commitment to organizational values			
Organizational values are supported by top management, organizational values are representing and consistent with the personal values of organizational members, etc.	Low	Low to Medium	High

The range [Low, Medium and High], used in the table, is simplified for the purpose of clarity.

This organizational assessment and classification technique was initially designed to formally specify the "perfect" organization (or organizational prerequisites) for the deployment of agile methods and techniques, based on organizational values, namely the *Dominant Superego*. Despite of this it, we expect it to be applicable in a broader context, including situations where the deployment of changes in organizational processes, products, etc., should be justified in terms of organizational values, when the strength of organizational values has to be measured, etc.

3   How to Build a Dominant Superego?

The Dominant Superego does not come for granted and additional efforts are needed in order to define, prioritize, select and propagate organizational values. As a result we had concerns about the possible utilization from the industry of agile deployment approaches, based on organizational values. To overcome these concerns, we looked for existing organizational value frameworks, which could be used by the organizations in their efforts to become Dominant Superegos. The high level requirements for these frameworks were to secure high utilization, providing a straightforward, ready to use and expandable instrumentation, applicable in a wide range of organizations. More specifically, we required the following elements to be part of the desired framework: (1) an expandable repository of formally defined and widely applicable organizational values, together with (2) an expandable repository of their associated organizational metrics; and (3) formally defined techniques for the prioritization, elicitation and propagation of organizational values. Starting from these requirements we reviewed many of the existing organizational value frameworks, including the Balanced Scorecards, Strategy Maps, Competing Values Framework, Corporate Transformation Tools, Actions-to-Value Framework and others [4, 11], together with some organizational value models and dimensions, as described in [4, 6, 11]. Although most of the required elements were fully or partially covered, there was no organizational value framework, currently existing in the research literature (to the extent of our knowledge), which provides all of these elements within a single and coherent instrumentation. To overcome this shortcoming, we have proposed a new organizational value framework.

The core elements of the proposed framework are the organizational values and metrics repositories. The *Organizational values repository* consists of concrete and formally defined organizational values and their interdependencies. Each *organization value* (e.g. Customer Satisfaction) is defined by specifying its name, type, associated concern and target, and the set of organizational metrics that could be used to assess organizational behavior in regards this value. On the other hand, each *target* (e.g. Customer), belongs to a specific *target group* (e.g. Organizational Stakeholders), has a set of desired *target characteristics* (e.g. Satisfaction) with their relevant measurable *target properties* (e.g. Purchase Rate). The set of measurable target properties (currently more than 80) compose the *organizational metrics repository*. A brief overview of the proposed organizational values, targets and target groups is shown in Table 3. These organizational values and targets (together with their associated characteristics and properties) were derived from the literature. The selection was based on well established criteria, requiring values to be (1) terminal (should describe desired end state [4]); (2) quantifiable (should be measurable); (3) scientific (should be subject of organizational studies); and (4) abstract (should be applicable in a wide organizational context), while the targets had to cover different aspects of organization life. The proposed values and metrics repositories are not comprehensive, but they could be easily extended as long as the selection criteria are followed. The other elements, included in the proposed framework, are a number of techniques used for the prioritization, elicitation and propagation of organizational values. For the prioritization of organizational values, *value game* was proposed. It constitutes of two sub processes (or game levels) – (1) the *target prioritization*, where the targets are prioritized at each hierarchical level of the organization using *target and point cards* and (2) the *values prioritization*, where the values associated with each target are prioritized at each hierarchical level using *value and point cards*. *Target and value cards* are used by the *Dealer* to describe targets and values, and to organize their allocated point cards, while *point cards* are used by the *Player* to actually estimate these targets and values. At the end of the value game, there should be a list of prioritized targets and organizational values, relevant for a particular hierarchical level. The final elicitation and propagation of organizational targets and values is done through the *value tournament* technique, where organizational values are further aligned at all levels of the organization and high acceptance rate from all stakeholders is ensured. This is achieved by gathering at least one player from each hierarchical level to participate in the tournament. Then the tournament itself is organized in way similar to the value game. At the end, the winning organizational values are officially announced and signed off. The monitoring and controlling of organizational values is organized through the use of so called *value signboard*, whose purpose is to visualize the organizational values including the current organizational values, their associated metrics, the decisions currently assessed in terms of organizational values and etc. As we are limited in size, we are leaving the thorough presentation of all these repositories and techniques for a separate paper.

Table 3. Organizational values, targets and target groups

Target	Organizational Values
Organizational Stakeholders Target Group	
Customer	Customer Satisfaction, Customer Delightment, Customer Enrichment, Customer Performance, Customer Trust, Customer Loyalty and Customer Engagement
Partner	Partner Satisfaction, Partner Trust, Partner Enrichment, Partner Performance, Partner Engagement and Partner Commitment
Employee	Cooperation, Respect, Discipline, Accountability, Competence, Creativity, Adaptability, Engagement, Commitment and Satisfaction
Shareholder	Shareholder Wealth, Shareholder Satisfaction and Shareholder Engagement
Society	Ecological Sustainability, Social Sustainability and Society Engagement
Organizational Glue Target Group	
Process	Focus, Resources Utilization, Communication, Shared Understanding, Performance, Continuous Improvement and Flexibility
Product	Product Functionality, Product Quality and Product Innovation

4   How Does the Dominant Superego Approach Agile Deployment?

In this section we will briefly describe how the Dominant Superego type of organization will approach the deployment of agile techniques. The process tasks and artifacts are graphically represented in Fig. 1, using BPMN 2.0. We call this approach to agile deployment *agile deployment by values*.

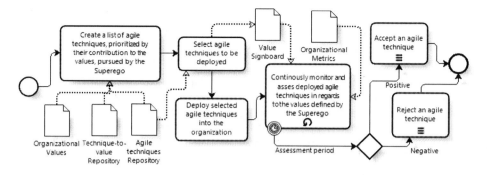

Fig. 1. Agile deployment by values, represented using BPMN 2.0

The first process task aims at creating a prioritized list of agile techniques in terms of their applicability to the organizational values, defined by the Superego. To do so, two process artifacts are additionally required – the agile techniques repository and the techniques-to-values repository. The *agile techniques repository* consists of formally defined agile techniques in a way that facilitates their deployment within the organization (including terms of use, constraints and limitations, interdependencies and other situational factors). The *techniques-to-values repository*, on the other hand, specifies the relation between each particular agile technique and different organizational values (their "fitness"). This relation could be a positive, neutral or negative contribution or a more complex conditional contribution and could be determined based on empirical evidence, expertise, etc. Such repositories already exist in the research literature as the evidence-based Agile Method Fragments (AMF) repository, proposed by Esfahani and Yu [8]. If the organizational value framework, introduced in the previous section is about to be used, these repositories need to be further adapted to suit the proposed organizational values. At the end of this process task, there should be a list of agile techniques, prioritized by their aggregated contribution in terms of organizational values as defined by the Superego. Only then the organization can further proceed with the selection of concrete agile techniques. During this selection process, the organization could take into account additional situational factors, as described in the agile techniques repository. Once the agile techniques are selected, they should be reflected on the value signboard, where the post-deployment monitoring will take place. After the actual deployment, assessment is continuously performed (on fixed time intervals) using the value signboard and the organizational metrics, associated with the pursued organizational values. After a predefined period of time, the assessment is finalized and depending on the results, the agile techniques are either accepted or rejected.

5   What Is Next?

In this paper we have briefly presented the deployment of agile techniques approached from organizational values perspective. This approach to agile deployment is quite unique, as none of the reviewed agile deployment frameworks introduces anything in this regard. We have briefly presented some of our initial results. This includes (1) a new organizational assessment and classification technique; and (2) a new organizational value framework. We have also discussed how a Dominant Superego type of organizations will approach the agile deployment. As a future work we are going to propose a complete framework for agile software deployment based on organizational values (or *agile deployment by values framework*). This will include not only the newly proposed techniques, but also concrete agile techniques and evidence-based techniques-to-values repositories, all welded together in a single structured process. The other major future work is the validation of the introduced techniques in a real industrial setting and the consequent experimentation of the deployment framework in real industrial cases.

Acknowledgments. The research presented in this paper was partially supported by the National research fund in Bulgaria, under contract No. DMU 03-40.

References

1. Agile adoption trends, http://www.rallydev.com/learn_agile/agile_for_executives/
2. State of agile development survey
   http://www.versionone.com/state_of_agile_development_survey/10
3. Abrahamsson, P., Conboy, K., Wang, X.: 'Lots done, more to do': the current state of agile systems development research. Eur. J. Info. Sys. 18, 281–284 (2009)
4. Jaakson, K.: Management by values: are some values better than others. Man. Dev. 29, 795–806 (2010)
5. Dolan, S., Garcia, S.: Managing by Values: Cultural redesign for strategic organizational change at the dawn of the twenty-first century. Man. Dev. 21, 101–117 (2002)
6. Iivari, J., Iivari, N.: The relationship between organizational culture and the deployment of agile methods. Info. Soft. Tech. 53, 509–520 (2011)
7. Pikkarainen, M., Salo, O., Kuusela, R., Abrahamsson, P.: Strengths and barriers behind the successful agile deployment—insights from the three software intensive companies in Finland. Empi. Software Eng., 1–28 (2011)
8. Esfahani, H.C., Yu, E., Annosi, M.C.: Strategically balanced process adoption. In: International Conference on Software and Systems Process, Hawaii, pp. 169–178 (2011)
9. Soundararajan, S., Arthur, J.D.: A Structured framework for assessing the "goodness" of agile methods. In: 18th IEEE International Conference and Workshops on Engineering of Computer-Based Systems, pp. 14–23. IEEE Press, Las Vegas (2011)
10. Krasteva, I., Ilieva, S., Dimov, A.: Experience-Based Approach for Adoption of Agile Practices in Software Development Projects. In: Pernici, B. (ed.) CAiSE 2010. LNCS, vol. 6051, pp. 266–280. Springer, Heidelberg (2010)
11. Jung, T., et al.: Instruments for exploring organizational culture: A review of the literature. Public Admin. Review 69, 1087–1096 (2009)
12. Freud, S.: The Ego and the Id. The Hogarth Press Ltd., London (1949)
13. The Aspen Institute: Deriving Value from Corporate Values (2005)
14. Kotter, J.P., Heskett, J.L.: Corporate culture and performance. Free Press (1992)
15. Cornelissen, J.P., Kafouros, M., Lock, A.R.: Metaphorical images of organization: How organizational researchers develop and select organizational metaphors. Human Relations 58, 1545–1578 (2005)

adVANTAGE: A Fair Pricing Model
for Agile Software Development Contracting

Matthias Book[1], Volker Gruhn[1], and Rüdiger Striemer[2]

[1] paluno – The Ruhr Institute for Software Technology, University of Duisburg-Essen
Gerlingstr. 16, 45127 Essen, Germany
{matthias.book,volker.gruhn}@paluno.uni-due.de
[2] adesso AG, Rotherstr. 19, 10245 Berlin, Germany
striemer@adesso.de

Abstract. Agile software development methods are harder to adopt by third-party software developers than by in-house software development teams, since traditional contractual frameworks can easily lead to unfair risk distributions between client and supplier when applied to agile projects. We therefore present a pricing model for agile software projects that distributes risks evenly between the partners, and encourages efficient, high-quality contributions on both sides.

Keywords: Agile processes, third-party developers, contracting, pricing.

1 Introduction

The development of complex information systems is typically subject to a number of common challenges – overrunning time and budget constraints, missing requirements and quality expectations, and dealing with continually evolving business environments and integration landscapes. As Curtis et al. already described almost 25 years ago, these problems mostly stem from insufficient communication between business and technology experts, or users and developers [1].

These challenges occur in in-house development projects, where a large company's IT department develops its own systems, as well as in external development projects where the software is developed by an outside contractor. Each project situation brings its own set of communication and collaboration challenges that contribute to the typical problems that complex software projects often face. In this paper, we will focus on one aspect that makes external software development even more conflict-prone, namely the contracting and pricing details of such projects.

1.1 Challenges in Traditional Project Contracting

In the experience of IT service providers who develop software solutions tailored to clients' individual requirements (e.g. building custom information systems for insurances or healthcare providers), most clients initially have only a rather coarse, high-level idea of the system they need. At the same time, however, they would like to negotiate a fixed price or budget ceiling for the project.

C. Wohlin (Ed.): XP 2012, LNBIP 111, pp. 193–200, 2012.

In theory, such a fixed price or ceiling could only be properly established based on a complete specification of the system to be built. However, creating such a complete specification typically is neither economical (since it requires considerable effort on both sides, before the actual project even begins), nor is it helpful (since the client typically remains unable to express all his requirements in sufficiently complete and consistent detail up front).

In practice, faced with the client's insistence on a fixed price despite the lack of a proper specification, service providers often end up trying to make a best guess of the price, trying to balance the expected project effort with the aim to under-bid any competing providers. Since this usually results in too low of a price, the contract will typically be won by a service provider who subsequently struggles with his too-low bid, or who is an expert in playing the inevitably ensuing change request game. Obviously, neither constellation is conducive to a lasting customer relationship.

1.2   Challenges in Agile Project Contracting

The recognized lack of helpfulness of complete up-front system specifications has led to the rise of agile development methods such as Scrum [2], where voluminous specifications are replaced by quick iteration cycles. At first sight, the continuous refinement of prototypes in tight collaboration of users and developers seems like an ideal solution to the difficulty of specifying a complete system beforehand. While the model lends itself naturally to in-house projects, clients and service providers have however found it hard to transfer to the commercial domain:

For an agile project, it is virtually impossible to set a fixed price – since the project scope and the required solutions materialize only gradually, and prototyping implies performing a considerable amount of work that does not make it into the final project, but is discarded, the actual effort is hardly foreseeable. A fixed-price contract would thus expose the service provider to the complete project risk, while the client is tempted to keep adding bells and whistles along the way at no additional cost.

On the other hand, running agile projects on pure time and materials (T&M) contracts is equally undesirable: While these seem more fair at first sight (since the payment corresponds exactly to the work done), they actually incentivize service providers to blow up the development effort and neglect quality control at the client's expense. The project risk thus lies fully with the client.

Again, neither situation is satisfactory for both parties. It would therefore be desirable to find a contracting model that has a built-in risk limitation mechanism for the service provider, and a built-in cost limitation mechanism for the client. In this paper, we will propose such a contracting model that ensures fair distribution of risks and encourages efficient work on both sides, without relaxing any of the contractual obligations (e.g. warranty) that parties in a large-scale development project would normally also expect from each other.

In the following section, we will review related works that we employ as building blocks of our approach. In Sect. 3, we will then introduce our agile contracting model adVANTAGE, and discuss initial practical experiences with it in Sect. 4.

2   Related Work

To improve the "thin spread of application domain knowledge" [1] and the inter-stakeholder communication issues that are at the heart of many troubled software engineering projects, numerous approaches, process models and tools have been introduced over the years. We believe it is necessary to find a pragmatic mix of these methods and tools for each project, since the solution often lies less in thorough formalization of a system than in solid understanding of its relevant aspects.

In our approach, we strive to reflect this conviction not just by choosing an agile process model, but also by supporting and encouraging it in the software project's contractual framework. The adVANTAGE approach is therefore grounded in two software project management concepts:

To focus on the relevant aspects of a system, Boehm and Huang introduced the notion of value-based software engineering [3] that integrates consideration of a feature's or component's value within a system into all software engineering activities. As detailed below, our contracting model enforces value orientation throughout the project's progress by attaching price tags to each user story.

As Lehman pointed out, stakeholders in every software project are bound to experience a considerable amount of uncertainty in their specifications and decisions [4]. Just as software engineering methods and tools should acknowledge these uncertainties by guiding stakeholders to resolve open questions, however not force them to fix answers prematurely, our contractual framework is designed to leave room for gradual elimination of initial uncertainty by allowing re-prioritization of the project deliverables and late detailing of user stories as the project progresses.

Beside the software engineering aspects, there is also a variety of suggestions for shaping the business and legal aspects of agile relationships: Van Cauwenberghe proposed a number of guidelines for reducing the risk in agile fixed price contracts [5]. As we will see below, adVANTAGE employs some similar mechanisms (e.g. letting the customer prioritize), however differs significantly in that it is not a fixed-price model. Sutherland also suggests mechanisms for risk sharing and ensuring sustained mutual involvement in his "money for nothing, change for free" approach [6], which we however deemed incompatible with the rather conservative client domains we are looking at.

Poppendieck and Poppendieck have presented a comprehensive classification of agile contracting schemes [7]. In their framework, adVANTAGE can be described as a multi-stage contract model with optional project scope. Larman and Vodde also discuss agile contracts in depth [8] – besides a strong focus on the legal details of agile contracts, they describe payment schemes that are similar to our approach, but more generic than the concrete model we present in the following section.

3   The adVANTAGE Contracting Model

To ensure fairness and efficiency for both parties in an agile development agreement, our contracting model combines elements of fixed-price and T&M contracting models: adVANTAGE strives to provide some idea of the overall project scope (in terms of requirements, time and budget) to users and developers, as they would have in a traditional, fixed-price project, however without exposing the service provider to the risk of being committed to that exact effort. Instead, adVANTAGE ensures that the client pays exactly for what is delivered, as he would in a T&M situation – however without exposing him to the risk of a runaway project that never gets done, as the service provider will be equally encouraged to complete the project efficiently.

The key commercial principles of our contracting model thus are risk distribution and efficiency incentives – for both project parties, and for the whole project duration. To enforce them, adVANTAGE does not try to shoehorn a complete software project into one contractual framework, as traditional approaches do, but instead breaks contracting, pricing, inspection and payment down to the elements of the agile process. In the following subsections, we will show how these commercial aspects tie in with the sprints and deliverables of an agile process model:

Step 0: Initial requirements collection and budget estimate. To obtain an initial overview of the project scope and cost, we collect all the client's requirements before the first iteration. Typically, these are "must-have" as well as "nice-to-have" features, business goals as well as business ideas. Acknowledging that clients are typically unable to define their requirements in detail (let alone in formal specifications), we only collect them as "user stories", i.e. individual, testable features with a coarse, non-technical description on the business level.

The service provider then estimates the effort required for implementing each of the user stories. Due to the coarse nature of the user stories, these estimates are naturally subject to some level of uncertainty. However, we expect this uncertainty to be no higher than it also is in traditional bidding situations that providers have to deal with, and the uncertainty is distributed over a large number of individual user stories, instead of accumulated in one fixed-price bid. Still, the service provider needs sufficient domain knowledge to make competent estimates, and should perform this step in close cooperation with the client to avoid misunderstandings.

In contrast to traditional contracting models, the total of all user stories' effort estimates is not used to calculate a fixed price tag in the adVANTAGE approach, but serves as a plausible point of orientation for the following (iterated) steps:

Step 1: User story prioritization and sprint definition. Based on the service provider's price estimates and the clients' internal budget ceiling, the client can now prioritize, eliminate or add user stories to match his means and needs. In doing so, the client needs to balance the importance of each user story with his available budget and desired timeframe. The transparency of these trade-offs to the client is an important difference from traditional fixed-price models that often tempt clients to force service providers into aggressive project scopes and schedules because they won't affect the price anyway. Instead, the continuous budget focus encourages clients to prioritize their desires by which user stories are most critical for putting the system into productive use, and which ones can be deferred. In addition, since this (re-)prioritization of user stories is possible after every sprint (as we will see below), the uncertainty in defining and detailing necessary system functionality is also distributed over the whole project duration (where its severity will gradually diminish), instead of being cast in stone at the beginning, when it is largest.

Based on the prioritized user stories, the client and service provider can now agree on the contents of the first sprint, i.e. the selection of the highest-prioritized user stories to be implemented next. To include users in the evaluation and prioritization of further sprints right from the beginning, we recommend that even the first sprint should include a sufficient selection of user stories that will yield a running – even if not complete – system.

Step 2: Sprint implementation. At the beginning of each sprint, its user stories are refined into more detailed specifications in close collaboration between the client and service provider. The implementation of these stories then progresses according to established agile development practices.

The duration of a sprint can be chosen flexibly based on the scope and nature of the project. However, given that our approach is aimed at large-scale projects, we recommend a sprint length of 4-6 weeks. Besides strict time-boxing of sprints, another rule is that the selection of user stories cannot be changed within a sprint, but only between sprints. This not only enables the developers to focus on a fixed set of requirements per sprint and arrive at a consistently integrated, thoroughly tested and running product after each iteration, but is also a prerequisite for the subsequent inspection and billing step.

Step 3: Sprint inspection and billing. In contrast to traditional contracting models, the adVANTAGE model ties the billing of services very closely to the agile process structure: At the end of each sprint, each user story is inspected individually for completion and acceptance (client sign-off), and the estimated and actual efforts of all accepted user stories are tallied. Depending on whether all user stories were implemented satisfactorily, and whether the sprint was completed within the estimated effort, this can lead to several different billing scenarios:

Underspend on sprint. As shown in the example in Table 1, the basis for the billing of each sprint is a lump sum for activities such as the requirements elaboration, the scrum master's work and other efforts that cannot be attributed to individual user stories (here, e.g., 22,000 EUR). Also on the bill is the initially estimated sprint effort, based on the service provider's usual daily rate (here, a total of 80 person days (PD) at 1,000 EUR each). We now contrast this to the sprint's actual implementation effort: If the team required less effort, only the actual effort is billed (in Table 1, for example, an underspend of four person-days leads to a 4,000 EUR reduction of charges).

Table 1. Underspend billing

Prio.	User Story	Completed & Accepted	Estimated Effort (PD)	Actual Effort
1	User Story A	yes	18	18
2	User Story B	yes	7	7
3	User Story C	yes	42	38
4	User Story D	yes	3	5
5	User Story E	yes	10	8
	Total Effort		**80**	**76**

Estimated price (80 x 1,000 EUR)	80,000 EUR
Underspend (4 x 1,000 EUR)	–4,000 EUR
Cross-cutting tasks (lump sum)	22,000 EUR
Sprint Bill	**98,000 EUR**

Overspend on sprint. On the other hand, if the effort was higher than expected, the additional effort is still billed, however at a considerably reduced rate that penalizes the service provider (in Table 2, for example, the five person-days of overspend are billed at only 600 EUR each). This way, the adVANTAGE model ensures a fair distribution of risks between both project parties: The client's risk is reduced since he is only billed for the actual effort, and the service provider's risk is reduced since he is still paid even if his initial estimate turned out to be too low.

Table 2. Overspend billing

Prio.	User Story	Completed & Accepted	Estimated Effort (PD)	Actual Effort
1	User Story A	yes	18	18
2	User Story B	yes	7	14
3	User Story C	yes	42	40
4	User Story D	yes	3	5
5	User Story E	yes	10	8
	Total Effort		**80**	**85**

Estimated price (80 x 1,000 EUR)	80,000 EUR
Overspend (5 x 600 EUR)	3,000 EUR
Cross-cutting tasks (lump sum)	22,000 EUR
Sprint Bill	**105,000 EUR**

One might wonder why we do not calculate the over- or underspend individually for each user story, but instead for the complete sprint. The reason is that this allows the service provider to spend effort saved on one user story on another story that needs more work, if necessary, without being penalized (as shown e.g. in user stories D and E). This is fair because what matters to the client at the end of a sprint is the overall state of the product and budget, not how the provider got to it.

Incomplete/unaccepted user stories. We still need to consider how to deal with user stories whose implementation was not completed in a sprint's time box, or whose delivered quality the client did not accept. In either case, the client has the choice of transferring these unfinished user stories to the next sprint, or to cancel them and thus eliminate them from the product.

As Table 3 shows, if a user story is transferred to the next sprint (e.g. user story B), neither its estimated nor its actual effort so far are included in this sprint's bill, but will instead show up on the next sprint's bill – then incurring an even higher actual effort (cumulated from both sprints), which will be penalized as described above. In case the client decides not to go ahead with an incomplete or unsatisfactorily completed user story and cancels it (example: user story E in Table 3), the work performed up to that point will still be billed as per the above rules.

This cancellation policy is reasonable as both parties know that work that was committed to also needs to be paid – and again, the risk is distributed as the service provider can rely on the client not cancelling already completed work on a whim, while the client has the option of cancelling work on user stories when he feels that their maturity is sufficient or further development on them is not economical.

Table 3. Partial billing

Prio.	User Story	Completed & Accepted	Estimated Effort (PD)	Actual Effort
1	User Story A	yes	18	18
2	User Story B	no, transfer	~~7~~	~~14~~
3	User Story C	yes	42	40
4	User Story D	yes	3	5
5	User Story E	no, cancel	10	8
	Total Effort		**73**	**71**

Estimated price (73 x 1,000 EUR)	73,000 EUR
Underspend (2 x 1,000 EUR)	–2,000 EUR
Cross-cutting tasks (lump sum)	22,000 EUR
Sprint Bill	**93,000 EUR**

Iteration or termination. After each sprint, the client then has the option to start the next iteration from Step 1 again, where he can re-prioritize all user stories, and also eliminate or add new stories. Change requests for already completed and accepted features will be treated as new user stories. Since this re-prioritization of the user stories will again be guided by the question of what is most critical for the system to enter productive use, and how this can be traded off with the available budget and time, the project will be focused on its overall goals and constraints in every iteration.

Alternatively, the client can terminate the project after any sprint, when he feels it has reached the required functionality and/or its budget limits. Since every sprint results in a running system, this exit strategy is again risk-free for the client.

4   Industry Example and Conclusion

The adVANTAGE model has been adopted in practice by adesso AG, a large German software development company mainly serving the public, financial and healthcare sector. In an ongoing large-scale project, adesso is building a new contract management system for a German life insurance company.

Given the complexity of the system – both in terms of its business requirements and its integration requirements with the legacy infrastructure – both partners agreed that a reliable up-front fixed price estimate would be very difficult. By employing the adVANTAGE model, the partners could however break the project down to the insurer's individual user stories, and proceed with incremental implementation and billing of more manageable chunks that could be prioritized according to the insurer's wishes for going live. With the project still ongoing, a visible benefit of the approach so far has been that the collaboration between adesso and its client is more focused on progress with the individual user stories, than on questions regarding components throughout the system (which could otherwise distract attention from the essentials as developers are drawn to problems that are interesting but not immediately relevant). As a formal basis for billing each sprint, staff members keep timesheets just as they would for traditional projects, so the administrative overhead is low. The actual efforts up to now also agree well with the initial estimates, indicating that adVANTAGE gives no incentive to either party to blow up efforts.

In discussing the above example and our approach in general, it should be noted that an understanding of the risks of agile software development, and a degree of mutual trust in the business partner's competence, quality standards and business ethics, and a commitment to open communication is still required for a flexible contracting model such as this to work. Given these prerequisites, however, we believe that the risk-sharing and fair billing provisions of adVANTAGE will help agile processes to be more readily adopted by third-party software suppliers and their clients alike.

References

1. Curtis, B., Krasner, H., Iscoe, N.: A Field Study of the Software Design Process for Large Systems. Comm. ACM 31(11), 1268–1287 (1988)
2. Schwaber, K., Beedle, M.: Agile Software Development with Scrum. Prentice Hall (2002)
3. Boehm, B., Huang, L.G.: Value-based Software Engineering: A Case Study. IEEE Computer 36(3), 33–41 (2003)
4. Lehman, M.M.: Uncertainty in Computer Application and its Control through the Engineering of Software. J. Softw. Maint: Res. Pract. 1(1), 3–27 (1989)
5. Van Cauwenberghe, P.: Succeeding with Agile Fixed Price Contracts. In: Aguanno, K. (ed.) Managing Agile Projects. Multi-Media Publications Inc. (2005)
6. Sutherland, J.: Money for Nothing and Your Change for Free: Agile Contracts. Agile 2008 talk, http://www.slideshare.net/gerrykirk/money-for-nothing-agile-2008-presentation
7. Poppendieck, M., Poppendieck, T.: Lean Software Development: An Agile Toolkit. Add. Wesley (2003)
8. Larman, C., Vodde, B.: Practices for Scaling Lean & Agile Development: Large, Multisite, and Offshore Product Development with Large-Scale Scrum. Pearson Education (2010)

Author Index